Retreat and Rearguard Dunkirk 1940

For my great uncle Lance Corporal Archie Goode
and my grandson Archie Proud

Retreat and Rearguard Dunkirk 1940

The Evacuation of the BEF to the Channel Ports

Jerry Murland

Pen & Sword
MILITARY

First published in Great Britain in 2016 by
Pen & Sword Military
an imprint of
Pen & Sword Books Ltd
47 Church Street
Barnsley
South Yorkshire
S70 2AS

Copyright © Jerry Murland 2016

ISBN 978 1 47382 366 2

The right of Jerry Murland to be identified as the Author of this Work
has been asserted by him in accordance with the Copyright, Designs and
Patents Act 1988.

Typeset in Ehrhardt by
Mac Style, Bridlington, East Yorkshire
Printed and bound in the UK by CPI Group (UK) Ltd, Croydon,
CRO 4YY

Pen & Sword Books Ltd incorporates the imprints of Pen & Sword
Archaeology, Atlas, Aviation, Battleground, Discovery, Family History,
History, Maritime, Military, Naval, Politics, Railways, Select, Transport,
True Crime, and Fiction, Frontline Books, Leo Cooper, Praetorian
Press, Seaforth Publishing and Wharncliffe.

For a complete list of Pen & Sword titles please contact
PEN & SWORD BOOKS LIMITED
47 Church Street, Barnsley, South Yorkshire, S70 2AS, England
E-mail: enquiries@pen-and-sword.co.uk
Website: www.pen-and-sword.co.uk

Contents

Author's Note

When describing the fighting in this book I have often referred to modern day road numbering in order to give the reader using current maps of the area a more precise location. While some of the abbreviations in the text are self explanatory others require a modicum of explanation. I have used a form of abbreviation when describing battalion formations, thus the 2nd Battalion Royal Norfolk Regiment becomes 2/Norfolks or more simply the Norfolks. German army units are a little more complex. Within the infantry regiment there were three battalions – each one approximately the size of a British battalion – and as with their British counterparts the battalion was broken down into four companies of riflemen who were given an Arabic numeral, for example, 3 *Kompanie*. Again, I have abbreviated when describing these units, thus Infantry Regiment 162 becomes IR 162 while the second battalion within that regiment is abbreviated to II/IR 162. Some of the other equivalent German and British ranks referred to in the text are as follows:

Colonel	*Oberst*
Lieutenant Colonel	*Oberstleutnant*
Major	*Major, Sturmbannführer*
Captain	*Hauptmann, Hauptsturmführer*
Lieutenant	*Oberleutnant*
Second Lieutenant	*Leutnant*
Sergeant	*Feldwebel*
Corporal	*Unteroffizier*
Lance Corporal	*Gefreiter*
Infantry Private	*Infanterist, Schütze*

Acknowledgements

In searching for personal accounts written by the men who fought in the France and Flanders campaign of 1940 I have examined archive collections across the country and it is to those archivists, librarians and keepers of collections that I am indebted. The National Archives at Kew continues to be a valuable source of material, particularly in respect of regimental war diaries and the rich source of accounts that flowed between veterans and the Army Historical Branch post-1945. These accounts, apart from revealing what exactly took place and where, have provided a fascinating insight into the true nature of the fighting at a tactical level. Other sources of material have been found in the Imperial War Museum collections and the Liddell Hart Centre for Military Archives.

I must also thank Eric Old the administrator at the Monmouth Castle Museum, Gavin Glass at the Royal Ulster Rifles Regimental Museum, Geoff Elson at the Staffordshire Regimental Museum, Lieutenant Colonel Colin Bulleid at the Hampshire Regimental Museum, Jim Pearson at the Soldiers of Oxfordshire Museum, Dr John Paddock at the Mercian Regimental Museum, General Jonathan Riley at the Royal Welch Fusiliers Museum, Kate Swann at the National Army Museum, Mike Galer at the 9/12 Lancers Museum, and the archivist at the Bovington Tank Museum.

I also extend my thanks to John Dixon for his help and Tim Lynch for sharing with me some of the material he used in *Dunkirk 1940 – Whereabouts Unknown*. Peter Caddick-Adams kindly gave permission to quote from his account of 143 Brigade, John Carbis allowed me to quote from *We Marched*, Major General Sir Lawrence New gave permission to quote from the *Pictorial History of the 4th and 7th Royal Tank Regiment*, Patrick Wilson kindly gave permission to use some of his material in *Dunkirk – From Disaster to Deliverance*, Guy Rommelaere was kind enough to allow me access to his sources and the Holdich family allowed me to quote from Neil Holdich's diary. I have also used extracts from several veterans' accounts and for these I must thank Ron Stilwell, Ian Laidler, Ricki Brandon Cliffe, Jim Garside, Peter Miller and Andrew Newson. Trefor Llewellyn very generously lent me his father's papers in which I found the account of the Welsh Guards at Arras and West Cappel.

Jim Tuckwell, the webmaster of the excellent Durham Light Infantry website read my material regarding the Durham Light Infantry and kindly sent me Michael Farr's diary along with other accounts of the St Venant fighting. Dave

O'Mara and Nick Watts advised me on aspects of the Arras counter-stroke while Dave Drew and others on the WW2 Talk website answered my numerous requests for information and very helpfully supplied me with material. Chris Baker saved me several trips to Kew and generously photographed material for me and Laura Dimmock at the RUSI library in Whitehall responded with her usual promptness to my many requests. Tom Waterer, Dave Rowland and Paul Webster have my gratitude for their excellent company on several battleground visits and for sharing in those delightful moments when the first beer is poured.

To Jon Cooksey I am eternally thankful, not only for his support and guidance in the preparation of this volume but for allowing me full access to his archive of material on Boulogne and Calais. He and I spent two days following the BEF retreat from Louvain to the Escaut trying to find obscure châteaux and scrambling around the pill boxes of the Gort Line, an activity that my eldest granddaughter Alisha found altogether easier than we did! It was she that remarked that we were often on ground that was fought over during the First World War, a sobering thought when visiting Commonwealth War Graves Commission (CWGC) cemeteries in search of 1940 casualties.

The maps have been drawn by Rebecca Jones of Glory Designs in Coventry who has made her usual suggestions as to how my scribbles can be improved. For her this book has been the catalyst that prompted the discovery of the military service of her grandfather, Gunner John Jones, who served in the 48th Division with 24/Field Regiment and was evacuated from Dunkirk on 2 June 1940.

While I have made every effort to trace the copyright holders of the material used, I crave the indulgence of literary executors or copyright holders where those efforts have so far failed and would encourage them to contact me through the publisher so any error can be rectified.

Finally I must once again thank my wife Joan for her tolerance in putting up with my absence, not only from home when visiting the battlefields and distant archives but also my absence from family life when surrounded by mountains of paper and dusty volumes of regimental histories. My only excuse is that it keeps me out of the pub and away from other activities of a more dubious nature.

Jerry Murland
Coventry

Introduction

This is the story of the retreat of the British Expeditionary Force (BEF) from the River Dyle to the channel coast of France from where Operation Dynamo began on 26 May 1940. Over the next nine days almost a quarter of a million men of the BEF were evacuated from the coast of France. The extensive history of the France and Flanders Campaign of 1940 is well documented by numerous authors and while all agree that the evacuation was a huge success and the numbers of men lifted from Dunkirk far exceeded expectations, they would also concur with Churchill's view, expressed at the time, that 'wars are not won by evacuations'. Dunkirk was the second occasion that British land forces had been defeated in Europe in as many weeks and although Norway was a costly campaign for Germany in terms of surface shipping, like France and Flanders, it was a decisive victory for the German military machine.

There is also a general agreement amongst British historians that the campaign in France and Flanders was lost almost before it had started. It was not so much a case of Germany winning the battle but of France throwing it away by their willingness to fall into the trap of planning to fight the battle on the basis of the experience of the previous war of 1914–18. While there is a great deal of truth in this, we cannot condemn the whole French Army for the disastrous events on the Meuse. There are innumerable occasions when French divisions fought well and courageously and we should remember that the Dunkirk bridgehead was defended between 29 May and 4 June by 8,000 soldiers of the The French 12th Motorised Infantry Division which had been at Gembloux fifteen days earlier. Their commanding officer, General Louis Janssen, was killed on 2 June during a rearguard action that is afforded little significance in British accounts of the fighting. Similarly in Lille, 35,000 French soldiers of the First Army held out against hugely superior German forces between 28 and 30 May, one regimental commander, Justin Dutrey, committing suicide rather than surrendering in an action that undoubtedly contributed to the successful evacuation at Dunkirk.

To some extent I am also guilty of sidelining the French Army but the story of *Retreat and Rearguard: Dunkirk 1940* does not attempt to retell the complete history of the campaign. Instead it focuses on the tactical realities experienced by British rearguard units during their withdrawal to Dunkirk. That said I have, of course, referred to the overall strategic picture where necessary in order to place actions in context and to provide the reader with an overview of the developing situation on the ground, although the astute amongst you will note that I have not included the events surrounding Army Group C along the Maginot Line as these did not impact directly on the Dunkirk evacuation.

In writing about soldiers and battlegrounds I have always sought to expose the emotions of war through the personal experiences of those who were there at the time, a task that continues to underline the frailty of man and to recognise that war is fought by individuals whose hopes and aspirations are no different from our own. Fortunately for us many of their personal accounts still exist and give us the soldier's eye view of the fighting and consequently provide greater access to the soldier's war in a battleground that is, at the time of writing, seventy-five years old.

I have confined this account to the area north of the Somme for the simple reason that the vast majority of the fighting I have described took place in Belgium and along the 'Dunkirk Corridor', an 'escape route' created by the British commander-in-chief through which the bulk of the British forces were able to reach the evacuation beaches at Dunkirk. The rearguard actions fought by those divisions in keeping this vital corridor open – in spite of determined assault by German forces – is perhaps the real story of the 'Miracle of Dunkirk'. This does not in any way reduce the importance of the desperate and magnificent rearguard action fought by Major General Victor Fortune's Highland Division at St-Valéry-en-Caux, but in books of this nature space often dictates the content. I have also omitted the work of the RAF in the Battle of France and their operations over the coast during the evacuation; an omission that does not denigrate their contribution to the campaign or the enormous losses sustained by the Advanced Air Striking Force in the defence of France. What is generally not appreciated is that the RAF were in action over the French mainland from 31 October 1939 when a 73 Squadron Hurricane was hit by flak over Bouzanville and over the next seven months, leading up to the German advance of 10 May, a further twenty-eight aircraft were lost in offensive action.

The decision as to which rearguard actions to include has always been governed by whether there are personal accounts through which to tell the story. Without the individual's perspective on events there is no story to tell and consequently many of the rearguard encounters I have written about have almost selected themselves. There are, however, some rearguard actions that, because of the impact they have already made on Britain's military history, cannot be ignored and others that will never find their way into the public domain because the individuals concerned were either killed or did not record their experiences. But to those men who did, I am eternally grateful that their story of the evacuation of the BEF to the channel coast in 1940 can be told in their own words.

Chapter One

Return

5 September 1939–10 May 1940

'We were led up to the edge of the cliffs by one of our officers and told, as he pointed towards France, 'That's where the enemy are …. shake your fists at them, like this!' Whereupon we obediently shook our fists at them in like manner, although I shouldn't think that it caused any misgiving amongst German armed forces!'
Private Bert Jones, B Company 5th Battalion
East Kent Regiment, 12th Division.

War became more of a reality for Captain Cyril Townsend and the 2/Durham Light Infantry (2/DLI), on 23 September 1939 when the 569 officers and men of the battalion crossed from Southampton to Cherbourg on a former 'Irish cross-channel boat packed with hundreds of RAF personnel and Brigade Headquarters'. Barely three weeks earlier the monotone voice of Neville Chamberlain announced to the nation that Germany's military incursion into Poland on 1 September 1939 had now resulted in a formal declaration of war. His address brought to an end the twenty-one years of uneasy peace that had elapsed since the Armistice of 11 November 1918 ended the First World War. For Chamberlain the declaration of war was also a personal failure ultimately leading to his resignation eight months later on 10 May, the very day German forces unleashed *Blitzkrieg* on the allied armies in the west.

Britain's undertaking to have two full army corps assembled in France thirty-three days after mobilization went remarkably smoothly and the Durhams were part of that initial movement of troops and equipment. With 6 Brigade Headquarters also on board the SS *Ulster* and a number of senior officers and NCOs wearing medal ribbons from the previous conflict, it would not have been far from Townsend's mind that the second battalion had made this short journey across the Channel in September 1914 en-route to joining the BEF in the Aisne Valley. Now, under the command of Lieutenant Colonel Victor Yate, who as a young man had served as a subaltern with the battalion in 1914, Townsend must have been well aware that history was repeating itself.

The stark reality of another war with Germany did not begin to surface amongst the British public until after the Munich Crisis of 1938. Rearmament then forced its way into the mindset of a population amongst which memories of 1914–18 still lingered. It also pushed its way onto the political agenda when the Territorial Army was doubled in size on 29 March 1939 by the War Minister, Leslie Hore-Belisha, by requiring each of the existing Territorial Army units to form duplicate units. A matter of weeks later he reintroduced conscription and so kitted out a new generation of young men in British uniform.

The question of just how a sudden influx of recruits were to be trained and equipped was one that had been very much on the minds of those entrusted with the formation and training of the Kitchener New Army units in 1914. The same question was now repeated as Territorial units began receiving a flood of willing volunteers. While the introduction of conscription and the increase in the numbers of Territorials served to accelerate the War Office's headache, in political terms the gesture bolstered the Franco-British Entente. The British were at last – albeit reluctantly – taking the prospect of war seriously.

Major Graham Brooks, commanding 366/Battery of 140/Field Regiment, found himself on the receiving end of an influx of these new recruits:

> *'On 1 May 1939 the Regiment had been formed as part of the doubling up of the Territorials. On that day it consisted of CO, Adjutant, and the expectation of recruits enlisted by the 'parent unit'. Joining as senior battery commander, I was given a list of two hundred and fifty names and the assurance that officers would be found. Soon the names materialized into bodies and the grand fun of building something out of nothing began.'*[1]

Brooks' light hearted attitude masked his apprehension at exactly how these men were to be equipped and trained and he was the first to admit that in those early days the battery was akin to a 'band of children' fumbling their way through a 'new world of black-out and adventure'. Even those who had served in the previous war found it strange, for soldiering was, as Brooks pointed out, 'vastly different to what it was twenty-five years ago'.

Whether the 53-year-old Commander-in-Chief of the BEF, General Lord Gort, shared this opinion is debatable, but he was a man who was certainly familiar with the battlefield. As a highly decorated Grenadier Guards officer he had served in the First World War with some distinction, wounded on four occasions he had been decorated with the Military Cross (MC) and the Distinguished Service Order (DSO) and two bars. His award of the coveted Victoria Cross (VC) came whilst he was commanding the 1st Battalion during the battle on the Canal du Nord in 1918.

Gort had certainly been a first class battalion commander, but as many such men did after the Armistice in 1918, he lost his command and reverted to his substantive rank of major. As promotion slowed to its pre-war pace, brigade command eluded him until 1928 when he was appointed General Officer Commanding the Guards Brigade. Thereafter his rise to the top was nothing if not spectacularly rapid. By 1935 he had been promoted to major general and three years later, after a short tenure as Military Secretary to Leslie Hore-Belisha, he was appointed Chief of the Imperial General Staff (CIGS). There is no doubt that his appointment as CIGS had a great deal to do with his war record and Hore-Belisha's misplaced desire for the army to be led by a man of proven courage on the battlefield.

If Gort's appointment as CIGS was met with a degree of bewilderment then his subsequent confirmation as Commander-in-Chief of the BEF on 1 September 1939, drew gasps of disbelief, particularly from General Sir Edmund Ironside who had been confidently expecting command of the BEF and now found himself appointed CIGS in Gort's place. 'The Army was certainly amazed', wrote Major General Bernard Montgomery, and was 'even more amazed when Ironside was made CIGS in place of Gort.'[2] But despite the barrage of criticism that greeted his appointment, it has to be said that whatever his faults may have been, when the situation facing the BEF became desperate in the last days of May, Gort maintained his composure and grasp of the situation.

As Cyril Townsend had noted, many of the men now landing in France with the BEF were wearing medal ribbons from the previous war. This was certainly the case with the two corps commanders, both of whom were older than Gort and had been senior to him before his recent promotion. Commanding I Corps was General Sir John Dill, an individual who had served with distinction under Douglas Haig and who many felt had been repeatedly passed over for the top appointments until he succeeded Ironside as CIGS on 27 May 1940. Dill, who was at Neuve Chapelle in 1915 as brigade major of 25 Brigade, was no stranger to the rigours of the battlefield and did not hide his anxieties over a possible attack by massed German armour.

After Dill's recall, command of I Corps was passed to Lieutenant General Michael Barker; an appointment that caused the outspoken Montgomery to remark that 'only a madman would give a corps to Barker', another comment that was to prove prophetic in the dark days ahead. Brigadier Charles Norman, commanding 1/Armoured Reconnaissance Brigade was no less complimentary and was of the opinion that Barker was only given the appointment because he was the next major general on the list, even though he was 'quite unsuited to command in the field'.

In command of II Corps was the energetic and able Lieutenant General Alan Brooke, a gunner who had risen from lieutenant to lieutenant colonel during the First World War. Brooke was not convinced that the Allies could hold a German offensive in the west, an observation not shared by Gort who regarded Brooke as too much of a pessimist. Both Brooke and Dill had drawn Gort's attention to the potential weaknesses of an advance into Belgium, views that were seemingly dismissed by the commander-in-chief. Dill is also known to have discussed his fears with Cyril Falls on his return to England in April 1940, but both men could never have anticipated the speed, ferocity and penetration of the German panzer advance.[3]

The BEF frontage in France took the form of a 45-mile-long salient formed by the Franco-Belgian frontier with its left flank on Armentières and the right flank resting on the village of Maulde, where the frontier cut across the River Escaut.[4] Within the salient lay the important industrial complexes of Lille and Roubaix. The French 51st Division, which had been placed under Gort's command, had already taken up position in the left half of the sector and was covering Tourcoing and Roubaix. This left the British II Corps (3rd and 4th Divisions) guarding the eastern approaches to Lille whereas I Corps (1st and 2nd Divisions) was deployed in more open country further to the east. Between the BEF and the Germans was neutral Belgium and in the months that followed the British Army settled down to build up its strength in both men and in fortifying the line of the frontier in depth – fortifications that became known as the Gort Line.

In overall command of allied forces was General Maurice Gamelin, who, like Gort, had excelled during the First World War. Gamelin was a small, plump individual whose vision for the defence of France was very much bound up with the static Maginot Line, construction of which began in earnest in 1930 along the Franco-German border. Political and financial considerations determined that it was 'incomplete' by 1939, however, the chain of mutually supportive fortifications petered out north of Montmedy, and therein lay the Achilles heel of French fortunes.

Consequently, when the BEF arrived in France, one of their principle tasks – along with the French – was to extend the Maginot Line defences along the border with Belgium to the North Sea. British General Headquarters (GHQ) was opened at Habarcq some 7 miles west of Arras and it was from there that the progress of the British military build-up in France was directed. By the end of 1939 a third regular division had been formed – the 5th Division – and in January 1940 the first of the Territorial divisions arrived – the 48th (South Midland) Division – followed closely by the 50th (Northumbrian) Division and the 51st (Highland) Division. April saw the arrival of the 42nd (East Lancashire) Division and the 44th (Home Counties) Division giving rise to the formation of III Corps under the command of the very capable Lieutenant General Sir Ronald Adam, an individual who was already well known to the commander-in-chief. When Gort was appointed CIGS, Adam was made Deputy Chief of the Imperial Staff and when Gort assumed command of the BEF in 1939 he understandably wanted Adam as his Chief of Staff but in the event Major General Henry Pownall was appointed, a man described as having an 'unruffled imperturbability'. Charles Moore in *The Road to Dunkirk* writes that Pownall brought with him an atmosphere of professionalism into a situation that increasingly became more and more chaotic and, given the huge strain on Gort, it is a tribute to Pownall that he was able to support his chief in those last desperate days of May 1940.

By the end of April 1940 the BEF had increased its strength to ten divisions, a force that had been added to by the departure from England of three incomplete Territorial divisions – 12th (Eastern), 23rd (Northumbrian) and 46th (North Midland) – to ease the manpower shortages. Neither equipped for a combat role nor fully trained, the intention was to use these divisions as pioneers in constructing marshalling yards, airfields and depots. Since there was no question of using such untrained units for fighting, it was stipulated that in each brigade one battalion should undertake training while the other two laboured. When the German attack opened on 10 May these 'digging divisions' which had allowed Hore-Belisha to claim in the House of Commons that Britain had fulfilled her military commitment to France, found themselves unavoidably drawn into the fighting.

~

The winter of 1939/40 was the period of the so-called Phoney War, a period which Second Lieutenant Anthony Irwin, serving with the 2/Essex Regiment (2/Essex), described as 'incredibly cold' as his battalion laboured each day building the Gort Line. Second Lieutenant Hugh Taylor, who commanded 7 Platoon in A Company, 1/Suffolk Regiment (1/Suffolks), was another who hated working on the Gort Line and, like his men, imagined this was where they would first encounter the Germans. 'We had been constructing pill-boxes and a large anti-tank ditch, the ditch being about fourteen feet deep and thirty feet across. It was defended by pill-boxes, there being one for every section of the infantry ... This was going to be the Battalion line.'[5]

While Irwin's and Taylor's experience was typical of the units who had arrived in the late Autumn of 1939, for Lieutenant Michael Duncan, a Territorial officer with the 4/Oxfordshire and Buckinghamshire Light Infantry (4/Ox and Bucks), it was 'a relatively pleasant interlude'. The 4/Ox and Bucks had only been in France since mid January 1940 and as one of the three battalions in 145 Brigade were part of the 48th Division. Based at Attiches, a few miles south of Lille, Duncan had joined up in 1934 for no better reason than he liked horses and most of his friends were already part-time soldiers. 'There was,' he wrote, 'the rather pleasant sensation of feeling that in some obscure way we were being heroes without having to do anything particularly unpleasant or dangerous to earn the title.' For 145 Brigade the unpleasant and dangerous task was yet to come.[6]

While the Maginot Line was under construction, Belgium was still an ally of France and any material extension of the line along the Franco-Belgian border was in danger of offending the Belgians and altering the balance of collaboration between the two countries. Critical to the French was the defence of the industrialised region around Lille, a region which had been denied them when the Germans seized and held it during the First World War. So when Belgium received a guarantee of neutrality from Germany in 1937 and attempted to steer a path away from any formal alliance with the French, it became clear in French military and political circles that, in the event of war, if the Germans entered Belgium from the east, their own forces would have to counter such a move from the west. The French were correct in suspecting a German attack would come through Belgium, a plan confirmed in January 1940 when a German Army major, Hellmuth Reinberger, crash-landed in a Messerschmitt Bf 108 near Mechelen-sur-Meuse, instigating the infamous Mechelen Affair.

Reinberger was carrying the first plans for the German invasion of Western Europe which, as Gamelin had expected, involved an advance which closely resembled the 1914 Schlieffen Plan and a German thrust through Belgium. Although the Belgians were suspicious and suspected deception they eventually concluded that the documents were genuine and even convinced the German government that the plans had been destroyed in the crash and thus remained unseen. At this point it was believed by Belgian military intelligence and Colonel Georges Goethals, the Belgian Military Attaché in Cologne, that the German High Command would not now pursue its original plan. Goethals even went as far as suggesting that a revised plan of attack might draw the Allied armies into north-eastern Belgium before the Germans redirected their main thrust further south.

Warning the French and British of their concerns, the Belgians at least expected some alteration to Allied strategy. But, despite the evidence to the contrary, Gamelin remained convinced that the main German effort would be between Maastricht and Liège, while Gort and the British Government – still apparently subservient to French military thinking – fell into step behind him by not questioning the wisdom of his decision.

In the circumstances it was hardly surprising that the Germans would rethink their invasion plans. German military planners now took the opportunity to issue a revised plan that not only caught the imagination of Adolf Hitler but reflected the boldness and momentum that came to be associated with *Blitzkrieg*. Alfred Jodl's personal diary records the drastic changes that were made to the German plans after the Mechelen Affair; plans which were masterminded by the 53-year-old Erich von Manstein. While Army Group B under General Fedor von Bock would continue to attack through north eastern Belgium as the French expected, the main thrust of the German panzer divisions – Army Group A – under Gerd von Rundstedt would be redirected through the Ardennes to turn north and cut through the British and French – exactly as predicted by Georges Goethals.[7] Dubbed 'the Matador's Cloak' by Basil Liddell Hart, Manstein's plan was masterly in its simplicity and was known as *Fall Gelb* – Plan Yellow.

With Gamelin continuing to ignore any thoughts of a German change of strategy, his first proposal for countering the threat of invasion focussed on the less risky 'Plan E' which called for Allied forces to advance to the line of the Escaut. Despite this plan being the more sensible, defending the line of the Escaut was discarded in favour of holding the line of the more easterly River Dyle; Gamelin successfully arguing that the anti-tank defences built by the Belgians would allow for a rapid deployment and facilitate the French Seventh Army linking-up with the Dutch via Breda.

Thus, the strategic plan – which became known as 'Plan D' – was for French and British forces to cross the border in the event of a German attack and occupy the line of the River Dyle, which runs roughly north and south about 30 miles east of Brussels. The BEF were to deploy between Louvain and Wavre with the French First Army under General Georges Blanchard on the right in the Gembloux Gap and the Belgians – who, it was anticipated, would fall back into the gap between the left wing of the BEF and the right of General Henri Giraud's Seventh Army.

It was a plan that certainly puzzled many in the BEF who had spent the whole of the previous winter preparing defences behind the Belgian frontier. Now as soon as Germany invaded Belgium all that was to be abandoned and the enemy was to be brought to battle from positions that were unfamiliar and where the defences were already thought to be of poor quality. If that wasn't bad enough, there was considerable doubt over the fighting quality of the Belgian forces and their ability to stage a stout resistance.

With the benefit of hindsight there is little doubt that Plan D was a fundamental flaw in the Allied strategy and must certainly be regarded as one of the principle factors in the Fall of France. As early as 13 May, three days after the advance into Belgium had begun, Captain Phillip Gribble, an air liaison officer with the Advanced Air Striking Force, was concerned as to why the *Luftwaffe* had been so restrained in their bombing. 'It looks almost as if the Germans want us where we are going. Has the French High Command forgotten that the encounter battle is the risk we have always been told to avoid at any cost?'[8]

It was a question that had also been put to Gamelin the previous day by his military advisor, Lieutenant Colonel Paul de Villelume, who apparently begged his commander-in-chief to halt the advance while there was still time to do so – a view shared by a number of officers in the BEF. Captain John Nelson, commanding 1/Guards Brigade Anti-Tank Company felt they had been 'enticed forward from well prepared positions on the French Frontier ... and now were to be cut off from our allies before we had a chance to strike a blow'.[9]

But whatever fears and concerns may have been apparent in the minds of the advancing British it was too late: the trap had been sprung and Gamelin's rather lame reply to de Villelume that it was a *fait accompli* was perhaps symptomatic of the air of helplessness that clouded French thinking. It was a response that would hardly have impressed Captain John Horsfall, commanding D Company of the 1/Royal Irish Fusiliers (1/RIF), whose opinion of Plan D was voiced in his diary. 'I have not yet seen strategic reasons ever given for that speculative unplanned [sic] surge into Belgium – reasons yes, but not military ones.' As a junior officer he kept his opinions to himself, expressing his amazement that the BEF, despite knowing that severe defensive fighting lay ahead, chose to leave 'the ground of our choosing and [take] up positions which offered only encounter battle at the enemy's bidding'.[10]

Chapter Two

The Dyle

11–16 May 1940

'In a stricken panic [the villagers] were obliged to leave their homes immediately. The old, the sick, women, children and babies just fled in terror. It was as if an avalanche had hit them.'

Lieutenant Michael Farr, 2/DLI at La Tombe,
14 May 1940.

Early on the morning of 10 May Lieutenant Anthony Rhodes, serving with Headquarters, 3rd Divisional Engineers, was woken when his bedroom door burst open. Standing in front of him was Mademoiselle Wecquier, the daughter of the house in which he was billeted. 'Lieutenant', she said, 'we have been invaded.' Rhodes confessed to be more absorbed by the fact the young lady in question was only wearing a silk nightdress and was 'charmingly silhouetted against the rays of the sun', it wasn't until a few moments later that he realized that the real war had begun and 'all hell was about to be let loose'.[1] Two hundred miles to the west Lieutenant Anthony Irwin of 2/Essex was just passing the Isle of Wight bound for Southampton on ten days leave when – much to the irritation of all those on board – the ship was turned around and returned to Boulogne where 'our presence confused the issue. No one knew what to do with us and no one much cared.' But as he candidly declared later, 'Thank God, we didn't know how much was to happen in the next ten days.'[2]

Operation David, the code word transmitted to every British Army unit on the Franco-Belgian border, signalled the end of the Phoney War and the move east to the River Dyle. The main fighting force was headed by motorcycle units of the 4/Royal Northumberland Fusiliers (4/RNF) and the Morris CS9 Armoured Cars of the 12th Lancers which were described in the Regimental History as 'under-engined, under-armed and under-armoured; being in fact the latest thing of its kind, already obsolescent'.[3] The 12/Lancers were commanded by 43-year-old Lieutenant Colonel Herbert Lumsden, a regular officer who had served with E Battery Royal Horse Artillery in the First World War, winning the MC in July 1918. Transferring to the 12/Lancers in June 1925, he had been in command of the regiment since 1938. When the move to the Dyle was confirmed Lumsden – like many of his colleagues – was still on leave in London but on hearing 'the balloon had gone up' was back in command by midnight on 10 May – six hours after the Lancers had taken up their positions on the Dyle! Considerably quicker than Anthony Irwin who took several days to find his unit.

The British move to the Dyle was carried out with little interference from the Germans and apart from the final few miles, the forward battalions were transported by the troop-carrying companies of the Royal Army Service Corps (RASC). There may not have been much enemy air activity in the darkness but navigating across 75 miles of Belgium proved for some to be more demanding than first thought. 21-year-old Hugh Taylor of the 1/Suffolks had two lorries allocated to his platoon and before long found himself in the driving seat with the RASC driver sound asleep next to him. Driving with only side lights and diligently following the axle light of the vehicle in front of him he rattled on 'through village and lanes, over bridges and through woods' by which time, he tells us, he had lost all sense of direction:

> *'After about four hours we entered a town and the light in front disappeared over a bridge, when I reached the crest of the rise I found to my horror that the tail light in front had gone and there was a cross road in front. I hastily looked for a guide, which the Provost Corps had put out when we deviate from the straight run, but saw none …I had not gone far before I realised that I was wrong, the road gave a twist to the right and I knew that I had gone in the wrong direction. I woke the driver up and told him to let me see the map as we were lost.'*[4]

Having turned around and knocked down a gate post in the process Taylor and his two lorries eventually came to a road junction where, to his relief, stood a Red Cap of the Provost Corps who directed him to a small convoy of vehicles directly ahead:

> 'They had stopped, so I pulled up behind them and found my Company Commander was just coming along to find out if anyone was lost. He found me on the tail of the convoy and directed me further up the road, where I found my own company and discovered to my delight that I had never been missed.'[5]

Gort's plan was to place the 1st and 2nd Divisions on the right flank and the 3rd Division on the left astride Louvain. By way of reserve the 48th Division was ordered to move east of Brussels and the 4th and 50th Divisions to the south. In addition the 44th Division was under orders to march to the Escaut south of Oudenaarde and the 42nd Division placed on readiness to take up station to their right if needed. After the initial move by motor transport, the leading infantry brigades completed the final approach on foot; for many of these men Saturday 11 May brought them into contact with the stream of refugees heading west ahead of the invading Germans. 20-year-old Private Ben Duncan, marching with the 2nd Battalion Hampshire Regiment (2/Hampshires) was horrified at the targeting of defenceless civilians by the *Luftwaffe*. 'One broke away and as he stumbled in our direction we could see that in his arms he carried a small body which we saw as he reached us that it was a little girl of some five or six years of age.'[6] The child was dead and there was little if anything Duncan and his mates could do as they marched on against the seemingly endless tide of humanity. But what was perhaps a little more worrying was the sight of Belgian Army units apparently in retreat. Hugh Taylor and the Suffolks noted they had 'very antiquated equipment and were struggling along the road on either side in all types of uniform, some armed, others not.'

The plight of refugees and indifferent Belgian soldiers was something that quickly became apparent to the 12/Lancers as they crossed the Dyle towards Diest. Tasked with linking up with the French Cavalry Corps in the Tirlemont area and reporting on the state of the Belgian defences on the River Ghette, they found no sign of the Belgians and were faced with a 4-mile gap between the French 3rd Light Mechanized Division (3/DLM) and units of the Belgian 1st Cavalry Division. Lumsden had little choice but to fill the gap himself, realising that 'the plans of the French 3/DLM and the Belgian units on the Ghette did not completely dovetail.' This was Lumsden's first indication that all was not well with the Belgian defence further east, a sentiment that was confirmed early on 12 May when German tanks were seen on the Tirlemont road.

Plan D had been based on the assumption that the Germans would, at the very least, take a week to force the Belgian border fortifications which ran along the Albert Canal and the Meuse. The Belgian defences were supported by strong positions on the near bank and all the bridging points had been prepared for demolition. The speed and audacity of the German attack was a major disaster for the Belgians who failed to demolish all the Meuse bridges and lost the Eben-Emael fortress to an airborne glider assault. It was the two Meuse bridges at Vroenhoven and Veldwezelt that the British Advanced Air Striking Force attacked on 12 May with Fairy Battles from 12 Squadron, a sortie which resulted in some damage to the bridges far outweighed by the loss of all five aircraft. Two posthumous VCs, awarded to Flying Officer Donald Garland and Sergeant Thomas Gray, testified to the ferocity of the encounter.

As the Belgians fell back onto the line of the River Ghette, Lumsden's men had some difficulty in getting the Belgian sappers to demolish the Ghette bridges. Lieutenant David Smith and his section of 101/Field Company Sappers who had been attached to the 12/Lancers, were now ordered up to the Ghette to ensure the bridges were ready for demolition. Smith found the Belgian attitude to blowing the bridges quite alarming. 'From the very outset of the campaign it was difficult to get the Belgian sappers to fire demolitions and quite often they seemed to have no settled plan for belts of demolitions.' His frustration was apparent in his 13 May diary entry when he wrote that despite successfully blowing the bridges along the Ghette, the Belgians retired from a position that could have been held successfully for much longer leaving the demolished bridging points 'uncovered by fire, thus leaving the enemy to employ with impunity whatever devices he wished to overcome the obstacle created'.

The 12/Lancers were by now engaged with the German 19th Division along the Ghette. A Squadron was involved in a sharp fire fight with a German motorcycle patrol from IR 17 and a fifteen-strong German mounted patrol which had swum the river was wiped out by Second Lieutenant Edward Miller-Mundy and 3 Troop. Despite losing three armoured cars from bombing and shellfire Lumsden was becoming increasingly concerned that the Belgians had no real intention of fighting for and holding the line of the Ghette; a suspicion already raised by David Smith. 'It was interesting,' wrote Lumsden, 'the number of anti-tank guns, in fact guns of all sorts, which were constantly on the move, when one would have expected them to be in position and dug in.'[7] At 1.00am on 14 May the Lancers began their withdrawal and by the afternoon were back across the Dyle and in reserve at Orphen. The infantry battle along the Dyle was about to begin.

∼

Hot on the heels of the 12/Lancers were the 3rd Division engineers who arrived at Eveberg around midnight on 10/11 May. Captain Dick Walker, the 3rd Division RE Adjutant, immediately left with the Chief Engineer Officer (CRE) Lieutenant Colonel Desmond Harrison, for Louvain. 'We drove through the town which was quite empty except for a few Belgian police, and had a look at the canal and bridges.' Intent on allocating the RE field companies to their areas of operation the two officers rapidly came to the conclusion that building any tank obstacles in the centre of Louvain was out of the question and the railway line to the east of the city would have to be the basis of any defence mounted by the infantry:

> *'Looking at the canal to the north of Louvain and the branches of the canal in Louvain itself the decision to use the railway as the main obstacle was strongly confirmed. The canal had three branches in Louvain and these were on average only 20 feet wide and the river was low ... no bridges had been prepared and very little defensive work had been done. I only saw one pillbox, there were, however some de Cointet obstacles, wire and rail obstacles.'*[8]

It was a view shared by Major General Bernard Montgomery when he arrived in Louvain. Initially frustrated in their attempt to garrison Louvain and its environs by the refusal of the Belgian 10th Division to hand over responsibility – an agreement that had been decided upon several weeks previously – British units waited rather impatiently in the wooded area of the Eikenbos to the west of the city. Montgomery, in a rare flash of tact, informed the Belgians that he was placing his 3rd Division under their command and would accordingly reinforce their line. 'I decided that the best way of getting the Belgians out and my division in was to use a little flattery.' His ruse appeared to work as the Belgians withdrew on 12 May 'when the Germans came within artillery range and the shelling began'.[9]

The medieval city of Louvain had already suffered badly at the hands of the Germans in 1914 and was about to bear the brunt of the German attack again. It came as no surprise to the 2/Royal Ulster Rifles (2/RUR) and the 2/Lincolnshire Regiment (2/Lincolnshire) as they advanced through the already badly damaged city to find the vast majority of the 32,000 inhabitants had already begun the move west, leaving them as the principle custodians of a rapidly emptying metropolis. Moving quickly to the eastern edge of the city the Ulster Rifles were allotted a front of some 2000 yards running from the communal cemetery on their right to a point just north of the bridge over the Diest-Louvain road. The Lincolnshires were on their right with D Company occupying the communal cemetery and the remaining companies deployed along the railway to a point west of the N251. To the north of the Ulster Rifles were 7 Guards Brigade deployed in what the Grenadiers' regimental historian described as an uncomfortable position forward of the Dyle Canal. 'The Germans had bombed the marshalling yards, the wreckage of engines and rolling stick was piled so high that many of the pill boxes had a view of no more than twenty yards and were therefore isolated one from the other.'[10]

The line of the railway occupied by the Ulster Rifles was another which was far from perfect. A wide boulevard, which was the continuation of that which encircled Louvain, ran along the southern edge of the city and along most of the western edge of the railway line. The railway line ran through a wide cutting in the south and along an embankment to the north. This inevitably made the positioning of section posts difficult as fields of fire nowhere exceeded 50 yards and those in the railway station were often considerably less. On the extreme left of the battalion – north of the station and close to the signal box – one A Company platoon post was perched on top of the railway embankment and only accessed via a ladder. Dubbed the Bala-Tiger post, it was named after the two subalterns who commanded it, Lieutenants Humphrey 'Bala' Bredin and William 'Tiger' Tighe-Wood. Bredin had already won the MC and bar in April 1938 while the battalion had been serving in Palestine and, despite being overlooked by a tall building some 20 yards away, was in no mood to allow his position to be overrun. Bredin's nickname 'Bala' is thought to have originated from the name of a fort in Peshawar and it was with some coincidence that on being posted to Palestine he found himself quartered in an Arab village named Bala.

The railway station, under the command of 22-year-old Lieutenant Pat Garstin, was situated at the eastern end of the wide Avenue des Allies. Garstin's men held the entrance hall and Platform 2 together with its subways and between them and Platform 1 was a thick belt of barbed wire which had been attached to the wooden sleepers, preventing movement across the rails. It was this unlikely battleground that prompted the *Daily Express* to use the headline '*The Battle Now Raging on Platform One*' in a later report of the fighting. Commanding the Ulstermen was 42-year-old Lieutenant Colonel Fergus 'Ghandi' Knox who had served as a second lieutenant with the battalion in the First World War. His command of the Ulster Rifles in 1940 was perhaps his finest hour and at Louvain, having adopted a motorcycle driven by Sergeant Norman Victor as his principle mode of transport, he directed the battle from the pillion seat earning a well deserved DSO in the process.

By dusk on 14 May the battalion was in contact with the enemy all along the railway line and for the majority it was their first real introduction to the German MG 34 machine gun – or 'Spandau' as it became known somewhat inaccurately – which succeeded in jangling the nerves of many of the less battle hardened of the Irish. The battalion historian remarked that 'after dark there was a tendency [for the forward posts] to continue firing rifles and Brens whether or not a target was visible.'[11] Nevertheless, it was just as well they were alert as in the closing hours of 14 May there were several attempts made by the Germans to penetrate the line, a situation that prompted Knox to move C Company and 29-year-old Captain Albert Ward into Louvain to counter any threat, a threat he took seriously enough the next morning to bring B Company and Captain Arthur Davis into the city as additional support.

A two hour German artillery barrage opened the fighting at dawn on 15 May countered by two batteries of 76/Field Regiment with the 7/Field Regiment's batteries of 25-pounders firing around 700 rounds in response. Undeterred, German infantry focussed their attack on the railway station and succeeded in penetrating the station yard. The problems around the station were exacerbated not only by the close proximity of the two platforms but also by the embankment and the buildings which overlooked the whole complex. To make matters worse German infantry had also taken up positions amongst the tangle of ruined railway rolling stock from where they directed a vicious curtain of machine gun fire.

Adding to these difficulties enemy infantry had also begun to infiltrate between the Bala-Tiger Post and the Guards' positions to their north and at one point got behind the station, cutting off many of A Company by firing down the Avenue des Allies into the station. The Irish reply was an instant counter-attack with grenades and Bren gun fire which – the war diary tells us – restored the status quo and resulted in a 'considerable reduction in fire'. So successful were these counter attacks that the German 19th Division was reinforced with units from IX Korps and the XVI *Panzer Korps*. Undeterred by the precarious nature of their position, Garstin's men used the subways to their advantage as the weight of German fire shattered the platform canopies above, showering them with shards of glass. Every so often the energetic Garstin would dart up from a subway, fire a burst from his Bren and vanish, only to reappear elsewhere to repeat the exercise, giving the impression the station was held by a much larger force.

At the Bala-Tiger post the defending garrison, despite their exposed position on the top of the embankment, had already inflicted a number of casualties on the attacking infantry. Overlooked by German snipers, the post – like the railway station – was continually under fire but even when surrounded, Lieutenant Bredin – who was usually armed with a rifle and his trademark blackthorn stick – refused to give way. Much to the chagrin of the Germans the narrow trench which nestled amongst the cinders and slag of the embankment remained firmly in Irish hands until the order was given to withdraw from Louvain.

Further north at Wilsele the initial enemy contact with the 1st Battalion the Coldstream Guards (1/Coldstream) on 14 May was easily brushed aside but as the attack gathered strength the outpost positions east of the canal were ordered to withdraw. No.2 Company posts were brought in without much difficulty but the No. 3 Company outposts had been penetrated resulting in Captain Richard Gooch and 24-year-old Lieutenant Richard Crichton together with Guardsman Lawrence Cook crossing the canal: 'By attacking with grenades they managed to get the forward sections out and back across the canal; but a number of men had to swim across – no easy matter in the dark – and two were drowned.'[12] Crichton was severely wounded in the action and almost lost an arm. Gooch and Crichton were both awarded the MC and Guardsman Cook the MM.

The next morning – 15 May – German infantry, reinforced by units from IX Korps, had moved machine guns and snipers into the houses on the east bank of the canal and attempted to cross it on No. 3 Company's frontage. Frustrated in this attempt by the Guards mortar platoon, orders were then received for No. 2 Company to retire in line with the 1st Battalion the Grenadier Guards (1/GG) which had reportedly pulled back in the face of a heavy artillery barrage. During the course of this retirement Captain Lord Frederick Cambridge was killed, but, as the regimental historian points out, the information was incorrect and it was only the outposts that the Grenadiers had withdrawn from:

> *'Since it was considered essential that the canal should still be held, the battalion was ordered to recapture the position from which 2 Company had withdrawn. The carriers under Lt. Tollemache, and the commanding officer* [Lieutenant Colonel Arnold Cazenove] *in a cavalry tank, went up to see how things were by the canal, and found not many of the enemy had yet got across. None the less, a heavy attack was laid on with the help of the tanks of the 5/Inniskilling Dragoons under the cover of which 1 Company (Maj Campbell) counter-attacked and succeeded in re-establishing themselves on the canal without losing any men.'*[13]

One further action of note on the 15th was that of Lance Corporal Percy Meredith who successfully dealt with a sniper who was giving the Coldstream posts some anxious moments. Crossing the open ground between his position and the buildings on the west bank of the canal, Meredith entered the building and silenced the sniper. His award of the Distinguished Conduct Medal (DCM) was presented to him by Montgomery at Roubaix on 26 May along with Gooch and Cook. Other recipients of gallantry awards that day were Fergus Knox who was awarded the DSO and Pat Garstin the MC.

~

Although British forces all along the length of the Dyle were engaged by the Germans, it appeared that the enemy's main attacks were concentrated on both flanks. Thirteen miles further south on Major General Henry 'Budget' Loyd's 2nd Division front, the sector ran from the left of Blanchard's French First Army, north along the Dyle through Wavre, before it linked up with Major General George Alexander's 1st Division. The 49-year-old Loyd was a former Coldstream Guardsman who had concluded the previous war as a decorated battalion commander. His three brigades – largely composed of regular troops – would see some of the bitterest fighting of the campaign. Sadly Loyd collapsed on 16 May and was replaced by Brigadier Noel Irwin, commanding 6 Brigade, who took command four days later – but not before the fighting around Gastuche had put the Durham Light Infantry on the front pages of the national newspapers with the award of the first VC of the ground war.

The three battalions of 6 Brigade began arriving on the Dyle in the early hours of 11 May and one of the first to arrive at La Tombe was Lieutenant Michael Farr serving with the 2/DLI. His diary betrays his evident dismay at the plight of the refugees who were flooding across the Dyle in great numbers. 'They were', he wrote, 'in a pitiable state, baggage, old carts, prams. Worst of all they did not know where they were going.'[14] Farr was a former Charterhouse schoolboy and recognising there would be no place for him in the family wine firm, decided on a career as a regular soldier, joining the battalion in 1938 from Sandhurst and at 21-years-old was now the battalion signals officer.

Looking across the river from their new positions the Durhams were without doubt uncomfortable with their deployment. The narrow river valley of the Dyle ran along the entire 2,000 yard frontage with the Louvain – Wavre railway line to the east crossing the river a little to the west of Gastuche. Beyond the river were several hundred yards of flat ground which eventually gave rise to thickly wooded steeper ground. With battalion headquarters at La Tombe, C Company was deployed to an outpost line on the high ground east of the river at Les Monts and Les Pres while the remaining three companies took up their positions along the line of the river. Townsend's diary detailed the deployment of the remaining companies:

'A Company on the right had two platoons forward on the railway embankment with one platoon in reserve in the woods … B Company in the centre also had two platoons forward, one on the railway and 10 Platoon on a broken tongue of ground where the river made a loop on the east and then ran away from the woods. This platoon position was even more overlooked than the other by the high ground of Gastuche immediately on the east side of the river. B Company HQ was in the old château with the reserve platoon. The right platoon of D Company had a blockhouse in its area and also covered the road and bridge. The left Platoon of D Company connected with the right company of The Royal Berkshires.'[15]

Their positions were not improved by the poor fields of fire which, in many places, was restricted by the trees and undergrowth making observation from behind the forward positions difficult. Dividing B and D Companies was a minor road – Drève de Laurensart – which crossed the railway line and the river over a narrow wooden bridge, described by Sergeant Martin McLane as 'about fifty yards long, eight yards wide and with ornamental balustrades on either side'. It was this bridge that was to become the focus of attention on 15 May.

The first contact with the German 31st Division came on 14 May on the east bank of the river at the roadblock manned by C Company on the N268. Although Captain Blackett's forward section soon dispersed the approaching armoured vehicles, the remaining German advance guard were able to maintain their observation of the Durhams from the safety of Gastuche from where they directed a hail of machine gun fire onto the forward positions. Private Dusty Miller and his mate George Blackburn from 16 Platoon were in foxholes on either side of the road when C Company withdrew across the wooden bridge. With news of their skirmish with the enemy ringing in his ears Miller was more concerned with making sure he and George Blackburn were not caught up in the blast when the bridge went up. A warning shout from behind was enough to send the two men scurrying back for cover. 'I went hell pelting out and we had just got into position when up went the bridge.'[16]

The 15 May opened with clear skies and a heavy mortar bombardment on the D Company positions at 6.00am during which the company commander, Captain Bill Hutton, was badly wounded. The bombardment quickly enveloped B Company and 10 Platoon, commanded by 24-year-old Second Lieutenant John Hyde-Thompson, came under a sustained attack as did the blockhouse in the nearby D Company sector. Garrisoned by Corporal Matthew Wilson and his section, their resistance collapsed when they ran out of ammunition and, unable to reach them through the heavy German machine-gun fire, the Durhams could only watch as the majority of Wilson's section were cut down attempting to escape. Only two men survived, one of which was Private Leslie Robinson who returned to the blockhouse under fire to retrieve the Bren gun which had been left behind. Originally recommended for the MM, Robinson's bravery was eventually downgraded to a mention in despatches.[17]

A counter-attack by 18 Platoon failed to recover the blockhouse but did manage to close the gap left by Corporal Wilson's section. In the meantime Hyde-Thompson's men were rushed from the cover of the paper mill, the enemy using a small weir to cross the river. Michael Farr's diary recorded the fight that followed:

> 'The bravery of Lt. John Hyde-Thompson was something never to be forgotten. With all his men killed the German officer called him to surrender. John's reply was to pull out his revolver and shoot him dead. He then fought off the attacking Germans singlehanded using grenades. Retreating quickly to another platoon [12 Platoon] on his left he attempted a sudden counter-attack which failed ... His great courage thus checking the advance.'[18]

Hyde-Thompson had in fact held on until 9.00am before he was overrun, earning a MC in the process. He was eventually taken prisoner but his repeated counter-attacks had stalled the German advance long enough for Lieutenant Colonel Robert Simpson to bring up C Company from reserve. Simpson had only been in command since March after Victor Yate had been sent home sick, but as the events of the next thirteen days would prove, he was the ideal replacement.

The situation was now in the balance. German infantry were across the river in front of D Company and were up to the railway embankment on B Company's front. Without immediate action by the Durhams the breach in the line created by this incursion would be exploited and their positions compromised. The Durhams' only possible reply was the counter-attack carried out by C Company at 11.00am; its partial success was observed by Townsend:

> [Platoon Sergeant Major (PSM)] *Ditchburn's platoon on the left had little cover and were almost wiped out by fire from the embankment. They did not succeed in reaching the railway. PSM Pinkey on the right had more cover and succeeded in reaching the railway from whence with 12 Platoon they forced the enemy back by enfilade fire. At this time heavy mortar fire was searching all cover around B Company and more enemy machine guns were firing from the high ground opposite. Captain [Frank] Tubbs was hit and evacuated, Lieutenant [John] Bonham taking over command.'[19]*

Although George Pinkey was later taken prisoner, he would have had some consolation that his award of the DCM was one of the first to be awarded in the campaign. But there is no doubt it had been a costly attack and according to the war diary both C and B Company lost heavily in the face of intense enemy machine-gun fire leaving the dead strewn across the battlefield. C Company's attack had restored the status quo to an extent and despite enemy gains making life difficult for the forward positions, the fire from 11 Platoon from the moated

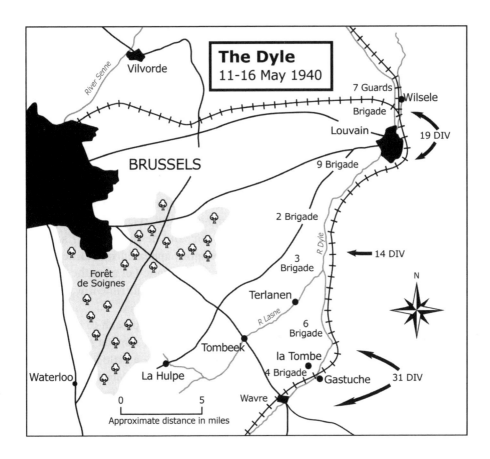

château and the arrival of Captain Anthony Lewis with his company of 1/Royal Welch Fusiliers put paid to any further enemy intentions for the time being.

Townsend's diary also records the action that was taking place on the D Company front, noting that the enemy were attempting to cross the river on the site of the demolished wooden bridge on the left flank. In position immediately in front of the bridge was 16 Platoon, commanded by 26-year-old Second Lieutenant Richard 'Dick' Annand. The Annand family were no strangers to the high personal cost of war. Annand's father, Lieutenant Commander Wallace Annand, had been killed in June 1915 serving with the Collingwood Battalion during the Gallipoli campaign and had Dora Annand known the circumstances in which her only son and his platoon now found themselves, she might well have thrown her hands up in horror.

Before it had been destroyed the wooden bridge had carried the narrow Drève de Laurensart over the river, which flowed at this point between steep muddy banks. German efforts to capture the bridge had so far been prevented by Dick Annand and his platoon, but just before dusk German engineers managed to establish a bridging party in the river bed. It was the beginning of a furious engagement that was recorded in Michael Farr's diary:

> *'The enemy came in great force and might. They ran into the withering fire of Dick's men; into an inferno of bullets; the enemy rolling down like ninepins. The dead and the dying met the same fate, on and on they came, heaps of dead and screaming men. The Hun had become wild and bewildered and could not shake Dick Annand and his men who were fighting with almost unreal guts. On they came again, clambering onto the parapets of the bridge and sliding down the banks.'*[20]

Amongst the defending Durhams was Sergeant Major Norman Metcalf who felt that although 'there must have been thousands of them' the enemy had been 'bumped off like ninepins in bundles of ten'. But despite Metcalf's rather encouraging view of the battle the heavy casualties appeared not to deter the enemy's ambitions regarding the bridge. After a short period of calm the crash of a heavy mortar barrage heralded another German attack, this time it was almost dark when Germans made their next attempt to cross the river.

Dusty Miller recalled German tracer lighting up the approach to the bridge and thought 'the approaching German army looked like a moving field of steel with the lights reflecting off their helmets.' Farr's diary – a little less colourful than Metcalf's account – acknowledges the extraordinary bravery demonstrated by Dick Annand as he 'personally fought off the Germans, throwing [grenades] from the parapet of the bridge'. Three times Annand returned for a further supply of grenades which he carried in a sandbag before he was hit. Finally, Farr tells us, 'came the order to withdraw. Dick brought his men out safely. It was then someone yelled to him that his batman [Private Joseph Hunter] was lying wounded near the bridge.' Miller thinks it was Sergeant O'Neill who alerted Annand to the plight of Joe Hunter, prompting the young lieutenant to return under fire and, despite his own wounds, attempt to bring his batman to safety using a wheelbarrow.[21] Sadly he collapsed from loss of blood before he was able to complete his mission and after being evacuated to the battalion aid post at La Tombe was unable to recall where he had left the unfortunate Hunter who was shortly afterwards taken prisoner. Unlike Joe Hunter, Dick Annand survived the fighting on the Dyle to be presented with the VC by King George V on 3 September 1940 – exactly one year after Great Britain had declared war on Germany.

Up until this point the battalion had been in action for over 24 hours and apart from some localized incursions, had held all the attacks made against it and it must have been with a mixture of relief and regret that Lieutenant Colonel Simpson received the order to retire behind the River Lasne at 11.00pm on 15 May. The Durhams' line had not been broken but events on the right flank in the French First Army sector had opened up a dangerous gap and Blanchard had ordered a retirement to avoid being outflanked. In effect this involved the British I Corps swinging their line back some 6 miles to conform to the French retirement. For the Durhams and the I Corps units dug in along the Dyle their initial surprise was replaced by the realization that the manoeuvre was to be carried out immediately and under the cover of darkness.

Withdrawing from battle positions is hard enough whilst under fire but even more so when the enemy is in close contact. The Durhams had great difficulty in getting away and, despite being supported by the machine guns from C Company of the 2/Manchester Regiment (2/Manchesters), Battalion Headquarters at La Tombe was almost cut off by enemy infantry who had moved forward under cover of darkness. In the fighting withdrawal that ensued, Anthony Lewis and D Company of the Royal Welch Fusiliers also came under fire in what the Manchesters' historian described as the 'entangled zone'.[22] Not only did the Durhams leave behind twenty-seven of their number, who are recorded in the CWGC database as being killed or missing over the three days of fighting on the Dyle, but the hurried departure meant a considerable quantity of stores and equipment was also left behind. Townsend felt that the battalion's labours in digging and sandbagging had been in vain and wrote 'there was not time to send back for the motor transport to come up and take the equipment and stores back. All kit had to be abandoned on the ground.'[23]

Further south at Wavre the fighting had enveloped the 1st Battalion the Royal Scots (1/Royal Scots) and D Company of the Manchesters who were holding the extreme right of the BEF line. Lieutenant Colonel Harold Money had already adjusted his front line to accommodate the withdrawal of the French 13/ *Tirailleurs* to the west bank of the river and on 13 May the 5/Field Company had blown the road bridge in the town after the last unit of the 4/7 Dragoon Guards had crossed. Twenty-four hours later the fighting, although 'firmly repulsed' was severe enough for Captain James Bruce, the battalion adjutant, to record in his diary that 'fairly heavy fighting had taken place on the A and C Company fronts.'

The road bridge at Wavre came under scrutiny again by the 2nd Divisional Engineers who, after receiving conflicting reports as to the state of the bridge, instructed Captain Mark Henniker to visit the site to ensure the structure had been properly demolished. Arriving after dark on 14 May to find 'several buildings were burning and the pavé streets deserted,' he finally found a company of Royal Scots and a sleepy subaltern called Thorburn 'with whom I had been a schoolboy long before, who was prepared to vouch for me'. Lieutenant Pat Hunter-Gordon, the subaltern from 5/Field Company who had been responsible for the first demolition, was of the view that not much more could be done and Henniker was of the same opinion: 'The bridge had leapt into the air from the river bed and returned as a pile of rubble to the river bed again.' The French expression *Faire sauter le pont* (make the bridge jump) exactly describes what happened and all that remained to be done was to make it jump again.

As they waited for the 5/Field Company sappers to arrive Henniker and his escort of Royal Scots were only too aware the Germans were just across the river. The fighting had died down but there were still stray shots ricocheting around the square; ahead of them the river bed was practically dry and the remains of the bridge lay in three pieces. It was a case of who would be the first to arrive, Pat Hunter-Gordon or the German Army:

> *'Just as we began to fix* [the explosives] *in place there was an air raid. Dive bombers, Stukas, made a dead set at the bridge, as though they had the same idea as us. We all dived for cover and several houses in the square collapsed in flames … presently the Stukas departed and Pat led his men back to work. People were popping off rifles and automatics promiscuously from both sides of the river.'*[24]

Eventually, writes Henniker, the bridge was ready for its second demolition and with the sappers safely out of range of falling debris, Hunter-Gordon depressed the exploder handle:

> *'There was a terrific explosion. The wreckage of the bridge jumped into the air. Stones, brickbats and bits of steel whistled all over the town, but the main bulk of the bridge eventually settled back more or less where it had come from, only in much smaller pieces … honour had been satisfied and none of us had been killed.'*[25]

Long after Henniker and the sappers had gone it became obvious to Harold Money that the 13th *Indigène Nord Africaine* Division on his right flank had retired without the courtesy of informing him. After establishing a defensive flank with B Company and the Carrier Platoon, Money received his orders to retire which placed him in a similar position to the Durhams. 'This meant very rapid verbal orders and the destruction of a certain amount of equipment.' Money does not share his thoughts as the battalion marched up the steep hill out of Wavre, preferring to leave James Bruce to write of his disgust at having to leave behind 'such things as 2-inch Mortars, some anti-tank rifles and in one case Bren Guns [which] had to be destroyed and abandoned'.[26] Equipment the battalion would sorely miss in the coming days.

Although the Lasne was a poor substitute for the larger Dyle, the BEF was intact and still full of fighting spirit, their movements now were dictated by a wider strategic picture which had reduced Gamelin's Plan D to ashes and begun to threaten the whole allied campaign. Unbeknown at the time to British commanders was the extent of the German thrust by Army Group A which had struck the French Second Army at Sedan. German infantry advances late on the 13th had hastened a disorganized French retreat, which 24 hours later, had become a rout. By 16 May armoured columns from Army Group A had advanced so rapidly into French territory that momentarily they lost contact with their headquarters because they had gone beyond field radio range.

Gort issued his orders for a general withdrawal to the line of the River Senne on the night of 16 May having first sent Major General Thomas Eastwood to Caudry to learn of General Billotte's intentions.[27] Even so it was several hours later before these orders were in the hands of battalion commanders. The Ulsters' move from Louvain was successfully carried out apparently without alerting the enemy which, given the close proximity of the Bala-Tiger post to the enemy, was quite remarkable. Nevertheless, the enemy must have realized a withdrawal was underway as British gunners loudly announced the tactic by expending their stockpiles of shells before falling back behind the armoured regiments.

The Guards withdrawal from Wilsele was a little more problematic. Their positions were under severe pressure from the enemy, the battalion historian observing that 'the order came as a relief to a battalion holding a position which had already become impossible.' The ground was far more open than further south in Louvain, continually under enemy observation and swept by machine gun fire. However, in small groups and with the protection of carriers the withdrawal was successfully carried out, the last troops of the 1/Coldstream Guards leaving on the vehicles of the Inniskilling Dragoon Guards.

Chapter Three

Towards the Escaut

15–18 May 1940

'The threat of tanks coloured all disposition. Water lines became all important and the obstacles they offered was deemed to outweigh the disadvantages imposed by the awkward alignment of a river and the holding of the forward slopes, portions of which were necessarily commanded from the high ground on the far bank.'

Lieutenant Colonel Charles Ryan, *Royal Artillery Journal*,
October 1943.

The German breakthrough at Sedan on the River Meuse was serious enough for the French Prime Minister Paul Reynaud to wake Winston Churchill at 7.30am on 15 May 1940. Churchill listened gravely as Reynaud told him that France was defeated. That morning, as the German panzer divisions began their breakout from the Meuse bridgehead, a weeping General Alphonse Georges had announced to his chief of staff that 'our front has been broken at Sedan'. Adding to the gloom and despondency that now gripped the French senior command was the surrender of Dutch forces after the bombing of Rotterdam – the first occasion in history that aerial bombing had prompted a national surrender.

Churchill's decision to fly to Paris with Sir John Dill, who was now Deputy CIGS, came a mere five days after he had formed a national coalition government. In Paris General Gamelin told him that German armour had broken through both north and south of Sedan on a 50-mile front and was advancing at incredible speed either towards Amiens and the coast or to Paris itself. Churchill's question as to the whereabouts of the French strategic reserve was met with a shrug from Gamelin – '*Aucun*' he replied (there is none). Churchill admitted to being taken aback by this rather blunt statement but was left with the distinct impression that there were no answers to be had.

While Churchill and Dill were in Paris the 2nd Division was reforming along its new line with 4 Brigade between Genval and Tombeek on the west bank of the River Lasne south-east of Brussels, while the units of 6 Brigade continued the line north-east to Terlaenen. Covering the right flank, which was still exposed to enemy incursion, were the three battalions of 5 Brigade positioned between Genval and Hanonsart. Fortunately the Germans did not follow the withdrawal too closely, only coming into contact on the morning of 16 May after announcing their arrival with artillery fire. But there was to be no fighting stand here as orders were soon received for a further withdrawal – this time to the line of the River Dendre, passing, en-route, through the 48th Division which had been brought forward in support.

The 48th Division – commanded by Major General Andrew 'Bulgy' Thorne – moved up towards the Dyle late on 13 May and after travelling all night were east of Hal by the next morning. The 2/Royal Warwicks of 144 Brigade were expecting to stand and fight in the Waterloo area and having made a reconnaissance of the ground in preparation for the battalion's move forward, Captain Dick Tomes, the battalion adjutant, was surprised to receive orders for an immediate move to Ohain Wood, 2 miles south west of Genval:

'We were told to withdraw to a ridge a mile behind us and hold it while the 2nd Division withdrew through us. I read the order and handed it to the CO. He remarked, "Dick, remember this day – 16 May. It will go down in history as the day on which another classic strategic withdrawal of the British Army began." I did not believe him at the time.'[1]

Lieutenant Colonel Piers Dunn's assessment of the situation may have come as a shock to Tomes, but to an old soldier like Dunn the rumours of an enemy breakthrough and the crumbling of the French line south of Wavre were classic signs that the chaos of retreat was not far away. It was a situation which he had seen before during the great German offensive of March 1918 and was certainly one which Lieutenant Colonel Ernest Whitfeld, commanding the 1/Ox and Bucks, would have recognised. Like Dunn he had been through most of the previous war and had won the MC in May 1915. The 43rd – as 1/Ox and Bucks liked to call themselves – were bivouacked in the woods north of Alsemberg where they were placed under the temporary command of the 2nd Division and ordered to move to the Hippodrome Racecourse in the centre of the Forêt de Soignes. Here they formed a check line with units of 5 Brigade along the line of the main road running south-east through the forest and awaited the appearance of German infantry.

Although they were never in direct contact with the enemy, the next morning they came under repeated air attack during which 'the tremendous scream from at least one diving machine' was enough to send the troops on the ground scurrying for shelter. For many this was their first introduction to the Junkers 87 Stuka dive bomber as they 'dropped like cormorants from about four thousand feet to within a few feet of the ground with an ear piercing scream'.[2]

The 2nd Division units which withdrew through the forest found the going difficult, their progress hindered by the inaccuracy of the maps they had been issued with resulting in brigade columns becoming mixed up and disorientated by the numerous tracks and paths in the forest. When the River Senne was eventually reached, the crossing points were blocked by a mass of terror-stricken refugees. 'It was', wrote Captain Edward Woolsey of 2/Manchesters, 'useless to attempt to force them out of the way, for we knew the column was twenty miles long and more.'

Rumours of a disaster along the French line had already been circulating amongst the staff of 145 Brigade as they crossed the Senne at Hal on 15 May. The 2/Gloucesters, under the command of Lieutenant Colonel Hon Nigel Somerset, continued to Alsemberg where they billeted on the ridge overlooking the town. It was to be Nigel Somerset's last day as commanding officer – an unexpected summons to brigade headquarters the next day resulted in his promotion to brigade command in place of Brigadier Archie Hughes, who joined the ranks of those elderly senior officers who were not up to the rigours of battlefield leadership. Somerset's return to the battalion not only confirmed Major Maurice Gilmore as commanding officer but corroborated the disturbing rumours that all was not well on the right flank of the Dyle. The not unexpected warning that a move was imminent to support the 2nd Division arrived shortly afterwards.

Captain Eric Jones remembered the order to move east was given at 11.00pm on 15 May, almost exactly the time that orders were received by the 2nd Division units to withdraw from the Dyle. 'The CO issued his orders – verbal. The battalion was to move to Joli Bois, 2 miles south of Waterloo by march route, and be in position by 7.00am, 16 May.' Jones recalls everything was in a state of flux when they arrived, no one knew if they were to remain there for long or whether a further move to the Forêt de Soignes was imminent. In the event A Company, which included Jones, was sent off to Waterloo to hold the eastern edge of the village and the battalion dispersed around Joli Bois.

The Gloucesters' front was so extensive that D Company of 1/Buckinghamshire Battalion was lent to the Gloucesters and C Company moved to the east side of Roussart. B Company occupied a large building complex known as *Les Six Maisons*, a building that can still be seen today on the N5b running south from Belle-Vue to Joli Bois. According to the war diary A Company were deployed to the west of the stone bridge at Waterloo where they were joined by the two batteries of 68/Field Regiment which established their headquarters in the luxurious Château d'Argenteuil along with Nigel Somerset and 145 Brigade. The war diary reported air attacks by Junkers 87 aircraft continuing through the day and the Gloucesters lost their first man that afternoon: Private Arthur Hammond killed by a bomb splinter.[3]

Lance Corporal Turner and his company of 4/Ox and Bucks found themselves in a small farm on 'the edge of a large wood'. Turner's account unfortunately lacks detail but he was probably east of Waterloo on the edge of the Forêt de Soignes where they came under air attack:

'I heard a drone in the sky and saw fifty German aircraft approaching in perfect formation, bombers in the centre with waves of fighter escort neatly dispersed in a protective screen. The aircraft passed to the right but soon returned with a vengeance. A very liberal supply of bombs was let loose and I felt anxious about the reserve ammunition.'[4]

Turner recalled that they soon came under attack from infantry before withdrawing to a small wood 3 miles to the west where there was a large country mansion. Here the battalion was shelled, the German gunners plastering 'the area of the country mansion with heavy shells and the margin by which we escaped their concussion and splinters must have been quite small.'

German advance units were certainly in evidence around the Waterloo area from late on 16 May and by early the next day had advanced in places up to the line of the railway. Although an attack was not immediately forthcoming, intelligence provided by the 12/Lancers patrols suggested to Lieutenant Colonel Lumsden that it was just a matter of time before a major effort would come from the build up of enemy forces in the southern corner of the Forêt de Soignes. As a result Lumsden instructed the bridges spanning the railway in his sector to be prepared for demolition. At Waterloo Lieutenant Smith and his detachment of Sappers from 101/Field Company began work on the stone bridge which crossed the railway line west of Waterloo. Smith's work that night was just beginning and still under random enemy fire he moved up the railway line to a second bridge that Sergeant Earl was working on. Earl had already laid the charges when Smith arrived with Lance Corporal Hourigan and Driver Roach. Pushing their way through the volume of retreating troops and civilian refugees, Smith decided to leave the bridge intact for the time being and moved up to the level crossing further north:

'Fortunately in this instance there were two very conveniently sited manholes, one each side of the crossing, and the charges were laid in these. L/Sgt Earl now returned to his bridge to await instructions to fire and [I] remained at the level crossing … In the early hours of the morning [17 May] the Germans tested the front at several points such as Waterloo and Braine l'Alleud, but [were] met at all points by our fire and withheld further attacks until [they were] able to make a large scale effort. Later in the morning, as soon as the British troops had withdrawn, the prepared demolitions were fired and the detachment withdrew with the 12/Lancers.'[5]

There is little doubt that there was considerable confusion as the 48th Division units deployed in and around the Forêt de Soignes. If Smith's recollections of the dates are accurate, then the German attacks on the 48th Division units on 16 May could only mean that they had already penetrated the tenuous British line. At Rixensart, some 8 miles to the east of Waterloo, two troops of C Squadron,

4/7 Royal Dragoon Guards with their Mark VIb light tanks were in action during the afternoon of 16 May on both flanks of the village. Reinforced by A Squadron the engagement was broken off with no casualties or vehicles lost but for a short time the war diary described the situation as 'unhealthy'. We also know that the 1/Ox and Bucks did not finally leave the Forêt de Soignes until early on 17 May by which time the Gloucesters – and presumably the 1/Buckinghams – were already under attack at Waterloo. Fortunately these attacks were not followed up in any great force and were fairly easily beaten off but they did indicate the degree to which the British line had been penetrated.

The 145 Brigade withdrawal began at 10.00pm on 16 May although it was after 8.00am on 17 May before Captain Bill Wilson and B Company of the Gloucesters arrived at Waterloo where they were greeted by an unseen enemy: 'We pushed on to the railway line running north, approaching which we were fired on from both sides.' Wilson and his men crossed the Senne by the Hal bridge 'just before it was blown'.[6] Presuming the diary account written by Second Lieutenant Wallis is correct, the whole of 145 Brigade was across the Senne at Hal by that afternoon. On two occasions during the march from Waterloo to Alsemberg the 4/Ox and Bucks reported being machine gunned by enemy aircraft, Turner recalling vividly 'the thud of machine gun bullets which entered the earth near my head. The holes in the ground were easily traceable when I got up.' Fortunately for Turner and his men there were very few casualties.[7]

Michael Duncan's memories of the withdrawal with the 4/Ox and Bucks to the Dendre were shrouded in a haze of exhaustion. 'Most of us were already drugged almost to a coma by lack of food and sleep and I remember the withdrawal as a series of vivid, but disjointed, pictures.' His fears for the wounded from the skirmish at Waterloo being pushed along in wheelbarrows and the dusty, sun-scorched road to Hal and Enghien were only eased when he crossed the river at Ath where the bridges were blown behind them.[8]

∽

Further north on the night of 16 May, the 1st Division units were withdrawing from the Dyle. The 3/Grenadier Guards were covering the departure of 3 Infantry Brigade and after seeing them across the Lasne, blew the bridges behind them:

'It was a nervous business, as the enemy were close on the heels of the 3rd Brigade and well forward on the battalion's right flank. At 11.50pm the forward companies began to thin out and successfully broke contact with the enemy after an exchange of a few shots in the darkness. The bridge at Huldenberg was blown up on schedule, and the battalion tramped back to the Forest of Soignes, to be greeted by a swelling chorus of nightingales. The commander of the 3rd Brigade, recorded Major [Allan] Adair, almost wept with relief when I reported that the battalion was safely away.'[9]

At the same time as Major General George Alexander's 1st Division units were leaving the Dyle valley the 3rd Division was leaving Louvain and heading towards Brussels. In 7 Guards Brigade 2/Grenadier Guards were detailed as rearguard and were waiting on the Brussels-Louvain road to check the units through. The withdrawal from the Guards' positions north of Louvain had been difficult and it was with some anxiety that Major Rupert Colvin, second-in-command of the battalion, waited for the Coldstream to arrive:

> '*It was a queer experience as one did not know if the first arrivals would be Guardsmen or Germans. I had two lambs with me who bleated pathetically, and all sorts of other animals turned up looking for a saviour who could give them food and water. The men were all tired and out of two Coldstream companies which had born the brunt of the fighting, no more than one officer and sixty-three men survived.*'[10]

In the event, Colvin's fears were unfounded. Captain Dick Walker, the 3rd Division RE adjutant, put the failure of any serious German opposition to the British withdrawal from Louvain down to the cratering of roads, which was carried out across the city. Walker does not give any further details but without doubt the delaying effect of the demolitions was very marked and the enemy almost completely lost touch with the rearguards during the night of 16 May as the 3rd Division approached Brussels.

But just as there was further south, a general and very disagreeable air of disappointment shrouded the retiring BEF. When the orders reached Lieutenant Colonel Lionel Bootle-Wilbraham at the 2/Coldstream Guards Headquarters his reaction was one of exasperation. Having witnessed the British Third Army's retreat in March 1918, whilst serving as adjutant of the 4th Battalion, his sardonic remark to Captain Roddy Hill, that the campaign was starting 'in the traditional British manner, with a retreat,' disguised his real concern as to what the next few days would bring. Giving orders for the battalion to begin the 17-mile march to Brussels, it crossed the Senne at Ruysbroeck, reaching Zuen just as day was breaking. The 44-year-old Bootle-Wilbraham lost little time in deploying his men:

> '*Nos 1, 2 and 3 Companies were on the line of the canal, while 4 Company was in reserve near Battalion Headquarters. There was a double obstacle on our front, where the River Senne ran to the east of the canal. In our area there were seven bridges to be prepared for demolition. The men were in good heart and showed no signs of weariness … A constant flow of refugee traffic over the bridges made it difficult to decide exactly when to blow them up. One could never be sure there were no British troops on the wrong side of the river. However, by 5.00pm the bridges were blown.*'[11]

Second Lieutenant Hugh Taylor had some difficulty explaining to his men of 7 Platoon that the Suffolks were withdrawing along with the rest of the 3rd

Division and to make matters worse, they would be getting no sleep that night. Taylor described the march to the outskirts of Brussels as one he would 'never forget'. Already exhausted, the monotony of the straight, dusty roads was only broken by bully beef and biscuits and the continual stream of refugees which accompanied them:

> '*About midday we reached Brussels where there were obvious signs of war. Machine gun marks could be seen across some of the houses, bomb craters had to be negotiated. And windows were broken by the dozen, in fact, as one walked along the road it was difficult to stop slipping on the broken glass. Here and there was a house completely demolished by a bomb and people looking for their belongings in the ruins. As we got further on, the roads became narrower and the inhabitants looked out of their doors and windows to watch us go past ... They seemed incredulous about our tales of the approach of the Germans, they laughed and said, why then were we retreating? We comforted them by telling them there were more of us behind and that the Germans were some way off yet, though we knew they were only twelve miles away.*'[12]

But there was to be no rest along the line of the Senne which, for the retreating British units, was only the first stage of three which would eventually see them fighting on the line of the River Escaut. The 2/Coldstream hardly had time to draw breath before fresh orders sent them towards Ninvove on the River Dendre. Arriving at 10.00am on Saturday 18 May the battalion at least had some rest before Bootle-Wilbraham received yet more orders to move to Pecq on the Escaut:

> '*I remember being appalled at the idea of withdrawing by daylight across the bare face of the hill under enemy observation ... My problem was to decide how best to withdraw over the open fields of a convex hill. It seemed likely that the enemy would be on the river* [Dendre] *by first light. The alternative was to slip away to a flank under cover of some trees and a village that was in the Hampshires' area.*'[13]

At 8.00am on 19 May the battalion moved quickly through Eychen and Bootle-Wilbraham confessed to being highly relieved when the withdrawal was completed successfully with the loss of only one man who was a victim of German air activity.[14]

The 2/Hampshires abandoned their positions on the Senne at midnight on 17 May and marched the 20 miles back to Ninvove deploying along the west bank of the canal where they were subjected to a violent mortar and machine-gun attack from across the water. Holding their positions all night in the expectation of an enemy attack, they finally abandoned the canal the next morning and marched to Nederbrakel where Ben Duncan and his mates found transport was waiting for them:

'The journey was long and tedious and made more so by the condition of the roads. The crowds of civilians that were packed on the road constantly held us up. Also the result of enemy bombing was very much in evidence. Horses lying by the side of the road and in some instances almost blocking it, their innards hanging out; small children sitting crying beside the torn bodies of their parents and too young to know how to fend for themselves.'[15]

The 4th Division had some trouble breaking clear of the enemy on the night of 17/18 May with 10 and 11 Brigades fighting hard to hold off advancing infantry units. Detailed as rearguard, the 15/19 King's Hussars were ordered to hold their positions west of Brussels until early on 18 May to allow 10 Brigade to retire through their lines. It was at 8.45am that permission was given for the regiment to move back to Assche and the first hint of 'trouble' – heard by C Squadron – was the unmistakeable sound of tracked vehicles coming from the direction of the main road from Vilvorde. Having failed to get in touch with the Belgian 5th Division, which was thought to be retiring north of Merchtem, it quickly dawned on Major Sir Henry Floyd, commanding C Squadron, just who was driving the tracked vehicles. Unbeknown to the British the Belgians were by now safely on the Dendre and the northern flank was wide open; circumstances the Germans were quick to exploit. The full extent of the German advance was discovered almost inadvertently by a patrol from the 5/Inniskilling Dragoon Guards who found Assche in German hands. It was in Assche that some of the most desperate fighting took place as four troops of A Squadron attempted to force their way through the town:

'As Squadron Headquarters entered the town, Major Frith's tank was destroyed by an anti-tank gun and he and his crew were killed. The rest of the force, under Captain Mytton, then tried to force a way through Assche and after twenty minutes' street fighting they succeeded in retaking nearly half the town and in reaching 4th Troop. By now every AFV of this force had been knocked out and the fighting developed into individual actions by small bodies of survivors. By the end Major Frith and his crew were all killed, Captain Mytton and SSM Laing were wounded and taken prisoner, and the main body of the Squadron was outnumbered and surrounded.'[16]

Major Colin Cokayne-Frith managed to warn the remaining squadrons that he was surrounded before he and his crew were knocked out but the regiment, in the words of Second Lieutenant Guy Courage, 'never stood a chance'. The 40-year-old Cokayne-Frith was the most senior officer of the regiment to be killed that day. He had served with Guy Courage's father in the 15/Hussars during the First World War and had celebrated the end of hostilities in November 1918 only 40 miles or so to the southeast of the town in which he lost his life.

Ordered to split up and break out in groups by the second-in command, Major 'Loony' Hinde – who himself was wounded and forced to swim the Dendre in order to return to British lines – the Hussars fought a very one-sided battle against German mobile infantry armed with the *Panzerabwehrkanone* (Pak) 36 anti-tank gun against which the lightly armoured vehicles of the 15/19 King's Hussars stood little chance. The commanding officer, Lieutenant Colonel Donald Frazer and the French liaison officer managed to evade capture for 24 hours before being taken prisoner. Of the reported 157 casualties, 21 officers and men were killed in action or died of wounds over the next twenty-four hours and that evening, as the remnants of the regiment gathered in a field at Alost, they could barely put together one squadron and were subsequently reorganized into a composite squadron under the command of Major Sir Henry Floyd. One remarkable episode involving Captain Anthony Taylor, the regimental adjutant, saw him escape from his German captors – he would be captured again on two further occasions and escape again – to finally reach Le Touquet on 5 June 1940 where he set sail and was picked up by the Royal Navy off the French coast. His award of the MC was well deserved.[17]

~

The I Corps retreat continued unabated and by nightfall on 17 May, 4 and 5 Brigades of the 2nd Division had reached the line of the Dendre where they were met by the welcome sight of transport. Not so fortunate were the men of 6 Brigade whose transport failed to materialise giving the luckless battalions little choice but to continue on foot. The exhaustion of these men who had fought so hard on the Dyle and had marched almost continuously since leaving their valley positions on 15 May was experienced by Michael Farr who was footslogging along with the Durhams:

'*The remnants marched on; it seemed about 35 miles in 48 hours. The men had become so tired, some were falling asleep on the march and it was difficult to get them on the march again. Each man carried his Lee Enfield .303 rifle (this was over 8lbs in weight), his gas mask, haversack, mess tin and water bottle, and of course, steel helmet. We marched on by day and by night. The troop-carrying vehicles which were supposed to lift us never arrived. We were now just four groups of 100 men. A half strength battalion, not properly organised either due to the sudden withdrawal.*'[18]

Farr failed to mention the additional weight of Bren guns and Boys anti-tank rifles which the Durhams clung to determinedly.[19] Captain Cyril Townsend recalls the battalion reaching Gammerages at dawn on 18 May and his estimation of the distance marched – 48 miles in 48 hours – is probably more accurate. Here the battalion finally fell into the waiting trucks and crossed the Dendre at Grammont to be off-loaded at Ogy. 'No one', wrote Townsend, 'quite knew how close the enemy was and how much the troops behind had delayed their advance.'

When the 2nd Division reached the Dendre orders were given that the line of the river should be held between Grammont and Lessines with the 48th Division holding the river below the latter settlement. Yet despite the urgency, Grammont – the key to the whole position – was undefended for several hours apart from a few section outposts manned by the 2/Royal Norfolks. In fact it was not until late that evening that troops arrived to hold the town. The Norfolks' war diary for 18 May notes wryly that 'there was a certain amount of excitement' at 7.00pm that evening when contact with the enemy was established. With no relief in sight, orders were just about to be sent out to companies to extend their frontage to include Grammont. Fortunately the Cameron Highlanders turned up at about 10.00pm allowing the Norfolks to hold fast in the positions they had already taken up. One can only guess the content and quantity of the 'banter' dished out to the newly-arrived Scotsmen by the weary wags in the ranks of the Norfolks.

But the story does not end there. It wasn't until the early hours of 19 May that Lieutenant Colonel Lumsden was summoned to the church at Ghoy where Brigadier Ian Gartland, commanding 5 Infantry Brigade, explained that all attempts to inform the Grammont garrison of the withdrawal had failed and requested Lumsden's help. With enemy infantry already in the wooded area to south of Grammont, Lumsden's men, together with a squadron of 13/18 Hussars, moved quickly to provide the necessary rearguard to allow all troops in the town to break contact with the Germans. Despite drawing a heavy fire onto his command Lumsden finally reported to Gartland that all troops were clear of Grammont by 12.05pm.

At Ath there was what Captain Mark Henniker called a hiccup over the demolition of the bridge north of the town. Apparently no one at 2nd Divisional R E Headquarters was sure that arrangements had been made to blow the bridge and Henniker was sent to ensure all was in order. Arriving at Ath he located the bridge a mile north of the town:

'The bridge was visible a few hundred yards down the road and it occurred to me that it might be on the point of demolition with the defenders taking cover to avoid the falling debris. I looked anxiously for some cover for myself and saw, to my relief, an armoured car from the Divisional Cavalry Regiment, the 4/7th Dragoon Guards. Sitting in a deck chair was the CO of the regiment. He was reading The Times *with a teacup in the other hand. He was a man of medium build, I should think in the mid-forties. His cap was pushed back and a pair of earphones were resting loosely around his neck … He was in fact the embodiment of a cavalry officer of the old school – perhaps a bit of a blimp.'*[20]

The 44-year-old Lieutenant Colonel Lawrence Misa was anything but a blimp. A veteran of the previous war, the calm exterior which so impressed Henniker belied the anxiety he was feeling for his regiment which was fighting hard against advancing enemy infantry between Ath and Lessines. Having reached the Dendre on 17 May the Dragoons were ordered to hold the river line until midday on 19th to allow the 48th Division time to withdraw.

Misa had deployed his squadrons along the 6 miles of the canalised Dendre between Ath and Lessines. Contact with the enemy was first reported at 8.45am that morning and B Squadron was soon in action against an 'enemy [who] kept on approaching the opposite bank of the canal in parties of 12 and 14 and attempted to inflate and launch rubber pontoons'. Finding no lack of targets the Hussars foiled further German attempts to cross the water. At 11.30am 3 Troop was pinned down by enemy machine-gun fire with Lieutenant Denis Atkinson and Corporal Edmundson still on an island in the middle of the canal. Unable to return, it was left to the bravery of Trooper Albert Argyle to paddle a boat across to the two men and bring them to safety. Argyle was awarded the MM but died later in the morning of wounds gained during his feat and Denis Atkinson was last seen in his carrier 'going over a fence and across a cropped field under heavy fire'. Those of his troop who were not killed were taken prisoner.[21]

The German assault across the canal was also being countered by A Squadron which, reinforced by a company of Cheshires machine gunners and a battery of anti-tank guns, was inflicting 'heavy casualties' on the enemy. The squadron diary recording a variety of targets which included infantry, cavalry patrols, artillery and rubber boats. At Lessines C Squadron were having 'a very sticky time with the Germans trying to enter the town by a bridge which was only partly blown and also working around the flank'. By 10.00am 3 Troop in particular was under severe pressure but despite reporting being 'harried considerably by 5th Column activities' still managed to put the weapon and crew of a German anti-tank gun out of action. Lieutenant Ian Gill was later awarded the MC whilst Trooper Alfred Charman received the MM for their part in 3 Troop's defence of Lessines.

It was at around this point in the battle that Henniker arrived at Ath to hear from Lawrence Misa that there was still a troop of his armoured cars on the far side of the canal and he was waiting for them to arrive. Sharing a cup of tea with the colonel 'which a trooper brought on a tray', Henniker quite rightly wondered for a second time that week if the Germans would arrive first:

'The CO was speaking to his rearguard troop commander, who told him there were some enemy in sight. The Colonel replied on his wireless; well you had better drive them away … Soon, however, the armoured cars started retreating over the bridge and the young officer in command waved cheerfully to us, saying he would tell the CO that he had got all the troops to our side of the river.'[22]

The bridge was blown with a deafening crash and 'the entire bridge sprang into the air', leaving a very happy Henniker to report to his headquarters and a much relieved Lawrence Misa to continue the retreat to the Escaut.

Meanwhile 2/Gloucesters were withdrawing towards Tournai when their convoy of lorried transport was held up by traffic congestion at Leuze. According to Captain Eric Jones the chaos was caused by the sheer volume of traffic. 'Vehicles were three and four abreast whenever the road permitted; pavements were driven along; drivers became separated from their columns, then anxious to rejoin them.'[23] Finally the Gloucesters' convoy got clear of the town and left the main Tournai road towards Ramecroix where they turned left for Bruyelle. At Ramecroix they met yet more traffic congestion which Jones says forced the drivers to decrease the gap between each vehicle in order not to become separated from the column. It was an error that was to cost the battalion dearly. There is no record of what first drew Captain Wilkinson's attention to the low flying aircraft but it was probably the drone of aircraft engines:

> *'I saw nine bombers at low level coming over our position, and had just decided that they were enemy aeroplanes and ordered the AA Bren in the truck behind me to fire, when the bombs started dropping. This was followed by machine-gun fire. An ammunition truck went up near me, and bombs seemed to explode on part of A Company, who were just behind me.'*[24]

Eric Jones' account points to the battalion being caught completely by surprise as the first three aircraft scored direct hits on five lorries, two of which were troop-carrying vehicles. Wilkinson was badly injured in the chest and arm and the road was completely blocked by blazing trucks, a situation rendered far more dangerous by exploding ammunition. Captain Bill Wilson, commanding B Company, felt the attack was the inevitable result of travelling in daylight: 'There was poor cover,' he wrote, 'for we were now in a village and no ditches on the road, but it was all there was.'

Unfortunately the accuracy of the casualty returns for this incident remains unclear. The war diary records 70 men killed, wounded or missing, David Scott Daniell in *Cap of Honour* writes that 194 men of the battalion were killed or wounded and the CWGC database identifies only 23 men of the 2nd Battalion recorded as being killed on 19 May, but has another three recorded as dying of wounds over the next two days. These figures do not take into account the unidentified that were either too badly burned or killed in the initial explosions.[25]

The BEF was now grouping on the Escaut, along a line running from Oudenaarde to Bléhairies but before examining the BEF's defence of the Escaut in more detail the focus must shift south, to the old Somme battlefields of the First World War, where the Territorial battalions of the 12th and 23rd Divisions were about to collide with Heinz Guderian's crack XIX *Panzer Korps*.

Chapter Four

Massacre of the Innocents

19–20 May 1940

'I lay doggo hoping that if night fell soon enough I might creep quietly away. This was not to be as I was finally rolled over by a German, who seemed to be making a very thorough job of examining the wounded. I think I managed a very sickly smile, rather like a small boy caught cheating at school and was promptly confronted by a large revolver.'

L/Cpl Wilson, A Company, 7/Royal Sussex at Amiens.

French Prime Minister Paul Reynaud's admission of defeat on 15 May was a devastating blow to the British. French high command was in turmoil, the Ninth Army's demise at Sedan had reduced General Georges to tears and still the German Army Group A was driving west from the Meuse, apparently without opposition. Adding to the weight of depression dogging the headquarters of French supreme commander General Gamelin was the news that Holland had surrendered on 15 May after the bombing of Rotterdam had shattered the will of the Dutch to resist. As Churchill and Dill left Paris after their meeting with Reynaud and Gamelin they had no accurate intelligence of the exact whereabouts of the German panzer divisions but at the Cabinet meeting later that day, the British government – probably for the first time – faced the realistic prospect that France was on the edge of defeat and Britain must either go down with her ally or withdraw and fight on alone. Indeed, as early as 17 May the Admiralty was asked to examine the logistics of assembling small boats in case an evacuation from the Channel beaches became necessary.

The German panzer advance was taking them not towards Paris as first suspected but due west – towards the coast. On 16 May the leading tanks of Heinz Guderian's XIX Korps covered 40 miles, reaching the River Oise at Guise, while on his right flank, Erwin Rommel's 7 Panzer Division was within sight of Le Cateau by dawn the next morning. The 17 May saw the first of the German 'Halt Orders' issued to the panzer divisions. Although short in duration it underlined Von Rundstedt's concern as to the vulnerability of his open southern flank and the rapidly extending supply lines that were becoming increasingly challenging. The order, which was lifted the next morning, aggravated an already impatient Guderian who threatened resignation if he was not allowed to continue his advance.

To the south General Georges was desperately attempting to assemble a new army corps to counter the threat from Army Group A that, together with a concerted effort from the north, would pinch out the panzer spearhead – assuming of course the necessary troops could be found. But it was far too late for Gamelin, who was replaced on 19 May by the 73-year-old General Maxime Weygand, the same day that Henri Giraud, the recently appointed commander of the French Seventh Army was captured.[1] Meanwhile seven panzer divisions were establishing themselves on the west bank of the Canal du Nord and the only BEF troops that stood between them and the sea were the British 12th and 23rd Divisions.

Private Bert Jones and the 5th Battalion Royal East Kent Regiment (5/Buffs) arrived in France on 20 April 1940. Jones writes with some optimism that their move to Fleury in Normandy would see them beginning their training with 36 Brigade, but if he and his comrades in B Company were expecting to be trained as soldiers they were to be disappointed. Numbered amongst the so-called digging divisions, the 12th Division was put to work building railway sidings around Rouen and developing the Abancourt rail centre.

The 23rd Division was detailed to begin work on airfields around St Pol and Béthune and serving with 1/Tyneside Scottish in 70 Brigade was 18-year-old Private James Laidler who began his army career at Newcastle on 15 March 1940. After a period of basic training the battalion moved to France and young 'Jim' found himself at Frévent north of Doullens 'employed in building an airfield, carrying bags of cement, mixing cement, anything except soldiering'.[2] Further south the 46th Division – a duplicate of the 49th (West Riding) Division – was dispatched to Brittany to begin similar tasks around Nantes and St Nazaire. Private Peter Walker joined 137 Brigade in May 1939 and 'having coughed for the MO' signed up for service in the 2/7 Duke of Wellington's Regiment. Within weeks he had been promoted to corporal and in August experienced his first live firing practice. His remaining training consisted of 'marching around Halifax, doing foot and bayonet drill with and without gas masks'. Nine days after 19-year-old Bert Jones first set foot in France, Peter Walker landed at Cherbourg where his battalion was transported to Blain near Nantes to begin work as loaders for the RASC.[3]

As far as military training was concerned each man had a rifle and bayonet but any heavier weapons, such as Bren guns and the Boys anti-tank rifle, had in some cases, not been issued and even if issued, they had certainly not been fired by the majority, even in practice. It was a situation that prompted General 'Tiny' Ironside to seek assurance from Gort that these men would not be deployed in an operational role until they had at least been issued with their full entitlement of equipment. But as British plans were rapidly overtaken by the speed of the

German advance, these early assurances were quickly forgotten as almost every available man was thrown into the front line.

On 12 May Gort's headquarters received a call from Major General Henry Curtis, commanding the 46th Division, offering his division as a battle-ready formation ready and able to take its place in the line. Incredibly this ridiculous assertion resulted a week later in the division being the first to be called to the front line and incorporated in 'Macforce', a formation being put together under the command of Major General Mason-Macfarlane to protect the rear of the

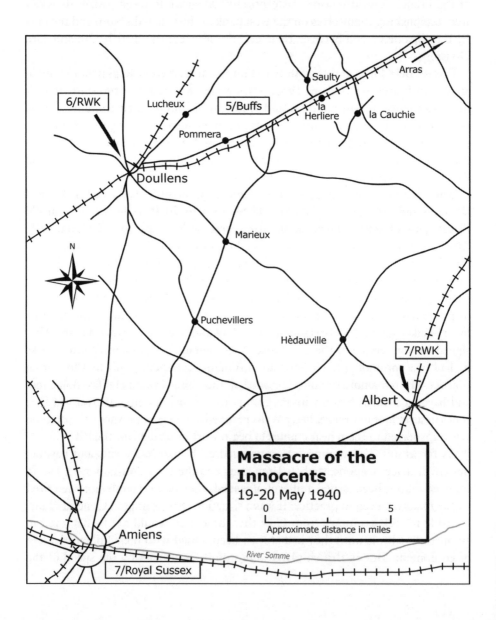

BEF. Perhaps of greater significance was the 23rd Division's move to the line of the Canal du Nord on the instructions of General Georges, an unexpected deployment that Gregory Blaxland felt came 'as a great shock to the senior General Staff Officer at Arras, Lieutenant Colonel Robert Bridgeman'. The fact that British troops were needed in this French sector was the first indication to British staff officers that Georges had, quite simply, insufficient fighting troops to contain the German breakthrough. Lacking the most basic fighting equipment, the largely untrained 23rd Division was hardly in a position to prevent the German armoured advance even now bearing down on them, particularly as most of the promised French troops failed to arrive.

The movements of the 12th Division were not helped by the absence of their divisional commander, Major General Roderick Petre, who had been summoned to Arras on 18 May to take command of the Arras garrison. Failing to inform the 12th Division that Petre was now commanding 'Petreforce', leaving it virtually leaderless, was just one example of a patchwork of ineptitude on the part of the Adjutant-General, Lieutenant General Sir Douglas Brownrigg, commanding BEF (Rear) GHQ at Arras. His ineptitude was to seal the fate of six of the division's battalions.

By the evening of 18 May the German 1st Panzer Division had reached the Canal du Nord and occupied Péronne where it was engaged by 7/Royal West Kents (RWK) from 36 Brigade which had been reinforced with four 18-pounder field guns cobbled together from the Royal Artillery School of Instruction. Twenty-four hours later the 7th Panzer Division had surrounded Cambrai and was approaching Marquion on the Cambrai-Arras road. As the 8th and 6th Panzer Divisions advanced either side of the Cambrai-Bapaume road towards Inchy-en-Artois and Beaumetz les Cambrai, the 1st Panzer Division was forming a bridgehead over the Canal du Nord at Péronne forcing the 23rd Division to fall back. Kirkup's 70 Brigade fell back along a 17-mile frontage astride the Arras-Cambrai road and 69 Brigade were ordered to take up positions along the River Scarpe, east of Arras.

Further south six of the Territorial battalions of the 12th Division were scattered across a wide area which took in part of the old Somme battlefields of 1916. The 6/RWK were strung out along the N29 Doullens-Arras road while the 7/RWK were in the vicinity of Albert. Of the two Royal Sussex battalions in 37 Brigade, the 7th was stranded in Amiens after the train which had been carrying it had been destroyed by enemy aircraft and the 6th was intact but completely isolated at Ailly-sur-Noye – more of which later.

The 7/RWK arrived at Albert in the early hours of 19 May with instructions to take up positions in the town using the River Ancre as an anti-tank obstacle. It was a locality that failed to impress 44-year-old Lieutenant Colonel Basil Clay who felt it was impossible to take up a position along the river as instructed 'as it was merely a ditch in parts and subterranean in the town'. Reacting to Brigadier

George Roupell's assurance that there were no German forces in the vicinity, Clay moved the battalion to the safety of the high ground northwest of Albert. The move was a short one, curt instructions arrived from Arras at 1.30am on 20 May ordering the battalion back to Albert to 'hold the position with a view to defence against AFVs'.

As Guderian's tanks crossed the Canal du Nord early on 20 May, Clay's men in Albert were being subjected to an attack by enemy aircraft machine gunning the town. Hardly had the smoke and debris of that attack cleared when a German motorcyclist made an appearance on 8 Platoon's front. Shot at by Sergeant Hill the enemy presence vanished in a hail of fire, but to an old soldier like Clay, who was fighting with the RWK in his second war, the motorcyclist was all the evidence he needed of an imminent attack. With a distinct premonition of trouble he began to issue his orders for the defence of the town.

Another officer who felt uneasy was Captain George Newbery commanding A Company. With hardly enough time to get his company in position on the eastern edge of the town, the arrival of General Friedrich Kirchner's 1st Panzer Division was announced by a runner from 7 Platoon bringing news of 30 enemy tanks advancing from the direction of Meaulte:

> *'I passed the information onto Battalion HQ but before I had a reply, a message arrived from 8 Platoon that twenty tanks were on their front. I looked into the market square to see if the CO was there and found him near the corner. I gave him the information. I cannot remember his reply as an enemy plane swooped on us at that moment. As we took cover an enemy tank entered the square behind us and firing broke out in all directions.'*[4]

It was 6.00am and Basil Clay's men were all but surrounded: British plans for the defence of Albert were in tatters before the battle had even begun. The opening attack from the south-east fell on D Company whose positions were on the left of the town. It was a brutal engagement in which Captain Edward Hill, the company commander, was killed before the remainder of the company took refuge in a nearby building, defending themselves until the survivors were forced to surrender. As the fighting became more desperate Clay sent out orders for the battalion to withdraw to the transport in the main square – but it was too late for many of the West Kents as enemy tanks burst through their positions demonstrating the absurdity of using Bren guns and rifles to repel an armoured assault.

Those who did manage to reach the transport were instructed to fight their way out and rendezvous at Bouzincourt but very few actually got away. It was in the main square that Second Lieutenant Michael Archer was seen firing a Boys anti-tank rifle under heavy fire and one of the RASC drivers, Private Val Hennam, covered the withdrawal by firing his Bren gun at the advancing tanks, at one point engaging two tanks at short range from the cover of a 30cwt lorry. Miraculously he managed to escape intact still carrying his weapon but later joined Archer in captivity.

Such acts of bravery were, however, to no avail. At 6.10am Second Lieutenant Brown, the battalion adjutant, witnessed the dispatch rider – who he had just sent to 36 Brigade Headquarters carrying news of the German incursion – 'immediately shot down before leaving the square' as German tanks 'arrived almost at once on two sides…making a withdrawal by M[otor] T[ransport] impossible'. Men were cut down by the all enveloping fire and those who were not killed were taken prisoner. Never seriously considered to be a fighting force, the battalion had practically ceased to exist.[5] However, Brown's account notes that three vehicles did manage to escape through the barrier of fire in the square, despite the fact the Germans 'were shelling and machine gunning at 30 yards range'. Amongst the more fortunate was Captain Newbery:

> *'The noise was terrific and it was quite impossible to judge what was happening. We waited ten minutes for 7 Platoon but there was no sign of them. A tank was then heard quite close to our left, so I ordered the 15cwt truck to be manned by PSM Ralph, my runner and two drivers – all that remained – and told the driver to try to pull out.'*[6]

Just after Newbery's vehicle got away towards Bouzincourt, Brown managed to get clear of the square with Basil Clay and the remaining transport that had evaded destruction. Six miles west of Albert he separated from the column and continued on the pillion seat of a Belgian refugee's motorcycle until held up by German infantry south of Doullens. 'At that moment I got on the saddle and rode off. The German fired two shots at me the first of which grazed my knee.' Despite his wound and running out of petrol, Brown evaded capture and eventually returned to England. Clay was amongst those who were later rounded up and taken prisoner but George Newbery and a party of seventy men did reach Boulogne. It was another six years before Michael Archer's MC and Val Hennam's MM were announced.

～

The experience of the two Royal Sussex battalions of 37 Brigade was typical of the disorganization that appeared to cloud the judgement of the 12th Divisional staff. On 18 May the 7/Royal Sussex, 263/Field Company and 182/Field Ambulance were met by Brigadier Richard Wyatt who gave verbal orders for the battalion to entrain for Lens. Routed towards Amiens the train was stopped just short of the station at St Roche on the western edge of the city before it slowly inched its way forward:

'The long train had hardly pulled into the station when it was attacked. The men were travelling in cattle trucks (about 40 in each) and most of them were lying asleep with their boots off, having been advised to get as much sleep as possible. The first thing they knew was being awakened by a heavy explosion at the front end of the train at 15.15 [3.15pm] hours. Then they heard the drone of dive-bombers and bursts of machine-gun fire. The train had been run into a siding and the engine had stopped at the buffer-stops, so it was a stationary target.'[7]

Travelling some distance behind was the train carrying 6/Royal Sussex and 264/Field Company which fortunately avoided the air attack and was run into the relative safety of a cutting where it remained until 6.30pm. Avoiding the carnage at St Roche the 6/Royal Sussex eventually continued to Ailly-sur-Noye where a lack of orders prompted them to continue to Paris where they were directed to Nantes to resume their labouring.

On board the 7/Royal Sussex train was Private Doug Swift, a 21-year-old gardener from Eastbourne. Called up in January 1940 he was in France four months later with 37 Brigade at Forges-les-Eaux, a small town 15 miles southwest of Aumale. Swift, like many of his comrades in A Company had not seen any reason to complete the will in the back of his pay book, reasoning that as a labour battalion there was little need. He was in for a rude awakening. Swift recalled the bombs falling and exploding amongst the trucks and sending showers of debris flying high into the air. 'We scrambled out of the trucks, diving underneath just before the Stukas came screaming down for a second attack, followed by a third.'

According to French historian Jacques Mercier one bomb fell between the tender and the first coach containing all the officers, killing ten and wounding, amongst others, Lieutenant Colonel Ronald Gethen the commanding officer. Gethen's account documents another twenty-five other ranks killed during the attack and some eighty more wounded, many of these wounded were taken to the nearby Hotel Dieu and treated by a French medical officer, Captain Lemoine, and 182/Field Ambulance staff. Once the wounded had been taken care of, Gethen's next priority was to move the remaining men to the shelter of a nearby wooded area around the Château Blanc a mile to the southwest on the Amiens–Poix road.[8]

Travelling on another troop train towards St Roche behind the Royal Sussex was Major Graeme Dalglish on his way to join the 1/8 Lancashire Fusiliers who were fighting with the 2nd Division. The first indication of trouble came at 2.30pm when German aircraft began bombing Amiens and Dalglish's train was shunted into a siding between two ammunition trains east of Pont-de-Metz! With the line ahead blocked and with little prospect of any further movement until the next morning, the train was evacuated.

Meanwhile Gethen had managed to contact British headquarters in Amiens and before long a staff officer arrived but was unable to offer much practical assistance. Irritated by the inability of the staff officer to provide further orders

Gethen informed his own officers that without further orders he intended to stay put. His situation was augmented by the addition of Major Dalglish's party which had by this time boarded a second train, only to be frustrated again at St Roche by yet another German air raid which blocked the line and destroyed the train. 'This was my first taste of dive bombing', wrote Dalglish, 'an unpleasant experience when it is such a one-sided show, as we had no LMGs [light machine guns] or rifle ammunition and as far as I could see there was no AA [anti-aircraft] fire of any kind.'[9]

At the Château Blanc the remaining men of the Sussex began to dig in and Second Lieutenant Garrick Bowyer was ordered by Gethen to establish a road block on the Poix road with his platoon which, apart from a single light tank, failed to persuade any retreating French infantry to remain with the Sussex. There is certainly some suggestion in the war diary account that Gethen was suffering from the effects of his head wound. This manifested itself in the form of flat denials – despite evidence to the contrary – of any enemy presence in the immediate area; whether his behaviour in this respect was an attempt to maintain the morale of his men and dispel any rumours we shall probably never know.

However, persistent reports from retiring French infantry of German forces heading in Gethen's direction could not be ignored. It was becoming clear to all concerned that there was an element of truth in the assertions, particularly after Major Dalglish observed enemy shells bursting on a ridge near the Amiens-Paris road about 11.00am on the morning of 20 May. Reporting this to Ronald Gethen he was dismissed by the irate colonel who accused him of 'romancing' but by this time Gethen must have realised that all was not well as Dalglish noted the Sussex positions were quickly changed to one of all round defence.

At 2.00pm machine-gun fire was heard on the right flank and Second Lieutenant Bower, who commanded 5 Platoon in B Company, watched as German tanks began to engage A and D Companies which were forward of the château grounds in the open fields to the north. This was the vanguard of Kirchner's 1st Panzer Division who had travelled the 17 miles from Albert and were en-route to the coast. Doug Swift remembered that the attack on A Company came almost without warning: 'A hail of machine-gun bullets came sweeping down amongst us from German tanks on the top road ... They were also hitting the château with heavy mortars causing considerable damage and the farm buildings on our right were on fire.' Moving forward to get a closer view of the battle now developing around the farm buildings, Bowyer and his company commander, Major Peter Miller, came under enemy machine-gun fire. Bowyer was wounded in the leg but managed to return to the Poix road where he witnessed Peter Miller's death in a shamefully unequal duel: tank versus revolver. Gethen's account provides more of a flavour of the battle as it unfolded:

'About this time [3.15pm] *the CO received a verbal message from A Company reporting they were pinned down by enemy MG, snipers and tanks. The CO and 2iC* [Major James Cassels] *reviewed the ground between the Amiens-Poix road and A Company and the farm. A good deal of fire of all sorts and one enemy tank visible … Decide to relieve pressure on A Company and drive out the enemy from their position by the advance of HQ Company, B Company to conform from the right flank … French tank got forward of the haystack in view of enemy tanks and it actually opened fire. The battle developed for probably an hour longer – until about 5.15pm when it seems tanks came right forward and cleaned up the remainder of HQ and B Company.'*[10]

A Company did not actually surrender until 6.15pm by which time Gethen had organised the reserve platoon of C Company to reinforce the beleaguered B Company, but the battle was almost over and Gethen was moments away from being taken prisoner. Dalglish writes that he and another officer – a Major Stannus en-route to join 1/6 Lancashire Fusiliers – attempted to reach the Sussex positions on both flanks but failed: 'As we attempted to move we got plastered with everything … to make things worse five light tanks had got round behind us on the slope the other side of the Amiens road and were firing into our backs.' Both officers were in the château grounds and in all probability witnessed Gethen and the remnants of the battalion he had rounded up, fix bayonets and advance across the fields towards the German tanks. It was the final act of defiance before the survivors were swept into oblivion or captivity.

The casualties had been horrendous. Pitted against tanks with no heavy weaponry and only lightly armed, the Sussex had been outgunned and out-manoeuvred by their German counterparts. In A Company alone only two men were left unwounded while overall there are at least 132 officers and men listed on the CWGC database as having being killed between 18–20 May or died of wounds later. Although some 160 officers and men, including Ronald Gethen, were taken prisoner, many did manage to escape and of these Garrick Bower was picked up by a French unit days later and finally managed to return to England. Major James Cassels initially escaped with Dalglish, but was later found shot near Aumale while Dalglish and his party stumbled into a patrol of the South Lancs and embarked for England on 4 June 1940.[11]

～

We must now move 18 miles north of Amiens to Doullens where 6/RWK under the command of Lieutenant Colonel William Nash arrived on 18 May after an exhausting eleven hour journey. In the town Nash found Lieutenant Colonel Hudson Allen and the 5/Buffs with Brigadier George Roupell who was waiting to give both battalion commanders new orders to move up to the La Bassée Canal. The 48-year-old Roupell was a First World War veteran and had been awarded the VC during the action on Hill 60 at Ypres in April 1915, but even he must have wondered if there was any clear overall strategy in place when these orders were rescinded an hour later, both battalions being instructed instead to remain in Doullens and construct road blocks at all the entrances to the town. According to Nash this was a process that was hampered by instructions not to crater the roads or fell any trees so as not to impede the retirement of the French!

Shortly after midnight on 20 May the movement orders were changed twice more forcing Nash to finally visit brigade headquarters for confirmation, resulting in the order Bert Jones was eventually given by his platoon commander to move out along the road to Arras:

> 'We moved up the Doullens-Arras road to take positions between Pommera and La Herliere. The road was choked with refugees blocking the way, but we [B Company] managed to get into place by the morning. We were very poorly equipped; besides our old Lee Enfield rifles we had a couple of Bren guns and a .55-inch Boys anti-tank rifle and a 2-inch trench-mortar.'[12]

If the Buffs considered themselves poorly equipped then the West Kents could scarcely be considered better off. According to Lieutenant Colonel Nash the only weapons the battalion possessed – apart from personal Lee Enfield rifles – were:

> '16 Bren guns and 12 Boys rifles: no hand grenades had been issued. Officers were not in possession of revolvers or maps and only a few had compasses. Very few NCOs or men had ever had an opportunity of firing an A/T rifle and some men, drafted to the battalion on the eve of proceeding overseas, of firing any weapon previous to going into action.'[13]

It was hardly a recipe for success, particularly as the battalion was now in the path of Georg-Hans Reinhardt's XLI Korps whose 6th and 8th Panzer Divisions were equipped with the heavier Czech designed *Panzerkampfwagen* 38(t) tanks.

News of the demise of the 7/RWKs at Albert arrived at 36 Brigade Headquarters in the form of a gunner officer, Second Lieutenant Larner, reporting the destruction of the four 18-pounders in the main square and heavy casualties. Shortly after this brigade headquarters was moved to the medieval château at Lucheux and Nash established his battle headquarters at Grouches-Luchuel. Three hours later shellfire from the direction of the D938 Albert road began to strike the roadblocks held by B and C Companies on the Arras road, while D Company, whose front extended from Beaurepaire Farm to the crossroads with the D24 west of Pommera, was attacked from the air. The battle was about to begin.

During the next hour tanks and troops with machine guns appeared from all sides, infiltrating along main and minor roads from the direction of Arras and

Albert putting B Company and the HQ Company roadblock at the junction of the Albert-Amiens road under pressure. Temporary respite was achieved at this roadblock when Second Lieutenant Pugh disabled the lead tank with a round from a Boys rifle and the enemy infantry attack was driven off by a party led by Captain Phillip Scott-Martin.

At 1.30pm the B Echelon transport managed to get away along the Abbeville road before the net began to close in around the town. Shortly afterwards battalion headquarters at Grouches came under attack, first by a single tank and later by a group of four of five, before they continued towards Doullens. Lieutenant Colonel Nash's diary records the final stages of the fight put up by the West Kents:

> '*By 2.30pm enemy AFVs appeared on the high ground both on the north and south of Doullens, but made no immediate attack, but as the houses occupied at the junction of the Albert and Amiens roads were now burning fiercely, they had to be evacuated and Captain Scott-Martin was obliged to withdraw his company* [HQ Company] *to the western side of the town. By 3.00pm the attack on the north side of Doullens developed and 2/Lt Henchie's road block on the St Pol-Arras road came under heavy mortar and 2-pounder fire and by 3.30pm 2/Lt Waters' platoon on the St Pol road was in action against enemy medium tanks and infantry. By 4.30pm D Company had been completely surrounded and their left platoon had suffered considerable casualties and all the Doullens road blocks had been under heavy fire.*'[14]

By 5.00pm the situation of the West Kents was critical as the surviving soldiers gradually withdrew to A Company headquarters on the Rue de Bourg near the main square. Completely surrounded and under heavy fire from tanks and machine guns, Captain Scott-Martin surrendered the remnants of the battalion at 8.30pm. Casualty figures are still difficult to ascertain. It would appear that no officers were killed during the engagement, and while several managed to get away with small parties of men, they were largely rounded up – in some cases days later – and taken prisoner. The CWGC database records twenty NCOs and men killed between 20–21 May and these are now buried at Doullens Communal Cemetery Extension No.1. At least sixteen officers were eventually taken prisoner including the commanding officer and although seventy-four officers and men returned to England some 503 were posted as missing.

∽

Lieutenant Colonel Hudson Allen, commanding 5/Buffs, had little choice but to create islands of defence along his 6½ -mile section of the Doullens-Arras road with his own headquarters in the small hamlet of La Bellevue. Running parallel and to the south of the road was the Achicourt-Doullens railway line which, in the absence of anything better, Roupell hoped would serve as some sort of anti-tank barrier. Roupell might not have considered Allen's battalion able enough to delay the panzer advance for any significant time but the comparative ease with which the battalion was overcome when it finally came under attack is almost shocking. The railway line offered little or no resistance to enemy tanks and although it was established much later that B Company at l'Arbret held out until 3.15pm, the Buffs were effectively swept aside by the German armoured attack.

At l'Arbret the company transport was parked near the mill where the modern day abattoir now stands and B Company set up its headquarters in the railway station building with 12 Platoon dug in between the railway and the main N25 road. Private Bert Jones was on the attic floor of the railway station on watch with Captain Rawlings:

'*From our vantage point we could see right across the fields to the south. The first sign of trouble was light glinting on metal. We could see lots of movement, and what looked like large numbers of vehicles moving along a road to the south. We reported to the officer* [presumably Captain Rawlings], *but he told us that it must be another refugee column, after all, the main German advance was supposed to be well away to the north of us.*'[15]

What Jones had seen was the advance of the 8th Panzer Division along the D1 at la Cauchie and it wasn't long before tanks were soon heading across the fields towards them. Lieutenant Colonel Allen's diary records that this information arrived at battalion headquarters at midday, at the same time as Captain Hilton's message reporting enemy shelling and tanks on C Company's front. The enemy attack was evidently enveloping the whole of the Buffs' defence line simultaneously.

According to Allen the forward platoon of B Company became engaged with enemy tanks at 1.15pm which, according to Jones, prompted men – probably of 10 and 11 Platoons – to retire swiftly to the railway buildings. André Colliot, a local French historian, writes that a single British soldier was left seriously wounded in the field and was later picked up by a German ambulance. Whether it was around this time that Corporal Alfred Carpenter took on two German tanks is unclear but firing the Boys anti-tank rifle for the first time he only withdrew after all his ammunition had been used. Attention was then directed towards the station:

'*One German tank drove down the street towards the railway station. A corporal called Ratcliffe* [E Ratcliffe] *I believe, opened fire on the advancing tank. I was told that he lost an eye, but was otherwise OK as far as I know.* [Private] *Sid Bartlett and I were still inside the station and I ran outside to drag a large box of .303 ammunition into the station. However, when the Germans started firing in our direction I thought it more prudent to get back in the station.*'[16]

In his account, Jones fails to mention Sergeant William Elson who, according to his citation for the MM, held the station with two rifle sections, repulsing two German attacks on the building and holding up the German advance for two hours. This suggests that Jones and Sid Bartlett got out of the back of the station before the final attacks. Crossing over the railway line they crawled into the long grass on the far side: 'While we lay there a German tank drove up the railway line and passed right beside us.' Ignoring the temptation to shoot the tank commander they watched German soldiers searching the abandoned goods wagons in the railway siding before setting off with three others to locate the remaining companies.

Neither Lieutenant Colonel Allen's diary nor Jones' account mention the heroic stand of Private John Lungley who had taken up position a few yards west of the D23E Saulty road. In the account given by the station master to André Colliot, Lungly's Bren gun fire held up the German advance and prevented their access to the Saulty road – this must have been around the time Elson was still fighting from the confines of the railway station. The station master remembers a German light armoured vehicle armed with two machine guns being brought up to machine gun Lungley's position at about 1.45pm. 'The firing ceased, a brave man was no longer.'[17] Carpenter and Elson's MMs were gazetted in 1945 but John Lungley's contribution went unrecognised although he is still remembered in the village and his grave in the nearby communal cemetery is often visited.

By 2.15pm the enemy had penetrated the gap between A and C Company and B Company was reported to be cut off. Allen's diary tells us it was at this point that he sent out orders for the battalion to withdraw north towards Lucheux but in the event only D Company and Major Tom Penlington with HQ Company managed to escape. Moving across country Lieutenant Colonel Allen and party reached Lucheux at 4.00pm:

> *'On arrival there the CO informed the brigadier of the situation and his reason for withdrawing. It appears that the brigadier did not realize the strength of the attack and appeared to think that only a few tanks were attacking. At this time a report was received that enemy tanks were in Gruche (HQ 6/RWK). A defensive position was taken up at the Château. About 6.30pm a light tank arrived in the square in front of Bde HQ and this was put out of action.'[18]*

The tank was hit by Private John Dexter of D Company who had been posted at the gate with instructions to cover the approach to the château. Opening fire with a Boys anti-tank gun – a weapon Dexter had never before fired – he hit the first tank before reloading and hitting another. His award of the MM was also announced in 1945. At 8.00pm Roupell ordered the château to be evacuated and the group were ordered to split into small parties and attempt to get back to British lines. Allen and his party were later captured but Roupell and Captain

Charles Gilbert, his brigade major, found their way to Rouen and spent nearly 15 months hiding on a farm before eventually escaping over the Pyrenees. The 5/Buffs had effectively ceased to exist, only 5 officers and 74 other ranks from C Company managed to return to England, the remainder were either killed or captured.[19] As for Bert Jones and Sid Bartlett, they remained at large until 17 June before they were taken prisoner near Namur.

~

If George Roupell had harboured any thoughts of units from the 23rd Division arriving in time to reinforce the Buffs along the Arras-Doullens road he was greatly disappointed. On 19 May the division was approximately 6 miles west of Cambrai along the Canal du Nord; 24 hours later, after their movement orders had been changed on four occasions, 70 Brigade was diverted from Thelus, north of Arras, to the Beaumetz – Saulty area from where they were to make contact with Roupell's 36 Brigade. As their route took them in a southwestly direction, Jim Laidler, marching with 1/Tyneside Scottish (The Black Watch), felt as if they had been marching 'all day and all night'. Thus as dawn broke on 20 May 1/Tyneside Scottish were at Neuville-Vitasse, 10/DLI at Mercatel and 11/DLI at Wancourt. Here at least there was some respite, with the nearest unit of the Buffs some 20 miles away to the west 47-year-old Brigadier Phillip Kirkup gave orders for the three battalions to rest while the RASC transport drove on ahead, dumped their loads and returned to assist in ferrying the infantry columns to their new destinations.

In command of 1/Tyneside Scottish was Lieutenant Colonel Hugh Swinburne who, prior to his promotion, had been second-in-command of the 9/DLI. Evidence suggests that he was a man who didn't suffer fools gladly and defined a fool as anyone who failed to live up to his expectations. His account of the battle – which was written post-war – conflicts with the 'official version' submitted by Captain John Burr as part of the war diary. Burr's account contains numerous corrections and additions in Swinburne's handwriting, one of which openly criticises the length of time the transport took in reaching Saulty and returning to Neuville-Vitasse. Swinburne writes they left at 3.00am and did not return from the 30-mile round trip until 9.00am that morning, citing this as a principle cause of the battalion's misfortune.[20]

Swinburne may well have been correct in his assertion but in mitigation author Tim Lynch suggests that the battalion transport was inevitably moving at the pace of the slowest vehicle on narrow country roads and possibly without the current editions of local maps. In addition the reliability of the vehicles – many being hired ex-civilian transport – was uncertain and the roads were undoubtedly heavily congested with refugee traffic. However, it must be said that two companies of the 11/DLI were successfully ferried into Beaumetz-les-Loges by 5.00am – leaving Lieutenant Colonel John Bramwell with the remaining men at

Wancourt. The distance was certainly shorter and whether their transport used a different route or was subjected to less refugee traffic is anyone's guess but, given the circumstances, Swinburne's criticism appears at the very least to be unfair.

Back at Neuville-Vitasse passing refugees had informed Swinburne at 6.50am of the presence of German tanks in the vicinity prompting him to give the order for the battalion to march towards Mercatel, each company moving through the other in a leapfrogging movement. With the battalion now on the move Swinburne left them to make contact with brigade HQ at Barly with a convoy of seven vehicles containing HQ Company and an assortment of men of the Pioneer Corps who had been picked up at Neuville-Vitasse.[21]

At approximately 9.15am Swinburne's party was ambushed in Ficheux by the 8/Motorised Battalion from Kuntzen's 8th Panzer Division and the lead vehicle containing Swinburne was immediately set on fire. Private Malcolm Armstrong remembered being in the rear of his vehicle and shouting for his mate Arthur Todhunter to get out:

> '*He couldn't as he was already dead. There was panic everywhere. I went round to the left and saw a small tank approaching. We were given orders to fix bayonets to attack. Surprised, I noticed that the cannon turned towards me but I escaped death when he changed direction, fired and one of the other lads fell. With Private Albert Foster, who was killed later, we advanced along the side of the Pronier Farm. I was going to go in when a bullet or something similar struck my rifle and I dropped it. As I bent down to pick it up I was again saved when something just missed me. I then ran to an area behind this building and saw a dozen of my comrades mown down by machine-gun fire.*'[22]

To Private Jim Laidler it felt as if the Germans had thrown 'everything possible at us – mortars, tanks, machine-gun fire and rifles. Our casualties were terrific. Out of 300 men who had arrived at Ficheaux, 150 were killed and many others wounded.'

Unaware of the disaster that had already overrtaken his battalion in the shape of the 7th Panzer Division, which had broken through south of Arras, Swinburne evaded capture for 48 hours before he was eventually taken prisoner at Avesnes-les-Comptes. In the meantime C Company – still at Neuville-Vitasse – had been surprised by an attack on both flanks at 8.15am. With ammunition expended and the line of withdrawal cut off on three sides, all were either killed or captured.

Having just passed through C Company – and realising Captain George Harker and C Company were under attack – Captain Esmond Adams commanding D Company, decided to remain with one platoon to assist Harker if necessary, while the remainder continued on towards the Arras-Albert railway line and battalion headquarters. Using commandeered vehicles, Adams soon rejoined the company, arriving just after Swinburne's party drove into the ambush. Leading his men round the right flank towards the firing they were eventually pinned down by enemy tanks and after heavy casualties had depleted his force, Adams split the survivors into small groups in the hope that they might evade capture.

It was now the turn of A Company, under the command of Captain Hilton Maugham, which had passed over the road junction at Mercatel and was moving towards the Arras-Albert railway line when enemy AFVs closed in on both flanks, catching the company in open ground. Despite anti-tank rifles being deployed the fight was over almost before it had begun. Half a mile up the road B Company had crossed the railway line where it came under hostile fire from the direction of Ficheux. A former soldier with the Machine Gun Corps in the previous war, 43-year-old Company Sergeant Major (CSM) Charles Baggs could see his men fighting with tanks all around them:

> *'What a terrible sight ... a German machine gun opened out on my left flank simply raking us with MG fire, and to complete his work, two tanks came up behind us and positioned themselves about 20 yards away. They opened out with their shells, and simply blasted us out of the* [railway] *embankment. We were at last surrounded, and within a minute or two, I had 14 killed and 6 wounded. To hear those lads moaning made me rather sick.'*[23]

As the battle became fragmented many of the Tynesiders continued fighting in the face of enormous odds. Provost Sergeant Dick Chambers was killed as he attempted to fire through the slits in a tank turret, Lance Corporal Frederick Laidler – no relation to Jim Laidler – continued to play his pipes until he was shot down and CSMs Alfred Parmenter and John Morris took over Boys anti-tank rifles after their crews had been killed until they too were overrun.

Two companies of the 10/DLI had also been caught on the outskirts of Ficheux. Not a single survivor remained from Captain John Kipling's C Company but the few survivors from B Company that managed to extricate themselves included Captain George Robinson and Private George Walton who finally reached the coast on 2 June. Both were captured two days later as they were launching a boat out to sea. The 11/DLI had also been hit hard by Rommel's 7th Panzers at Wancourt and, after a short engagement, were all either killed or captured. In due course the surviving Durhams were gathered together by Lieutenant Colonel David Marley commanding 10/DLI at Lattre-St-Quentin. When 70 Brigade finally reconvened at Houdain a few days later only 233 officers and men answered their names.[24]

～

If the 36 Brigade orders had lacked clarity then those issued to 35 Brigade smacked of almost total incompetence. Consisting of three Queen's Royal Regiment (West Surrey) battalions, they had been labouring at Abancourt since mid-April. On 17

May the 2/6 and 2/7 Queen's – possibly mistaken by Movement Control for the 46th Division – were ordered to Abbeville where they were surprised to discover they had been diverted to Lens. Reaching Lens in the midst of an air raid they learned to their dismay that the original orders had been a mistake and they were to return to Abbeville where at least they were reunited with the 2/5 Queens. On 20 May it was decided to withdraw the brigade across the Somme, but in the confusion of the 2nd Panzer Division assault on Abbeville, Brigadier Vivian Cordova's orders went astray.

Trouble began when Lieutenant Colonel Edward Bolton commanding the 2/6 Queens, noted that the tanks he had seen crossing the airfield south east of le Plessiel were not British, as first thought, but German, and what's more, were heading for the mouth of the Somme. Having failed to make contact with the 2/7 Queens he wisely decided to lie low and remain where he was until darkness fell before he led the battalion across the Somme at Port-le-Grand. Apart from the rearguard platoon, which was surprised by German tanks crossing the St Omer road, the battalion was south of the river by dawn.

The 2/7 was less fortunate. Deployed around Vauchelles the same German tanks were first seen approaching the lines at 5.30pm and after a short engagement with all the available anti-tank ammunition Lieutenant Colonel Francis Girling gave orders to retire. In the confusion of battle those orders only reached HQ Company in addition to two platoons which succeeded in crossing the river, the remainder being killed or captured. The only battalion that received Cordova's orders to retire was the 2/5 which was told to wait until the 2/7 had crossed the Somme before moving. The battalion was eventually split into small groups by Lieutenant Colonel Alex Young and told to make their own way to the river. About 120 officers and men escaped death or captivity. By midnight on 20 May 35 Brigade had practically ceased to exist as a viable formation, a tragedy that may have been avoided if the 6 and 7/Royal Sussex battalions had been deployed on the south bank of the Somme opposite Abbeville as originally intended, where they might have been able to assist the Queen's brigade by holding the high ground which overlooks Abbeville from the south.

Corporal Peter Walker's adventures with the 2/7 Duke of Wellington's Regiment began on 18 May when the battalion left St Nazaire by train for Arras via Amiens. After several delays around Rouen their destination was altered to Béthune. Walker's account betrays the almost total confusion caused by the fast approaching panzer divisions:

'The battalion travelled to Rouen and met up with the rest of 137 Brigade and another battalion, the 2/4 KOYLI from 138 Brigade. They were bound for Béthune via Amiens but the railway bridge over the Somme had been destroyed by the enemy so were diverted [with us] through Dieppe to Abbeville.'[25]

Eventually four trains were travelling in convoy towards Abbeville, Walker and the 2/7 were in the last train with the 271/Field Company sappers:

> *'In the near distance the bombing and fires in Abbeville could plainly be seen and it became obvious the Germans had occupied the town. The only way we could go now was backwards towards Dieppe. The KOYLI made their way back on foot. The trains carrying the [2/5 & 2/7] Duke of Wellingtons had come to a halt on an embankment and could not be unloaded without being moved and to make matters worse, night had fallen and it had become dark.'*[26]

Unbeknown to Walker the first train carrying the 2/5 West Yorkshires and 137 Brigade Headquarters staff had carried straight on through Abbeville and finally ended up at Béthune on 21 May. Meanwhile, 11 miles west of Abbeville at Chépy, the Dukes had unloaded two utility trucks and dispatched reconnaissance parties to get some idea of exactly what was taking place around them. The death of Second Lieutenant Kenneth Smith near Abbeville confirmed that the town was in enemy hands prompting Lieutenant Colonel George Taylor to deploy the battalion in a defensive position around the train. As Walker recounts, they were hardly in a position to meet a determined German attack:

> *'The position took the form of a line of soldiers lying on the ground armed with a rifle and 50 rounds of small arms ammunition per man, with a Bren gun, with only one magazine per platoon. We were lying flat on the ground, because we had neither pick, shovel nor entrenching tool.'*[27]

Given the options open to him, Taylor had little choice but to withdraw on foot in the direction of Eu to find a better defensive position. But fortune was clearly smiling as at Fressenville, behind a jumble of wreckage, they discovered two trains that had remained intact:

> *'We were, however, able to free some horses from what was evidently a train transporting either French or Belgian cavalry ... a dog which we freed from the train quickly became attached to the battalion and they say it remained with us to the end. The last train was a hospital train containing French wounded. The CO promised to get help and the battalion took up a defensive position in a wood near the railway line.'*[28]

Eventually the line was cleared with assistance from a large crane and on 27 May the battalion steamed into Dieppe. Peter Walker was wounded and captured on 10 June at the seaside town of Veules-les-Roses while waiting to be evacuated.

The German advance to the channel coast had not only deprived Curtis of a large proportion of the 46th Division by effectively cutting the Allied armies in half but had destroyed 70 Brigade in the process. The 21 May also marked the end of the 12th Division's war. It is hard to find another division that was so badly led and deployed and while there is little doubt that the 12th Division would have eventually been sucked into the battle regardless, it was certainly not fit to engage anything like *a panzer korps*. The loss of six of the division's nine battalions in a single day was an appalling tally that might have been significantly reduced if these raw Territorials had been used to maintain a house-to-house defence of Amiens and Abbeville such as the Home Guard was trained to carry out after the Dunkirk evacuation – but in May 1940 that was unimaginable!

Gort, now faced with the urgent need to strengthen his line on the southern front, ordered two divisions to move south, the 50th Division occupied the Vimy Ridge on 19 May and were joined by the 5th Division and 1 Tank Brigade a day later. Major General Howard Franklyn now assumed command of these units which, together, bore his name and would fight as 'Frankforce'.

Chapter Five

The Escaut

19–23 May 1940

'News from the south reassuring. We stand and fight. Tell your men.'
Message from Lord Gort on 21 May to all units on the Escaut.

Even as 'Frankforce' was being formed at Arras, 53 miles to the north-east the 44th (Home Counties) Division, under the command of 55-year-old Major General Edmund 'Sigs' Osborne, began arriving on the Escaut on 14 May. Osborne, a former Royal Engineers officer, was commanding the extreme left of the BEF at the junction with the Belgian Army. With the ridge of high ground between Anzegem and Knok centre stage in his sector, he was left in no doubt by Sir Ronald Adam that the high ground was of critical importance: its loss to the enemy would compromise the whole Escaut position.[1]

Given the critical nature of his sector, Osborne's deployment focused on localities rather than a more continuous line of defence, which certainly raised eyebrows at the time and continues to be questioned today. Placing 132 (Royal West Kent) Brigade on the left flank and 131 (Queen's) Brigade on the right, he left Brigadier Noel Whitty's 133 (Royal Sussex) Brigade in reserve around Knock. With four battalions on the canal and another five behind, his dispositions looked fine on paper but as Gregory Blaxland remarked in *Destination Dunkirk*, Osborne's strategy 'provided the least firepower forward'.

The Escaut was some twenty yards wide and ten feet in depth with the tow paths ten feet above the water, effectively obscuring any meaningful observation of the last 300 yards on the opposite bank. Even with the forward posts on the tow path itself, observation was still limited. The first contact with the enemy came at 10.00am on 19 May, not from across the river, but from the air as Stukas attacked the bridges at Eine and Oudenaarde and the railway station, providing 132 Brigade with their first battle casualties of the war. Lieutenant Colonel Arthur Chitty, commanding the 4/RWK, recalled thirty bombs being dropped and an ammunition truck parked on the bridge being completely obliterated along with the personnel of an artillery observation post. The other casualties were noted by Captain Stanley Clark to be mainly from A and B Companies who were in the forward posts near the bridges:

'It was a nasty shake up and our first taste of war, but there was too much to do to repair the damage done to think then. The brigade commander ordered the bridges to be blown and by the afternoon there was no contact from the other side … that evening several shells fell near the town and the first sight was seen of the enemy.'[2]

It was not until the next morning that the first German soldiers appeared in any real force and were dealt with by a C Company patrol led by Lance Corporal Brookes who crossed the river and returned with a prisoner. But the German breakthrough came two miles downstream in the 2/Buffs sector.

The Buffs held a frontage of over 2,500 yards and although they were half a mile from the river itself, a drainage canal running in front of their positions was considered enough to stop German armoured vehicles. At 12.30pm the first German units were seen on the hill behind Melden, a presence which developed into artillery fire by late afternoon and an attempted crossing of the river was reported by A Company in the vicinity of the canal loop to the south west. This was the 1/6 Queen's sector and although Captain Richard Rutherford and D Company quickly dealt with this initial incursion, enemy attempts to cross continued into the night.[3] Nevertheless, despite the level of the river dropping some four feet – partly due to the fine weather and partly the result of closing the sluice gates at Valenciennes – the advantage was still with the men of the 1/6 Queens who 'dominated the open ground on its front'.

Concerned by the strength of the German incursion Brigadier John Utterson-Kelso, commanding 131 Brigade, now involved the 2/Buffs Reserve Company to reinforce the 1/6 Queen's. This movement of Captain Francis Crozier's B Company completely unbalanced the defensive jigsaw that had been created by the battalions of 131 Brigade and allowed the German assault to penetrate the Queen's line. This error of judgement ultimately opened up the western bank of the Escaut and effectively sealed the fate of the 44th Division. The Buffs were already under attack from German infantry who, under the cover of a heavy mortar and artillery bombardment, had crossed the river at the point where the wooded area surrounding Scheltekant Château met the river bank. Attacking the forward positions of A Company, which was pushed back to the ridge of high ground behind the reserve trenches, the enemy were soon in occupation of the Buffs' positions in Huiwede and Petegem, ground which may well have been held had Crozier's B Company not been elsewhere! There is certainly evidence of confusion and inexperience hampering operations at this stage. Lieutenant Robert Hodgins, the 131 Brigade Intelligence Officer, wrote that 'no plan was established or received from division necessitating continual reference' to the senior staff officer 'for help and guidance'. What was more worrying was the opinion of Gregory Blaxland who felt his company commander had no views on how his company should be deployed in battle.

Hodgins also felt that the German use of the MP 38 machine pistol in close-quarter fighting tactics had taken the British by surprise, a factor that may have adversely impacted on the British troops who had little or no experience of automatic small-arms fire. That said, the British reply came quickly, in the shape of a section from the 1/5 Queen's Carrier Platoon with orders to clear up isolated pockets of enemy troops. After a somewhat wild and inconclusive exchange with the enemy the carriers returned just in time to join Major Lord Edward Sysonby's carrier attack on Petegem from the west. Advancing with two sections through the village Sysonby found the village burning fiercely but apart from the 'main street being a shambles of dead men and animals' no Germans were seen until Sysonby's carriers turned left at the crossroads. At this point they came face to face with a column of marching Germans. Opening fire on the enemy with their Bren guns, Sysonby remembers one German firing an anti-tank rifle at him:

> *'I shot him in the face with my revolver which was a very fluky shot as we were travelling at about 20mph. We then proceeded on our course for about a mile and a half into the enemy's lines shooting all and sundry we saw.'*[4]

The return trip was not without drama. Corporal Arthur Peters was hit and his carrier was knocked out leaving him with a shattered thigh. Temporarily taken prisoner he and two others were rescued by Sergeant Reginald Wynn under heavy fire. Wynn was awarded the DCM and Sysonby, who was the godson of King George VII, received the DSO. Sadly, Peters died of his wounds five days later.[5] Following the carrier attack two companies of the 1/5 Queen's did manage to establish themselves east of Petegem which returned control of the so-called Petegem gap – between themselves and the château at Scheltekant – to the British, who could now bring flanking fire to bear on any attempted enemy advance. But it was a situation that was not to last.

A little to the southwest of Petegem, 16 Platoon and the Buffs' headquarters staff were still grimly defending the Scheldekant Château grounds as the 1/RWK launched another counter-attack towards Petegem from Eekhout. Hopes of closing the gap were dashed when they were brought to a standstill on the railway line. For a few hours there was stalemate before the German gunners turned their bombardment on the 1/5 Queen's still clinging to ground east of Petegem. Inevitably the hapless defenders were pushed back to new positions behind the railway line and the waiting German infantry flooded through the gap.

Enemy infantry quickly outflanked the Buffs and turned their attentions to the 1/6 Queen's who rapidly became engaged by an enemy that appeared to have them almost surrounded:

> *'The enemy could be seen to be working round the left and rear of B Company. Kwaadestraat Château grounds were badly shelled by guns in the rear, presumably*

our own, and small parties of enemy penetrated the grounds, but were driven out by a counter-attack by members of Battalion Headquarters. The recaptured posts were occupied by C Company, 1/5 Queen's, which had just arrived as a reinforcement. About 8.00pm the Germans reached Elsegem and were firing into the flank and rear of the Kwaadestraat Château grounds. At the same time news arrived that the enemy was also across the Escaut on the right of the 1/6 Queen's front, and this appeared to be confirmed by a display of white Very lights to the north and west of Eekhout ... Firing was now continuous; several fresh parties of the enemy had again got a foothold in the Château grounds and no more reserves were left to deal with them, so at 9.15pm Lieut-Colonel Hughes decided to extricate the remainder of the battalion before the position was completely surrounded.'[6]

As night fell the remnants of 131 Brigade fought their way back over the railway line, where they met units of 2/Royal Sussex who had been brought forward to fill the gap. 131 Brigade reformed north of Courtrai late on 22 May where the 1/5 numbered 22 officers and 447 other ranks while the 1/6 were reorganised into three companies. Of the reported 400 other rank casualties in the 1/6, over 130 were taken prisoner but, like their sister battalion, the number of wounded remained imprecise. Amongst those captured was Sergeant Alex Horwood who was serving with B Company 1/6 Queen's. Horwood's escape from captivity and subsequent evacuation from Dunkirk (see Chapter 15) was emblazoned over the front pages of the popular press and resulted in the award of the DCM.

Meanwhile at Oudenaarde the enemy incursions on the front of 2/Buffs had put pressure on the 4/RWK headquarters at Kasteelwijk Château and although well defended by Major Marcus Keane, two companies were overrun before the order to withdraw was given. Keane, along with two companies of 5/RWK had been ordered to cover the flank of the battalion as it broke contact with the enemy at 8.00pm on 21 May. Sergeant Jezard, the MT Transport Sergeant, was at Kasteelwijk Château when the order to withdraw was relayed to all ranks:

'First of all we loaded all the casualties into a carrier ... having got them safely on board PSM Chapman said, "well boys here we go", and we made our way to the main gate. We reached the gate and decided the best way out would be round the back and through the grounds and fields. We had not gone far when someone asked, "who can drive a truck?" Everyone looked round and then I saw a 15cwt beneath a tree. It had been plastered all day along one side with shrapnel – one rear tyre had been ripped open but this didn't worry us.'[7]

Jezard's account of the fighting around the château differs slightly from that of Lieutenant Colonel Chitty who reported that 'the men fought to the end and twenty signallers, the officer's mess cooks and drivers were among the casualties.' Clearly some managed to escape as Jezard says there were 20 men in his party including Sergeant Humphrey, the Cook Sergeant, and PSM Arthur Chapman, commanding 5 Platoon, who was later singled out for the award of the DCM. Whether some fought on to the end is uncertain but we do know Marcus Keane was killed while commanding the rearguard.[8]

~

Major General Dudley Johnson was already the recipient of the DSO and bar and the MC when he was awarded the VC whilst in command of the 2/Royal Sussex in November 1918. Appointed to command the 4th Division in 1938 he was responsible for a six mile sector of the Escaut on the right of the 44th Division, a sector that included the Kerkhove bridge. Dug in around the bridge was A Company of the 1/East Surrey Regiment which occupied the village and was in touch with B Company on the left along the river bank. Across the river at Berchem C and D Companies with the battalion's carriers were tasked with preventing enemy patrols from reaching the bridge. Overlooking the Surreys' position was Mont de l'Enclus, a high point from which enemy artillery observers had an uninterrupted view. Lieutenant Colonel Reginald Boxshall later remarked that it 'gave the German gunners, good observation, and we were heavily and accurately shelled'.

Working alongside 11 Brigade were the sappers of 7/Field Company who, in addition to preparing the bridge at Kerkhove for demolition, were also fortifying the riverside buildings. Second Lieutenant Curtis was at the bridge:

> *'Road blocks had been erected east of the bridge and a light screen of the Surreys were ready to hold back the Germans if they appeared. Assault boats were issued to the Surreys so they could return across the river after the bridge was blown. Shortly after 23.00hours* [11.00pm] *on May 19, the Adjutant of 3 Div rearguard arrived to say the rear-most battalion was some miles away, and that the bridge should not be blown until it had crossed. It was now a question of waiting to see who would arrive first, 3 Div or the enemy.'*[9]

Lieutenant Colonel Boxshall had no doubt that *he* gave the order that delayed the blowing of the bridge and writes that it was a battalion of Sherwood Foresters that were the last to cross the river before the order was given for its destruction.[10] At what point Boxshall brought C and D Companies back is not clear but 'eventually', he wrote, 'the Germans occupied all the east bank of the River Escaut.'

The battle at the bridge continued for most of the day as the Germans tried to cross the river under a curtain of heavy shellfire. The Regimental Aid Post (RAP) received a direct hit killing or wounding everyone who was working there; fortunately Lieutenant Donald Bird, the battalion medical officer, was dealing with casualties elsewhere at the time. Boxshall observed with some alarm that all the battalion's anti-tank guns were also knocked out. On the Surreys' right flank the 2/Lancashire Fusiliers were also under a heavy artillery and mortar bombardment. Major Lawrence Manly, noting the remarkable, accuracy of the blizzard of fire, noted that 'Battalion Headquarters, A Company and B Company suffered the most'. Yet, despite the bombardment the East Surreys and Lancashire Fusiliers were managing to hold their own, a state of affairs that was not replicated on the left flank as Lieutenant Colonel Bill Green's 5/Northamptons came under increasing pressure.

The 42-year-old Green was a decorated RFC flying ace in the First World War and credited with nine victories between January and September 1918. Transferring to the Northamptonshire Regiment in 1921 he assumed command of the battalion in 1938. Now, with D Company in touch with the Queen's on the left, the battalion was strung out along 2,000 yards of the Escaut. Although Boxshall makes no mention of this in his account, A Company of the Northamptons under the command of Captain Hart were dug in along the eastern edge of Berchem and it was there that the battalion had their first contact with the enemy:

> *'A Company were well hidden in scattered houses on the edge of the village … At about 11.00am a group of about twelve apparent refugees approached. To Captain Hart it seemed that they were walking with a somewhat martial stride and his suspicions were confirmed when they were followed by about twenty cyclists, riding in pairs, and a lorry. The section covering the road held their fire until the cyclists were a good target at close range and opened fire with Bren and rifles.'* [11]

The first burst of fire took down the majority of the cyclists prompting the marching 'refugees' to break for cover and return fire. As the attack became more determined the company were withdrawn across the river by boat. Hart was given an immediate award of the MC and Privates Sharpe and Herbert the MM.

The bombardment that was causing havoc at Kerkhove was also being directed at the Northamptons and after some very fierce fighting the Germans managed to establish themselves in a small orchard on D Company's front. Although they were discouraged from widening their foothold by a Northamptonshire bayonet charge, D Company sustained heavy casualties reducing the effective strength to less than two platoons. Brought into the fight as support, C Company lost around a third of its strength before the battalion front was readjusted and it was only the arrival of the 6/Black Watch during the night that prevented the enemy from working found the flank and surrounding the battalion.

Early on 22 May patrols from A Company established the Germans were now across the river in some strength and it wasn't long before they directed their attentions towards Captain John Johnson's C Company positions. After Johnson was killed by a direct hit, the company – by now very much reduced in numbers – got away only after Green ordered up the carrier platoon to hold the enemy, an order that resulted in five of the carriers being destroyed and eleven of its twenty-eight men being killed. Surrounded and out of ammunition, the remaining men of the carrier platoon fought their way clear with grenades. The orders to withdraw came not a moment too soon. The battalion had suffered enormously and, with eleven officers killed or wounded and C Company less than forty strong, the remaining rifle companies could only muster some sixty-five men apiece. Worse still was the news that Lieutenant Colonel Green had been killed at Teighen.[12]

Back on the 1/East Surrey's front at Kerkhove the Germans had also got across the river and with the battalion's left flank turned it looked very much as if the situation was fast becoming untenable; a situation that did not prevent Captain Ricketts from leading a counter-attack with C Company:

> '*It all started with a sergeant arriving at my position very much out of breath and with a revolver in his hand to tell me A Company were surrounded and they needed the reserve company to get them out … I went in deployed in Y formation. The only opposition met on our way came from a house and a party of apparent Fifth Columnists which we despatched, with me on the Bren and PSM Bob Gibson bowling a couple of Mills bombs. I eventually arrived at A Company's position and found Captain Finch White who told me he was intact, but was receiving a belting and could do with some help.*'[13]

Ricketts was wounded along with Second Lieutenant Meredith in the attack which, in the event, turned out not to be needed – it was later in the day that A Company would have appreciated Rickett's assistance! Shortly after the C Company counter-attack the brigade major arrived at battalion headquarters with orders to withdraw immediately. Boxshall recalled that he was unhappy with the order as it meant 'moving men over open ground exposed to full view from enemy observation points. However, as both flank battalions were on the move I had no choice. I issued orders by runner (all lines had been cut), and backed them up with liaison officers in carriers. Three companies got the orders, but A Company on the right did not.'[14]

Pinned down by enemy fire and finding themselves isolated and outflanked, Captain Finch White realised the Germans were now across the river on both flanks and waited until dark to find out for himself what was taking place:

> '*After going a short distance I was fired upon from what had been the position of Battalion Headquarters and it was clear we had to get out quickly …We withdrew with the Germans advancing parallel to us on each flank. Fortunately they took no notice of us. We did come under heavy machine-gun fire from our own rearguard, not the Surreys, and had to take cover … We then got a lift in some transport and rejoined the battalion.*'[15]

The Surreys' withdrawal was not without cost. Machine gunned by low flying aircraft as they retired out of the Escaut valley, Boxshall's carrier was hit by anti-tank tracer which penetrated the vehicle, badly bruising him and wounding his second-in-command, Major Ken Lawton.

It was a similar story on the sector held by the Lancashire Fusiliers. At 3.00pm on 22 May news that the right flank had given way prompted Lieutenant Colonel Leslie Rougier to push Captain Hugh Woollatt's carrier platoon into play to form a defensive flank. Last seen at B Company Headquarters, Woollatt was taken prisoner shortly before the orders to retire to the Gort line were received, a move that cost the 44-year-old Rougier his life when he was killed by shellfire near the railway cutting south of the Tie(gham Ridge. Command was assumed by Lawrence Manly who brought the battalion out of action with over 175 officers and men either killed wounded or missing.[16]

At Avelgem Lieutenant Colonel James Birch commanding the 2/Bedfordshire and Hertfordshires had established his headquarters in a small café close to the main cross roads. Deploying C Company at Escanaffles on the eastern bank of the river with orders that the bridge was not to fall into enemy hands, the remaining companies – presumably under orders from Brigadier Evelyn Barker commanding 10 Brigade – were directed to positions on the forward edge of Mont de l'Enclus. In his account Birch writes that he met Barker and Major General Johnston on Mont de l'Enclus and was immediately told to move his men to the east and south faces of the hill, leaving him to wonder just how he was going to hold the position with so few men. However, sanity appears to have prevailed as the orders were changed yet again resulting in the battalion taking up new positions on the western bank of the river.

Nevertheless there was still a sticky moment or two before C Company was finally brought back across the bridge:

> '*Eventually the last section under the command of Lance Corporal Major came doubling back over the bridge followed at a distance by the head of a column of refugees. The sapper sergeant called upon the civilians to go back but they paid no heed. He then told the troops to run flat out and he would press the plunger in a minute. Lance Corporal Major and his section then completed an Olympic 100 metre dash when there was a deafening roar as one and a half tons of explosive charge erupted and bits and pieces of the bridge were thrown high in the sky.*'[17]

Lieutenant Colonel Birch's account is quite critical of the 'marching and counter-marching' his battalion had been subjected to on 19 May, writing that, 'I have no doubt that there was good reason for it, but I did regret that I had no opportunity of making a good recce of the canal bank on such a vast front before the enemy arrived.' Birch neglects to mention that the flat and featureless ground between the river and Avelgem gave his forward platoons little cover from German artillery and mortar fire.

As they had done further north, German troops made their first appearance on the far bank on the morning of 20 May. Birch's unease at the extent to which the battalion's positions were overlooked was not improved by the first casualties at the hands of enemy snipers lodged in the industrial buildings at Escanaffles. At 11.00am 12 Platoon was subjected to a heavy mortar attack, during which PSM Warren was badly wounded, adding to Birch's overall apprehension as to the vulnerability of his canal side defences. In reality he was between a rock and a hard place. If he remained where he was the battalion would continue to take heavy casualties but if he withdrew to a safer line German infantry would be given the opportunity of crossing the river and establishing themselves on the western bank:

> 'The very exposed positions on the edge of the canal could not be held and I was much concerned. I moved some carriers to increase the fire power in this area and that night fresh positions were dug. I had made a thorough reconnaissance of our side of the 'billiard table' and with the brigadier decided to make our main defence along the courant about 1,000 yards back from the canal with the forward platoons still close to the canal.'[18]

All troops were in their new positions by dawn on 21 May and it was not long before German troops – as expected – began filtering over the blown bridge.

The British reply was a counter-attack launched by one platoon of C Company supported by artillery. The plan involved Second Lieutenant David Muirhead and 15 Platoon approaching the enemy from a flank and, with support from 13 Platoon and the guns of 22/Field Regiment, checking the German incursion. Second Lieutenant Robin Medley witnessed the attack:

> 'The guns fired bang on time and the ground around the target area erupted with explosions, but as yet the attacking troops could not be seen as they were hidden from view. After some eight minutes the attacking platoon came into view with the soldiers advancing steadily, rifles and bayonets across their chests … it was a splendid sight and, as far as could be seen there were no gaps in the lines. Meanwhile, the artillery was pounding the objective and 13 Platoon was firing onto the enemy bank of the canal with their Brens. Bang on time the assault charged as the guns lifted … giving 15 Platoon time to deploy and firm up its objective. After sixteen minutes the guns stopped firing and there was a sudden silence.'[19]

Birch is more matter-of-fact than Medley in his account and simply tells us the enemy 'cleared off when they saw the attack was on' but Muirhead's counter-attack clearly had the desired effect and the battalion was not bothered by German infantry again during its short occupation of the canal.

The orders to withdraw arrived later that night and with the carrier platoon forming the rearguard the Beds and Herts began their move west at 9.00pm under cover of darkness. Quite why the 4th Division withdrawal from the Escaut was begun in daylight is anyone's guess. Blaxland suggests it may have been connected to the intensity of the shelling but it was that very shelling that killed two commanding officers and accounted for further significant losses, losses that Birch's battalion appeared to avoid.

~

North of Pecq Hugh Taylor and the 1/Suffolks had taken up their positions along the line of the river on 20 May. As we know, much of the 1st and 3rd Divisional sector was overlooked by the prominence of Mont St Aubert on the eastern side of the river, a feature that had not gone unnoticed by Lieutenant Colonel Lionel Bootle-Wilbraham commanding the 2/Coldstream Guards. An early indication that the German gunners were using the hill for artillery observation was confirmed when the Suffolks' commanding officer, Lieutenant Colonel Eric Frazer, was wounded by shellfire along with Captain John Trelawney during their initial reconnaissance of the river. Once in position on the river line Taylor confessed to being a little surprised at the close proximity of the enemy across the water:

> '*Now that we were in the forward area we could see the enemy's line, he was occupying a row of houses to our front and we could see very easily where he was … The range was too great for our weapons* [to be used with effect but] *through field glasses we could see DRs* [Dispatch Riders], *runners and all kinds of people moving about. They were very rash as they lit fires in certain houses. We could see the snipers crawling through the long grass towards us on the other side of the river, so I told our company commander and he sent for one of ours, and I think he was successful as we did not see the German snipers again.*'[20]

Fortunately the Suffolks got away from the Escaut on 22 May relatively unscathed, but it proved to be a different story a little further south. The 3/ Grenadier Guards were deployed south of Pecq with three companies on the river bank and one in reserve. To their left, in the village of Pecq itself, were the 2/Coldstream Guards with the 2/Hampshires in reserve a mile to the west at Estaimbourg. Lionel Bootle-Wilbraham arrived in the early afternoon of 19 May, noting the sappers were already preparing the bridge for demolition. Deploying 1 and 3 Companies along the river he kept 2 Company in reserve with the roads leading into the village covered by 4 Company.

Apart from the blowing of the Pecq bridge at 2.00am on 20 May there was very little enemy activity to interfere with the Grenadiers' preparations for the arrival of the German 31st Infantry Division. The first contact came on the 1 Company front with the death of Captain Evelyn Boscawen who was sniped during the

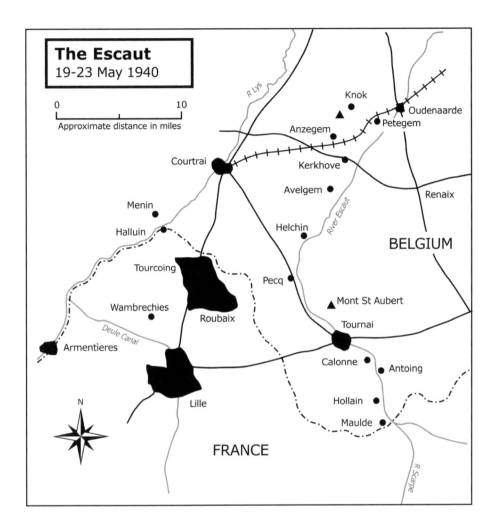

The Escaut
19-23 May 1940

0   10
Approximate distance in miles

R Lys

Knok

Oudenaarde

Petegem

Anzegem

Courtrai

Kerkhove

Avelgem

Renaix

Menin

Helchin

Halluin

River Escaut

BELGIUM

Tourcoing

Pecq

Wambrechies

Roubaix

Mont St Aubert

Deule Canal

Tournai

Armentieres

Calonne

Antoing

N

Lille

Hollain

Maulde

FRANCE

R. Scarpe

night from the opposite bank where an unseen enemy was mustering for a major attack the following morning. It came shortly before dawn: a sudden and violent assault – undoubtedly being directed from Mont St Aubert – which succeeded in establishing a bridgehead at the boundary between the two Guards battalions.

The first Bootle-Wilbraham heard of the enemy incursion was around midday. After a rapid reorganization of the defences around battalion headquarters at the château on the N510 Lille road, Captain Charles Fane was ordered to take his carriers up to the rising ground on the right of 1 Company to form a defensive flank. He was killed shortly afterwards by shellfire:

'In the meantime a gun had opened fire to our right rear and shells from it were landing 150 yards north of Battalion Headquarters. I could not help wondering

whether the Germans had not succeeded in getting an infantry gun across the river and were working their way up between the Grenadiers and ourselves to Estaimbourg. Bunty Stewart-Brown went forward to take command of 1 and 2 Companies and the carrier platoon. Sometime later he reported the Pecq-Pont-a-Chin road was held and there did not appear to be any enemy between the road and the canal ... For five minutes the road to the château was searched by a battery of medium guns. There was one direct hit amongst pioneers and a number of men were killed and wounded, the latter including CQMS Burnett. One of the signallers, a very young boy, burst into tears, not so much from fright as because two of his pals had been killed and he was splattered with their blood. That was the climax of the battle. From then on things improved.'[21]

Meanwhile on the Grenadiers' front, Guardsman Les Drinkwater of 4 Company was in a large barn which was screened from enemy observation by the riverside vegetation. Drinkwater's company was at the critical junction of the two Guards battalions, a position which was giving Major Reggie Alston-Roberts-West, commanding the company, some anxious moments. Sending Drinkwater and Sergeant Bullock – presumably to report on the situation on the left flank – the two men found themselves in the thick of the fighting with enemy infantry from IR 12 forming the German spearhead and establishing themselves in the wood on the ridge of high ground known today as Poplar Ridge:

'When we arrived we realised the enemy was determined to wipe out this flank. We were lying down behind a bush, bullets were cracking over our bodies, trench mortar bombs and shrapnel shells were exploding. The din was terrible. To our amazement, through all this noise, we could hear the familiar sound of a Bren gun firing as if it was defying the whole German Army.'[22]

It may not have been the whole German Army but if the account of *Hauptmann* Lothar Ambrosius – commanding the IR 12 assault – is correct, the Guards were inflicting a considerable number of casualties on his infantry attempting to cross the river. Ambrosius reporting nearly 200 casualties inflicted on his men by the Guards with some 66 killed in the action.[23] Drinkwater writes that his admiration for the two men firing the Bren gun was shattered by a direct hit which blew Guardsman Arthur Rice 'clean through the bush' and badly wounded Guardsman George Button who was firing the Bren. Dragging a blinded Button by the hand and shouting for Drinkwater to follow him, Bullock was last seen 'running like blazes'. Despite Rice pleading to be left, Drinkwater remained with the badly wounded guardsman convinced he would soon become a prisoner. But fortune was smiling that day and they both eventually arrived back at the barn where Rice was loaded onto one of the two company trucks:

'We were very fortunate, the large double doors faced the bank – the enemy were closing in from the rear. A decision had been made for the first truck to turn left, the other right. On clearing the barn we ran straight into the enemy – the essence of surprise was with us. At this stage the enemy dared not fire in case they hit each other; we were through, a hail of bullets hit our truck wounding the driver, but we continued and were soon over a ridge of high ground and out of sight of the enemy.'[24]

Les Drinkwater may have escaped captivity but the venom of the German advance was still threatening the left flank, giving Major Allan Adair little choice but to counter-attack with his reserve company. At 11.30am Captain Lewis Starkey's 3 Company, supported by three carriers led by Lieutenant Reynall-Pack, advanced towards the German positions now established at the base of Poplar Ridge. 'It was', wrote Allan Adair, 'a magnificent and inspiring sight to see the company dash forward through the cornfield and vanish out of sight over the ridge.' Suicidal was the word that immediately sprang to Guardsman Bill Lewcock's mind as he and his comrades advanced across the cornfield in open formation. Met with a hail of machine-gun fire 3 Company was soon taking significant casualties which included Captain Robert Abel-Smith the second-in-command.. Lewcock saw Lieutenant the Duke of Northumberland go down at the head of his platoon and recalled the attack was in great danger of stalling in the face of mounting casualties:

'At this stage the attack would probably not have been successful had it not been for the action of two individual Grenadiers. The first was Lieutenant [Heber] Reynell-Pack, in command of the carrier platoon, who took his carriers across the bullet-swept ground, using them as though they were tanks, and silenced the machine guns on the left by hurling grenades into the midst of the crews: he was killed in his carrier immediately afterwards. The second was L/Cpl [Harry] Nicholls.'[25]

Harry Nicholls was on the right of the 3 Company advance; having already been wounded in the arm by shrapnel he seized the initiative as the company suffered mounting casualties and became bogged down. Running forward with a Bren gun and firing from the hip he silenced three enemy machine-gun posts, during which time he was again wounded in the head. Moving forward he continued to bring fire to bear on the Germans until his ammunition ran out.

Guardsman Percy Nash was with Nicholls as he dashed forward, he remembered feeding Nicholls with ammunition for the Bren gun as they advanced in short rushes towards the enemy. After silencing the machine gun posts at Poplar Ridge, Nash says Nicholls then began firing on the enemy who were crossing the river and sunk at least two boats before their ammunition ran out. Nash was Mentioned in Despatches and promoted to Sergeant while Nicholls – on Nash's evidence – was reported as missing believed killed and his 'posthumous' VC was subsequently received by his wife Connie. It was only after the presentation at Buckingham Palace that it was learnt Nicholls was a prisoner and in hospital in Germany and he was finally presented with his cross at Buckingham Palace in June 1945.

But the fight here was not entirely a Guards affair. The counter attack was supported by A Company of the 2/North Staffordshires under the command of 41-year-old Major Frederick Matthews, who was ordered to attack with two platoons and the battalion's carriers in the direction of Esquelmes – a plan which failed to manifest itself fully but did in the event prevent any German advance penetrating beyond the main N50 road. Sadly Matthews was killed during the attack and although his body was not recovered at the time, he was later found during the battlefield clear-up.[26]

The counter attack – which had accounted for some 60 Germans killed and over 130 wounded – forced the IR 12 bridgehead from the west bank of the river and restored some semblance of calm to the battlefield. Understandably the greater number of casualties suffered in the fighting were in the ranks of the 3/Grenadier Guards where twenty men were taken prisoner and six officers and fifty-one other ranks were either killed in action, missing or died of wounds. Amongst the wounded, Arthur Rice was safely evacuated along with Les Drinkwater who was hit by shellfire after arriving at the RAP with Rice. Both men survived the war. The Coldstream suffered two officers and twenty men killed or missing while the 2/North Staffs lost six officers and men from A Company. It was during the course of this battle that Bootle-Wilbraham remembered, with some irony, receiving an order of the day from the Commander-in-Chief, 'in which he said the British Army had to withdraw through no fault of its own and was to now stand and fight on the line of the [Escaut]'.

～

Lieutenant General Barker's deployment of I Corps along the Escaut appeared to bear out the poor opinon of him held by some of his subordinates – the 3rd Division's commander, Major General Bernard Montgomery, amongst them. Alan Brooke later confided in his diary that Barker 'cannot make up his mind on any points ... and changes his mind shortly afterwards'. During the withdrawal from the River Dendre Barker's three divisions had retreated along one road, communication between brigade and division was almost non-existent and delayed messages were contradicted by new orders that themselves were often rescinded as British and French units became inextricably muddled. So chaotic was the situation on the roads that Private Ben Duncan was moved to remark, with more than a hint of sarcasm, that the 'modern French Army did a great deal to add to the general confusion with horse-drawn kitchens and guns.' Little wonder then there were misunderstandings as to who was to be deployed where. Certainly inadequate staff work was largely responsible for the 2nd Division being squeezed in between the the 42nd and 48th Divisions with the unfortunate 6 Brigade originally ordered to hold the river line between Chercq and Calonne. On arrival they found units of 126 Brigade from the 42nd Division already in possession of part of the sector, resulting in 126 Brigade remaining and the 6th moving into reserve at Willemeau. As Bell remarked in his *History of the Manchester Regiment*, it was, 'quite impossible to trace all the consequences of the orders and counter-orders that were issued to the three brigades' [of 2nd Division] on 20 May.

But it was in the I Corps sector that another VC was awarded south of Tournai, where the 2/Norfolks, under the command of Major Nicholas Charlton, had positioned three companies along the river frontage at Chercq. Charlton had only been in command since 18 May after Gerald de Wilton had been evacuated following a mental breakdown. But at least the Norfolks and 1/8 Lancashire Fusiliers had arrived in time to relieve 6 Brigade before the German assault began, a scenario that was unfortunately not repeated further south at Calonne.

Deployed on the right of the Norfolks' sector – with some of his platoon positions in the grounds of the Château de Chartreaux – Captain Peter Barclay – who had been awarded the MC for his patrol work on the Maginot Line – had established the remainder of his men in the cover of buildings along the river. Private Ernie Leggett remembered his section was concealed extremely well amongst the ruins of an old cement factory. It was from these hidden positions that Barclay and his men observed German infantry making a determined effort to cross the water by laying wooden hurdles across the rubble of the demolished bridge:

'*I reckoned we'd wait until there were as many as we could contend with on our side of the canal before opening fire. There were SS with black helmets and they started to come across and were standing about in little groups waiting. When we'd enough, about 25, I blew my hunting horn. Then of course all the soldiers opened fire with consummate accuracy and disposed of all the enemy personnel on our side of the canal and also the ones on the bank at the far side – which brought the hostile proceedings to an abrupt halt.*'[27]

The accuracy of the resulting artillery and mortar fire indicated to Barclay that the German gunners had guessed correctly as to their positions and were now using their superior fire power as a prelude to a more determined attempt to cross the river. This same bombardment was also searching the battalion's rear areas; a lucky round succeeded in hitting battalion HQ, wounding Charlton and his adjutant thus placing the battalion in the hands of Major Lisle Ryder. It was around this time that Barclay was wounded in the stomach and thigh and with no stretcher available he insisted on being tied to a door and carried by four stretcher bearers to deal with what he described as 'a very threatening situation'.

Barclay had spotted German infantry crossing the river on the company's right flank but in spite of his rising number of casualties he hit back with the meagre reserves available to him – the company clerk, radio operator and other personnel from company headquarters – led by Sergeant Major George Gristock with orders to cover the flank and deal with a German machine gun that had established itself 'not very far off' on Barclay's right. His plan hinted at more than a touch of desperation and, of course, he had no idea it would result in the award of a VC, but it worked:

> '*He* [Gristock] *placed some of his men in position to curtail the activities of the post so effectively that they wiped them out. While this was going on fire came from another German post on our side of the canal. Gristock spotted where this was and he left two men to give him covering fire. He went forward with a Tommy gun and grenades to dispose of this party which was in position behind a pile of stones on the bank of the canal itself. When he was about 20–30 yards from this position, which hadn't seen him, he was spotted by another machine-gun post on the enemy's side. They opened fire on him and raked him through – smashed both knees. In spite of this he dragged himself till he was within grenade lobbing range, then lay on his side and lobbed the grenade over the pile of stones* [and] *belted the three Germans.*'[28]

The arrival of B Company secured the right flank and Barclay and Gristock were evacuated to the RAP. The Norfolks' war diary makes no mention of Gristock's action or his award of the VC which was announced – along with that of Richard Annand – in the *London Gazette* of 23 August – sadly after Gristock's death. Sharing a corner of the RAP with George Gristock was Ernie Leggett who had been badly wounded in the cement factory by enemy mortar fire. Initially left for dead he was rescued by 'Lance Corporal John Woodrow and a chap named "Bunt" Bloxham'. Fortunately all three men were evacuated well before the orders were received on 22 May to retire to the Gort Line. Gristock and Leggett would meet again in the Royal County Hospital in Brighton where Leggett was horrified to learn the CSM had had both legs amputated at the hip. 'I used to stay with him for half an hour or an hour. Every day they'd wheel me through. Then that horrible morning came on 16 June when they hadn't come and got me.'[29]

Some of the most desperate fighting along the Escaut was on the 48th Divisional front south of Tournai where Major General 'Bulgy' Thorne – a former Grenadier Guards officer who had fought with the 1st Battalion at Gheluvelt during the First Battle of Ypres in 1914 – must have despaired at the indecisiveness displayed by General Barker and his staff as they struggled to deploy I Corps. There is no doubt that the delay in relieving the territorial battalions of 143 Brigade resulted in disastrous consequences for the 8/Warwicks who were still on the Escaut long after Douglas Money and the 1/Royal Scots had arrived to take over the 1/7 Warwicks' positions on the night of 20 May.

The 1/7 Warwicks, under Lieutenant Colonel Gerard Mole's command, were a little to the north of Calonne holding a front of some 1,000 yards with two companies deployed in buildings along the river and two in reserve on the sloping ground to the west. The 8th Battalion was in and to the south of Calonne and held a slightly longer frontage, again amongst buildings along the river side. Lieutenant Colonel Reginald Baker moved three companies forward, keeping D Company in reserve at battalion headquarters at Warnaffles Farm. The regular 2nd Battalion from 144 Brigade was at Hollain where Captain Dick Tomes thought the battalion's position on the river was too open on the right flank and provided the enemy with a 'covered approach' on the left:

> *'We had sunk some barges the day before but the stream* [Escaut] *was not wide, only some 30 yards. The ground was flat by the river and the slope on which the town of Hollain stood, which did in fact overlook the far bank in a few places, was not adaptable to defence on account of the houses; we could not have stopped the crossing of the river from it.'*[30]

Although there had been desultory firing the previous day, the fighting increased in intensity during the morning of 20 May. At Hollain German infantry from the 253rd Division began crossing in the afternoon under the cover of intense shelling, making their most determined effort opposite D Company where a sharp bend in the river offered more concealment – exactly the point where Tomes had anticipated the enemy might give them trouble. Tomes' account tells us this was largely thwarted, although 'a few men with LMGs had succeeded in gaining a foothold on our side and were shooting from gardens in front of A Company'. By the time darkness fell the battalion was still holding its positions.

On the 1/7 Battalion front a number of men had been killed or wounded by enemy shellfire before the relief by the 1/Royal Scots went ahead as planned, although the shelling did give Harold Money some anxious moments before the battalion were established at midnight. However, the intended relief of the 8/Warwicks by the 2/Dorsets never took place, much to the chagrin of the men from the 'Heart of England'. All the evidence points towards the confusion of 'orders and counter-orders' which had dogged the Dorsets on 20 May, so much so that by early next morning the battalion was still east of St Maur attempting to extricate itself from the seemingly Gordian knot of units from 4 Brigade which were 'milling around in the early morning mist'.

In the meantime the 8/Warwicks were having a hard time of it due to German mortars and machine guns; one casualty being the battalion medical officer, Captain Neil Robinson who was killed whilst loading wounded into an ambulance. Battalion headquarters and the B Echelon transport also came under fire but the forward companies did manage to prevent the enemy from crossing the river after dark – or so they thought. At midnight a C Company patrol was fired upon from a building on the west bank: evidently units of IR 54 had managed to gain a foothold. Darkness also meant that any relief that might have been planned could not now take place until the following night. Lieutenant Colonel Baker's men resigned themselves to yet another day of hard fighting.

The 21 May was, in the words of the Royal Scots Adjutant, Major James Bruce, 'a hellish day! We were mortared and shelled heavily.' The German lodgement on the 8/Warwicks' front held by C Company was also proving troublesome but not as troublesome as the pressure now being brought to bear on B Company on the battalion's left flank. Under cover of a high explosive bombardment some German soldiers managed to get across but the bayonets of the Royal Scots dispatched them quickly. However, despite the efforts of their neighbours, the Warwicks' forward companies were slowly pushed back into an enclave on the edge of Calonne, giving further opportunity to the infantry of IR 54 to cross at the junction of A and B Companies. The situation now hung in the balance. The surviving Warwicks were all but cut off from battalion headquarters and were in great danger of envelopment. Decisive action was needed and needed quickly.

Lieutenant Colonel Baker's next course of action was undoubtedly decisive but whether his decision to lead the attack himself was altogether wise is open to debate. Instead of bringing his reserve company into the fight, he assembled an assaulting force from battalion headquarters and led them forward into the teeth of the German menace, now firmly established on the west bank in some strength. Captain Neil Holdich, commanding C Company of the 1/7 Warwicks felt the whole exercise to be several hours too late:

> 'Now followed one of the most fantastic affairs since the Light Brigade, albeit on a much smaller scale. Their CO removed his helmet and equipment, put on his orange and blue regimental forage cap, took up his swagger stick and formed up the men of his Battalion HQ in one extended arrowhead on the open ground behind Calonne. Himself at 'point', and supported by a couple of Bren gun carriers, the whole show moved like part of a peacetime Tattoo towards the village. As they descended the slope into the village, the carriers' guns ceased to bear on the enemy and, unhindered, the Germans blazed away. It was all over very quickly, a crash of flame and smoke and all went, three officers and 50 men, only two surviving.'[31]

The attack was a disaster. Baker was killed along with the majority of his men, leaving the British dead strewn across the battlefield and only two survivors to return to Warnaffles Farm. Undoubtedly courageous but ultimately foolhardy, Baker's attack had made very little difference to the situation apart from depriving the battalion of its commanding officer.

The 1/Cameron Highlanders' counter-attack later in the morning did manage to partially re-establish the line which certainly eased the lot of the Royal Scots. Captain Ronald Leah commanding B Company recalled being 'shelled all the way between Merlin and the main road' over ground that was unpleasantly exposed. From Leah's account it would appear that his company headquarters was for a short time situated in the wooded area around the Château de Lannoy and the B Company platoons formed up on either side of the Rue de L'Aire. With their objective being the small bridge near the cement works, Leah's men managed to clear the broken ground behind the works – although he says the area was a 'death trap' with 12 Platoon losing a lot of men. The attack hit Leah's company very hard and he was particularly saddened by the death of Lieutenant Peter Grant, his second-in-command. Yet it may well have been the Cameron Highlanders' counter attack – together with the dogged resistance elsewhere – that finally saw the Germans being pulled back over the canal that night, a retirement that allowed the surviving 8/Warwicks to begin their own withdrawal. Although more rejoined later, that evening at roll call only 366 men answered their names.

On the 2/Warwicks' front 21 May opened with another determined attack on D Company's positions resulting on enemy troops gaining what Dick Tomes termed as 'a considerable footing on our side of the river'. Shortly after this, a runner arrived at battalion headquarters with the news that Major Phillip Morley had been killed leading an attack on a German machine-gun post – leaving 21-year-old Second Lieutenant Kenneth Hope-Jones in command of the company. The attack on D Company was renewed just after midday and although they held on to their positions, enemy troops managed to get into the small wood immediately behind them. Relief arrived in the form of a counter attack by three companies of the 1/Ox and Bucks:

'The plan entailed B Company advancing 15 minutes ahead of the remaining companies to secure the right flank of the attack, a difficult task which was carried out at some cost, including another very good young officer, Second Lieutenant [George] Duncan. The carriers supported the attack from the west while the 3-inch mortars fired a hundred bombs into the wood.'[32]

As far as Dick Tomes was concerned the attack came at just the right moment:

'With the assistance of A Company's covering fire [they] drove the enemy back a considerable distance – though not over the river – and captured about a dozen prisoners. But D Company suffered heavily and the remaining two subalterns, Hope-Jones and Goodliffe, [Goodliffe was later found to have survived] and a great many men had been killed. PSM Perkins was wounded and later died together with the majority of his platoon taken prisoner. No officers and 30 men remained out of two platoons.'[33]

The situation around Calonne and Tournai still remained tense despite the numerous counter-attacks which appeared to contain enemy incursions. But the constant pressure and superior firepower from an enemy intent on crossing the river was taking its toll. The enemy footholds gained along the Escaut – however small – were disturbing enough but the breakthrough on the 44th Division front at Oudenaarde had compromised the whole of the Escaut line leaving Gort and his commanders in an unenviable situation. As with the BEF units further north, instructions ordering the withdrawal arrived on 22 May and set in motion the retirement from the I Corps sector which was 'successfully carried out', wrote Harold Money, 'to the accompaniment of mortars, shells and last, but not least, the song of the nightingales singing as though to drown out the former'. Nevertheless, the Royal Scots had suffered heavily, losing over 150 men, one of which was Major George Byam-Shaw who had been frozen to his Bren gun five months previously on the Maginot line.

The decision to abandon the Escaut was confirmed at the GHQ conference at Brooke's headquarters at Wambrechies on the late afternoon of 21 May which, according to Brooke, was marked by Gort's rather gloomy account of the situation facing the BEF. The Arras counter-stroke – dealt with in the next chapter – had failed, the Germans were reported to be close to Boulogne and there were enormous difficulties in the resupply of ammunition to the fighting divisions. 'We decided', wrote Brooke, 'that we should have to come back to the line of the frontier defences tomorrow evening. Namely to occupy the defences we spent the winter preparing.' Brooke's diary does not mention if the possibility of a British evacuation from the channel ports was discussed at this meeting but I find it hard to accept that it was not: surely Gort and his commanders must have been aware that the chances of the BEF remaining on the French mainland were receding with every hour that passed.[34]

Chapter Six

Arras

21–24 May 1940

'I realized there was no hope of an organized withdrawal, nor could I expect to receive any further orders from 6/DLI. I therefore determined to hang on as long as possible, the persistent but receding sound of firing to the flank and rear emphasising the value of such a course. By now the light was failing quickly but nearby fires enabled us to inflict severe casualties on the Germans until we were overwhelmed.'
Major Kenneth Clark, Y Company 4/RNF,
at the crossroads east of Achicourt.

On 20 May Gort found himself fending off the British cabinet's view that the BEF should move south to avoid being cut off in the north. Patiently outlining his deployment on the Escaut to the CIGS, General Tiny Ironside, Gort explained that seven of the nine BEF divisions were currently engaged on the Escaut and withdrawal from the river line would not only expose the Belgians but would introduce another gap which would rapidly be exploited by the German Army Group B. All that could realistically be done was to use the remaining two divisions to extend the line south of Arras and, with the aid of tanks, support a major French offensive from the south – provided that General Weygand had the means and enthusiasm to mount an offensive in the first place. Ironside's subsequent conversation with Billotte and Blanchard at Lens left him with the distinct impression that little French assistance would be forthcoming. In the event General René Prioux – one of the few French commanders whose morale had remained intact – could only support the subsequent Arras counter-stroke attack with elements of the 3/DLM equipped with Somua S35 tanks and 13/Battalion *Chars de Combat* with their smaller Hotchkiss H35 tanks.

Against this background Gort carried on with his plans independently. Any pride that Howard Franklyn may have felt in his appointment, on 20 May, as commander of Frankforce was dented slightly by Gort's failure to put him fully in the picture. His orders to block the roads south of Arras to cut off German lines of communication from the east and gain as 'much elbow room as possible south of the town' did little to shed light on the task now being entrusted to Franklyn:

'To the best of my memory he [Gort] *used the term 'mopping up'. I certainly got the impression that I was only likely to encounter weak German detachments … I am still unable to understand why he painted such a distorted picture. At the time there were seven German armoured divisions operating between Arras and the River Somme twenty miles further south: rather a tall order for me to mop up.'*[1]

Herbert Lumsden, whose Morris armoured cars had spotted the tanks of 8th Panzer near Beaumetz-les-Loges and those of 5th Panzer on the Cambrai road, adopted a more realistic and pragmatic view of the job in hand, an assessment he relayed to Franklyn in no uncertain terms: '[Lumsden] painted a very different picture of the opposition I was likely to encounter south of Arras', leaving little doubt in Franklyn's mind that his task was going to be 'far more difficult than one of mopping up'. It is also likely that Franklyn's attention had already been drawn to the whereabouts of Rommel's 7th Panzers who had made their presence felt at Ficheux the previous day and whose forward units had clashed with Cook's Light Tanks from the 2nd Light Reconnaissance Brigade on the outskirts of Arras.

The most immediate question that springs to mind is why Gort did not give Franklyn fresh orders in the light of what was known about the strength of German opposition? Franklyn already knew a larger Allied offensive strike had been planned as he had previously met Altmayer, the commander of the French V Corps, who had asked for British co-operation – a request that Franklyn declined as he had 'received no orders to do so'. It is interesting that in his initial briefing early on 21 May to Brigadier Douglas Pratt, the commander of the tank brigade, and the two commanders of the Royal Artillery (CRA) of the 5th and 50th Divisions, Major General Giffard Le Quesne Martel, commanding 50th Division, made light of the opposition they were about to face. Whether this was intentional on the part of Martel or possibly because Franklyn had not passed on Lumsden's intelligence is unclear but it was symptomatic of a very hurried operation thrown together at the last moment.

On paper Frankforce was composed of the two brigades of the 5th Division together with Martel's 50th Division less the 1st Tank Brigade and 25 Brigade which was on the La Bassée Canal. In reality, with the 5th Division deployed on the Scarpe east of Arras, Franklyn only had Brigadier John Churchill's 151 Brigade and two battalions of the tank brigade available, although once the semi-circular attack around the south of Arras had been accomplished, it was intended that 13 Brigade from the 5th Division would cross the River Scarpe and join the operation.

The men of the three infantry battalions were all Geordies from 151 Brigade comprising the 6, 9 and 8/DLI under the command of Brigadier John 'Jackie' Churchill. A former commanding officer of the 1st Battalion, Churchill had been awarded the MC in 1915 and had finished that war with the rank of major. Described as an energetic officer he was without doubt the ideal brigade commander and one who endeared himself to officers and men alike. But the

Durhams were already tired and footsore having marched back from Grammont in Belgium via the La Bassée Canal and were now being thrown into a mobile battle they had not been trained for and were in ignorance of the enemy's strength and dispositions. It did not bode well.

The Royal Tank Regiment (RTR) began life as the Heavy Section Machine Gun Corps which had gone into battle with the first tanks on the Somme in September 1916. Twenty-four years later the regiment had adopted the mantle of armoured warfare professionals and wore the badge of a First World War tank on their black berets. By the time the Arras offensive was conceived Britain only had the 1st Tank Brigade deployed in France consisting of 4/RTR equipped with the 11-ton Mark 1 Infantry Tank – also known as Matilda 1s – and 7/RTR which had some of the larger 26-ton Mark II Matildas.

Commanding 4/RTR was a veteran of the 1917 Cambrai tank offensive, Lieutenant Colonel James Fitzmaurice MC. His thirty-five Mark 1s were armed with a brutish .05-inch machine gun and limited by a top speed of 8mph. 7/RTR was commanded by Lieutenant Colonel Hector Heyland DSO and had twenty-three Mark 1s and sixteen Matilda Mark II tanks armed with a 2-pounder main armament gun and a .303 machine gun. With a top speed of 15mph, six of these Mark IIs, along with their squadron commander, 47-year-old Major Gerald Hedderwick, were loaned to 4/RTR. Thus, in total the brigade had some sixteen Mark IIs and fifty-six Mark 1s as well as a dozen or so light tanks which had the advantage of a top speed of 30–35mph.

The artillery support, such as it was, was provided by two batteries from 92/Field Regiment and two Anti-Tank batteries from 52 and 65/Anti-Tank Regiments equipped with 2-pounder guns. Reconnaissance was entrusted to the motorcycles and Daimler Scout Cars from 4/RNF. Air support – despite Franklyn's request for an air umbrella over Arras – was not forthcoming and the only recorded RAF air activity was from 15 and 18 Squadron Blenheim IVs who were tasked with attacking enemy armour in the Boulogne area. It is a sad fact that the only air umbrella on 21 May was provided by the *Luftwaffe* who bombed and strafed British units with impunity.

Command of the attack itself was given to Giffard Martel who, as a former Royal Engineers officer with the DSO and MC had developed a keen interest in armoured fighting vehicles as early as 1916. Martel proposed to attack with two mobile columns during the afternoon of 21 May. On the right flank the 8/DLI and 7/RTR – with the support of 3/DLM on the right flank – would attack towards Warlus and Wailly while on the left 6/DLI and 4/RTR were tasked to attack towards Achicourt and Beaurains. By a strange twist of symmetry 4/RTR was to attack over the same ground as D Battalion of the Tank Corps on 9 April 1917 when it was brought to a standstill on Telegraph Hill.

Both columns left Petit Vimy at 11.00am on the way to the start line on the Arras-Doullens road where the attack was planned to begin at roughly 2.00pm.

In the opinion of Second Lieutenant Ian English, the 8/DLI carrier platoon commander, it was 'a hectic rush with very few managing to get any rest. There were few maps, no reconnaissance; orders were rushed and many went without a hot meal.' Second Lieutenant Tom Craig, a tank commander with 7/RTR, arrived at Petit Vimy in his Matilda II exhausted and without time to compose himself. He was 'given a map by my company commander and told to start up and follow him. The wireless was not working; there was no tie up with the infantry and no clear orders.' Ian English's comments mirrored those of Craig, both men having concerns that the attack was going ahead before units had got to know each other:

> '*It was a force of all arms on paper only. There had been no combined training between tanks, infantry and artillery. Many of the DLI had never seen a tank until they were going into action with them. The left hand column was desultory and* [with] *largely ineffective artillery support, and only in the later stages. The right hand column had no artillery support whatever because the guns could not be brought near enough to the action due to the thousands of refugees blocking the roads. There were no communications between tanks and infantry due to the breakdown of R/T sets.*'[2]

English had highlighted the most serious misconception of all which concerned the thorny problem of who was in command of each column. Both infantry commanders understood the tanks were under their command while the tank commanders thought they were only in a support role, all of which eventually played into the hands of the Germans.

The left hand column was the first to make contact. Commanding the 6/DLI was 47-year-old Lieutenant Colonel Harry Miller who realized early on that his men were not going to keep up with the tanks of 4/RTR as they crossed over the railway line south of the Arras-Doullens road towards Achicourt. He knew only too well from his service with tanks in 1917 that the work of armoured vehicles could quickly be undone if not followed up promptly by infantry, but first his men had a more pressing task:

> '*I now decided it would be desirable for us to clear Agny as it occupied a prominent position overlooking the road between Achicourt and Beaurains, so I walked across and told Major Perry to continue on that line and take in Agny and the wood northwest of it. It was very fortunate this step was taken as the bulk of our prisoners were captured in Agtny. When I returned to my advanced HQ, I was met by Major* [Peter] *Jeffreys and he reported that touch was being lost with the tanks and suggested that we should send forward the carriers to keep in contact. I agreed to this and gave orders to go forward and prevent enemy infantry re-organizing after the tanks had passed through.*'[3]

At Achicourt the tanks found the exposed flank of Rommel's 6/Rifle Regiment. Sergeant 'Diddy' Reid was commanding a Mark 1 Matilda:

'After picking up a crewman from a broken down tank we crossed a railway line with difficulty, and this brought us under fire again. Ahead of me I saw a railway embankment and a road beyond it on which German vehicles were moving about. Everyone was firing away briskly and I claimed a side-car machine gun outfit which divided itself round a tree and a lorry.'[4]

Second Lieutenant Peter Vaux commanding the 4/RTR Reconnaissance Troop almost whooped with joy as he realized they had come straight into the flank of a German mechanized column:

'They were just as surprised as we were and we were right in amongst them before they knew what was going on. For a quarter of an hour or so there was a glorious free-for-all in which we knocked out quite a lot of their lorries: there were Germans running all over the place. For the most part they were too scared to do very much but some of them had a go at jumping on our tanks and I remember that a German who climbed on the outside of mine was very kindly removed by another tank which turned its machine gun on me and removed him.'[5]

Growing in confidence, Vaux was particularly impressed by the German gunners' inability to penetrate the armour on the Matildas. 'I don't know how many Germans we killed', he wrote afterwards, 'nor how many vehicles we destroyed, at that moment we did not see why we shouldn't go all the way to Berlin.'

At Dainville Y Company 4/RNF made the first ever mounted motorcycle attack together with Captain David Hunt of C Company when they ambushed a German column in the sunken road just south of the D59 where it passes underneath the Maroeuil-Achicourt railway line. Positioning one of his tanks by the bridge to block the route into Dainville, his tanks destroyed most of the enemy halftracks and took some forty prisoners.

As the tanks continued southeast towards Wancourt elation turned to shock as two companies of tanks ran into the range of German guns on Telegraph Hill. The heavier shells of the German 78/Artillery Regiment with 4 and 5/Batteries astride the wood on Telegraph Hill and 6/Battery south of Tilloy, were working together with the 88mm guns north of Mercatel. It was a deadly combination, the results of which horrified Peter Vaux as he moved from the Beaurains-Tilly road towards Telegraph Hill:

'The Colonel's tank was down there, a little in front of them – I could see it quite clearly, it was stationary and I could see the flag flying from it ... I went forward through those tanks of A Squadron and I thought it was very odd they weren't

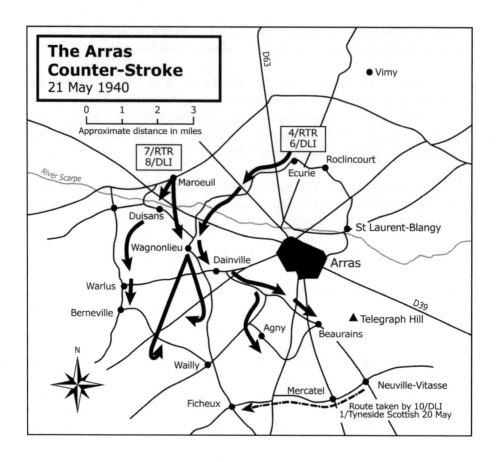

moving and they weren't shooting, and then I noticed that there was something even
odder about them – because their guns were pointing at all angles; a lot of them
had the turret hatches open and some of the crews were half in and half out of the
tanks, lying wounded and dead – and I realized suddenly, with a shock, that all
these twenty tanks had been knocked out and they had all been knocked out by these
big guns and they were in fact, all dead – all these tanks'.[6]

Although Vaux hadn't realized it at the time Lieutenant Colonel Fitzmaurice was
dead along with his operator, 23-year-old Corporal Alan Moorhouse – as was
Major Gerald Hedderwick. Command was now in the hands of Major Stuart
Fernie who immediately called up his reserve C Company tanks to attack the
German guns. SSM Jock Armit and his troop were amongst those who responded:

'I advanced over the crest of a small ridge and ran smack into six anti-tank guns.
They were not camouflaged and their only cover was a fold in the ground. My .50
MG was brought into action and before [they] realized, I was on them – the range
was approximately 200 yards. The other guns started on me now and one hit the gun

housing. This caused the recoil slot pin of my gun to snap and shook the gun back into the turret jamming me between the shoulder piece onto the back of the turret.[7]

Having destroyed two of the 37mm guns he managed to reverse his damaged tank into cover and in desperation ignited a smoke generator to provide some sort of cover, to his horror he found the turret flap had jammed:

'*It was quite a shock to have the smoke generator burning in the tank with the flap jammed, but after a few moments struggle I managed to get the flap open and throw it out. It seemed like hours before we regained the cover of the ridge but all of this must have happened within the space of eight to ten minutes. … I got my gun going again, and, thirsting for revenge, I returned to the attack. They must have thought I was finished because I caught the guns limbering up to move to another position, and revenge was sweet.*'[8]

Revenge may have been sweet but the advance had been brought to its knees, the ripple effect of which impacted on Colonel Miller and the 6/DLI who were ordered not to advance beyond Beaurains. To make matters worse the 5th Panzer Division was putting in an appearance across Telegraph Hill having swung southwest from the Arras-Cambrai road. Understandably, Miller, who was in complete ignorance of the events on Telegraph Hill, was by now a little uneasy with the general situation around him, particularly as enemy machine-gun posts were still apparent in the woods between Achicourt and Agny and there were reports of enemy tanks – the advanced units of 5th Panzer – approaching Beaurains:

'*It became evident from this, and reports of encircling movements by the enemy, that it would be impossible to continue to hold Beaurains, and at 8.15pm I decided to withdraw to Achicourt. A Company took up a position covering the railway, B Company was already in position covering the railway east of Agny and C and D Companies were ordered to withdraw from Beaurains to Achicourt through 4/ Northumberland Fusiliers who were already holding a position on the road St. Martin-Arras.*'[9]

Commanding Y Company of the Fusiliers was 29-year-old Major Kenneth Clark whose brother was serving in Z Company with the right hand column. Positioned around the road junction where the tree lined D919 intersected the Achicourt-Beaurains road, Fusiliers were soon subjected to a heavy tank and artillery attack from units of the 5th Panzer Division:

'*I deployed two platoons forward, 4 on the right and 5 on the left and withdrew 6 into reserve some distance behind. A section of scout cars was allotted to each forward platoon. The Germans appeared to be active, not only ahead but on both flanks ... The leading tanks advanced up a sunken road and could not at first deploy out into the open ground, or at any rate they hesitated to do so. I had already got my mechanics to explore the possibilities of an abandoned anti-tank gun nearby, and with only two remaining rounds of ammunition, siezed my opportunity and opened fire on the leading tank. I secured a direct hit and successfully blocked the sunken road.'*[10]

But as darkness fell the enemy attack was renewed, this time supported by flamethrowers. During this attack Lieutenant Thomas Bland commanding the Scout Car Platoon was badly wounded along with Corporal Winder who continued to command his section despite the wounds to both legs. Late in the evening, with his meagre force surrounded and taking heavy casualties, Clark realized that an organized withdrawal was impossible and gave orders for the survivors to withdraw in small groups. Although a few individuals escaped from 6 Platoon, the bulk of 4 and 5 Platoons and the Scout Platoon were either killed or captured. Clark – by now wounded in the arm – was taken prisoner along with two officers while 166 other ranks were recorded as killed, wounded or missing, losses which accounted for over half the battalion's fighting men.[11]

It was after leaving the crossroads that the withdrawing Durhams and a few tanks from 4/RTR bumped into 5th Panzer in the darkness. 'It was dark with the moon just rising,' wrote Peter Vaux, 'there were flames, smoke, our vehicles, the carriers of 6/DLI, soldiers of 6/DLI on foot; there were German soldiers, some doubtless prisoners, but others on motorcycles.' Chaos ensued for some minutes before both sides extricated themselves from the confusion, the survivors of the left hand column eventually finding their way back to Vimy Ridge.

⁓

The right hand column also left Petit Vimy at 11.00am but without their Northumberland Fusiliers motorcycle reconnaissance or artillery which had been held up on the gridlocked roads to the north. Commanding 8/DLI was 46-year-old Lieutenant Colonel Tim Beart, a regular soldier who had arrived in France with the 2/DLI in September 1939 and been awarded the MC in 1919. Issuing his orders while the battalion was on the move, they came under fire near Maroeuil where German gunners were ranging on the village. Here Ian English tells us the column was delayed and the tanks of 7/RTR soon disappeared off in the distance:

'That was the last the rest of the column saw of them. Contact was lost with the officer commanding the tanks and his liaison officer with the battalion was unable to get in touch with him at any period during the battle.'[12]

As the battalion crossed the Arras–St Pol road (N39) the burnt out wreckage of a column of German 5.9-inch howitzers and a staff car from the 8th Panzer Division were scattered around the road along with dead Germans soldiers who had fallen prey to the 12/Lancers and tanks from 3/DLM. C Company was soon in action around the CWGC Cemetery on the D339 to the west of Duisans where a number of Germans had taken refuge. Corporal George Self, fighting with C Company, remembered they were fired on from the cemetery and with the assistance of three French tanks lead by a French officer on foot, cleared it:

> *'This Frenchman came down the road with these three tanks, walking in front of them, and then he turned into the field and led the tanks against the cemetery ... He cleared them out and some of our lads followed behind ... one of our boys was shot in the back by one of these Germans who was supposed to be dead. I suppose they* [the Durhams] *lost their heads and if there was anyone else alive apart from this German they weren't alive very long.'*[13]

Some of the crews from the burnt-out enemy vehicles had also made for the woods around Duisans Château but were soon rooted out by B Company who then took up defensive positions with C Company around the village under the command of Major Ross McLaren.

Pressing on ahead of the infantry 7/RTR appeared to lose direction and moved southeast towards Wailly, apparently not realizing that Warlus was one of the objectives. Had they kept to the agreed route they would certainly have found the 25th Panzer Regiment between Warlus and Wanquentin on its way to Acq and although the German division possessed more tanks their machines would have been hard pressed against the thicker armour of 7/RTR's Matilda IIs. As it was, the German panzers continued almost unopposed but it is hard to believe that the level of dust thrown up by the panzers went entirely unnoticed by 7/RTR. Unfortunately for 12 Platoon of the RNF they did find the panzers between Warlus and Wanquetin and in the ensuing skirmish lost practically all their number.

Having lost direction, the tanks of 7/RTR now found themselves entwined with the rear units of 4/RTR, a state of affairs which only served to underline how far off course they had strayed. Despite none of the radio sets working, Colonel Heyland managed to get the regiment back on course, although both he and the adjutant, Captain Herman Kauter, were killed in the process as they attempted to redirect the confused tank commanders. As 7/RTR spread out in fan formation from Dainville they were without their CO and, it appears, without their system of command. B Company now headed down the Doullens road before turning towards Wailly at le Bac du Nord, D Company trundled towards Ficheux and A Company – such as it was – moved towards Mercatel.

The column was now split and the DLI were completely without reliable information as to the dispositions of German forces, let alone their own. Accordingly, Colonel Beart with A and D Companies, accompanied by the Carrier Platoon, marched on towards Warlus leaving Ross McLaren in command of B and C Companies at Duisans. Advancing through Warlus Captain Francis Goodenough and A Company ran into a heavy barrage of fire from enemy units on the Arras-Doullens road which minutes later gave way to an air attack by Junkers JU 87s:

> *'For twenty minutes there was the high pitched whine of the Stukas, the whistle of falling bombs and the clatter of machine guns as the planes came down low to strafe. The first air attack coincided with an attack by German tanks coming from the front and right flank. The French tank crews were taking cover under their tanks from the low flying planes and knew nothing about the German threat until Major Raine dragged one of the gunners out feet first and indicated the danger in no uncertain terms.'* [14]

Although the enemy armour was kept at a distance by a battery of 65/Anti-Tank Regiment, the advance had ground to a halt and by dusk the three companies were in a defensive position in and around Warlus. With the darkness came another strong attack with tanks and infantry from the 25th Panzer Regiment which had been recalled by Rommel but delayed by the 260/Battery Anti-Tank guns that had destroyed several Panzer IIIs and three Mark IVs.

With Beart now wounded, this fresh attack ultimately forced the Durhams to withdraw into the village where the battle raged on amidst the burning buildings. Efforts to get in touch with the besieged village failed until Second Lieutenant Redvers Potts, the mortar officer, rode a motorcycle flat-out through the German lines to reach brigade headquarters at Maroeuil in the small hours of 22 May. Then, with Brigadier Churchill's orders for the Durhams to withdraw safely tucked into his tunic, he arrived at Major McLaren's headquarters in the Château at Duisans but failed to make it back to Warlus. With the 7th Panzers on the Duisans-Warlus road McLaren assumed Beart and his men were either killed or captured and concentrated on getting his own force away.

Beart's men must have felt like the end was close; with ammunition running low and the noise of German reinforcements apparent all around them, they prepared themselves for the inevitable. Then, at midnight six French tanks and two APCs smashed their way through a very surprised German cordon around the village and 'rumbled into the village'. The only way out was to run the gauntlet of German fire with the French tanks covering. With surprise on their side and the darkness concealing their movement, the remaining Durhams crowded into the serviceable carriers and broke out to head north reaching Vimy at 6.00am.

But what of 7/RTR who had lost their CO and were now dispersed in and around Wailly, Mercatel and Ficheux? Lieutenant Tom Craig in his Matilda II was ordered to move on to Wailly after a brief halt at Achicourt:

'I was entirely on my own as the other troops had not caught up. About 500 yards from [Wailly] *I was fired on by a large armoured car with a small gun on it; 20mm I suppose, with no effect on my tank. I fired back and the car burst into flames. One of the crew must have had guts, as although wounded he continued to fire as I closed in and eventually I saw him climb out and fall in the gutter, badly burned. I moved past the blazing armoured car nearly up to the crossroads in the village which was full of German infantry.'*[15]

What Tom Craig didn't know when he burst into Wailly was that he was only 1,000 yards from Rommel and his ADC *Leutnant* Most, but he and his crew were too preoccupied with firing on the disorganized units of the SS *Totenkoph* Division to worry about anything else.

Had Rommel not been on hand to personally direct the German response the evident panic may well have become a rout. Establishing himself on the high point west of Wailly he must have realized the battle was at its critical point. A knocked out Panzer III was evidence enough that tanks from D Company 7/RTR had already crossed the minor Wailly-Berneville road and some of B Company's tanks were moving up from the Doullens road sending German gunners running for their lives. Dealing first with the attack from the north before turning his attention to the threat from the west, Rommel turned every available gun onto the oncoming tanks. His divisional report provides an insight into the chaos and confusion the British attack caused:

'While the 25th Panzer is making its attack [on the 8/DLI at Warlus], *the main body of the division is subjected to a surprise attack by a strong force of tanks followed by infantry down the line at Dainville ... Heavy fighting continued between 15.30 and 19.00hours against hundreds* [sic] *of the enemy's tanks ... our own anti-tank guns were not powerful enough, even at short range, to defeat the English tanks. The defensive front built by the anti-tank guns was broken through by the enemy, the guns destroyed or over-run, the crews mostly killed. Finally it was possible to hold this heavy attack by the defensive fire of all batteries ... and after the loss of many tanks the enemy drew back to Arras.'*[16]

Rommel had managed to bring the tank advance to a halt by firmly demonstrating the importance of forward command but, as the death of *Leutnant* Most – who was standing by his side – underlined, it was a style of command that carried risks.

There was one audacious attack by two Matilda IIs from A Company 7/RTR carried out by Major John King and Sergeant Ben Doyle. Whilst this may have highlighted the bravery of these two tank commanders it also drew sharp attention to the vulnerability of tanks without the close support of artillery and infantry. Having begun the day with seven Matilda IIs the two remaining tanks of King's Company careered through German held territory shooting at everything that moved and no doubt causing innumerable German gunners considerable anxiety as their anti-tank rounds failed to penetrate the British armour. King recalled running over several guns:

> 'Suddenly we came under fire of 3 or 4 guns about 300 yards to our front. They did not penetrate, so we went straight at them, and put them out of action. My tank ran over one, and I saw another suffer the same fate. Small parties of enemy machine gunners and infantry now kept getting up in front of us, and retreating rapidly, giving us good MG targets for about 10 minutes.'[17]

Further on they came across four enemy tanks and a roadblock. King wrote that the tanks were about the same size as his Matilta II and were armed with a gun and machine gun. These tanks may well have been Panzer IIIs:

> 'They were firing at the Matilda 1s and when they saw me, the two rear tanks swung their guns round in my direction. We opened fire together, and I advanced up the road, Sgt Doyle following, but unfortunately with his fire masked by my tank. Their shells did not penetrate … my 2-pounders went right through them. By the time I reached them, two were in flames and some men from one of the others were running over the fields. I passed between them and went hard at the weakest part of the roadblock.'[18]

Isolated but still moving King called up Doyle and, reassured to find he was still intact, they both pressed on, by now fully aware they were outnumbered and had a slim chance of survival. Doyle recounts the events of the next hour:

> 'Then the fun started. I know at least five German tanks he put out of action and a number of trucks etc. You see we met a convoy, and we did have some fun. We paid the Jerry back for the loss of the rest of the company, and about 8.00pm, I saw him get hit in the front locker, but he still kept going. I myself was then on fire, but he must have been on fire for an hour or so. He would not leave his tank because we were surrounded by German tanks, so we just kept on, letting them have it.'[19]

Despite their tanks being finally hit and rendered unserviceable both crews survived and for a short time evaded capture until they were rounded up.

The British had paid a very heavy price for their defeat and, as is often the case, exact casualty numbers are imprecise. Apart from the seventeen men of the two tank regiments, the CWGC database records twenty-three identified men from the two DLI battalions killed on 21 May, five of which are commemorated on the Dunkirk Memorial. The RNF have identified six deaths on the same date from Y and Z Companies. Ian English maintains that 6/DLI suffered over 200 casualties and 8/DLI had over 100 killed, wounded or missing, largely from A and D Companies. What these figures do not tell us is the number of wounded who escaped capture or how many later died of their wounds like the unfortunate Lieutenant Bland of the 4/RNF on 30 May. However, we do know that the day cost Rommel's 7th Panzer Division 30 to 40 tanks and 378 officers and men, and according to German sources, 43 British tanks were destroyed, 28 of them being destroyed by the guns of 78/Artillery Regiment.[20]

Many historians are of the opinion that the foundations of the so-called miracle of Dunkirk were laid at Arras on 21 May 1940, a notion that is not entirely true as the action on the Ypres-Comines Canal also played a significant role in delaying the advance of the German Sixth Army from the east. The counter-stroke is often cited as the sole reason for building doubts in the minds of German High Command and generating the subsequent delay imposed by Hitler's 'Halt Order' – of which more in Chapter 9 – that allowed the British to escape from Dunkirk. This rather simplistic view of the situation is not altogether accurate as the counter-stroke was only one part of the defence of Arras and the defence itself did not persuade von Rundstedt to relax the pressure. What it succeeded in doing was relieving the pressure on Boulogne and Calais – delaying the move of three panzer divisions towards Dunkirk until 27 May; by which time a more robust defence of the latter port had been organized to cover the evacuation.

~

While the tanks were burning around Arras, General Weygand was at Ypres with King Leopold of the Belgians and Admiral Sir Roger Keyes together with General Billotte – commanding First Army Group – and General Bertrand Falgade, commanding the French VI Corps. Gort's headquarters had moved that day to Prémesques and he was unable to be contacted; by the time he had arrived Weygand had left for Paris convinced he had been formally snubbed by the British. However, the meeting did confirm Gort's willingness to join a Franco-British offensive designed to cut through the panzer corridor. The BEF and the French First Army would attack southwest towards Bapaume and Cambrai to link up with the new French Army Group striking northwards from the Somme.[21] Weygand's Plan could not apparently take place before 26 May to allow for a withdrawal from the Escaut and the subsequent movement of allied forces. Although an attractive proposition to the politicians, there were few in British military circles who had any faith in its chance of success.

The question as to why Gort left his headquarters without ensuring he was able to be contacted is overshadowed by Weygand's quite astounding underestimation of the military reality. While the myth of allied strength and German vulnerability lingered on in the minds of Weygand and the politicians, the notion of a French assault on the panzer corridor from the south existed only on paper and died almost before it had begun when the fatal injuries to Billotte in a car accident later that day effectively removed the one man who was in any way capable of coordinating such an attack.

If further evidence was needed of the inability of the French to mount a serious counter-attack against the enemy it came on 22 May when a very much reduced force of French armour attacked towards Cambrai. Despite a promising start in which the French 121st Infantry Regiment hit the Germans hard and even penetrated the outskirts of Cambrai, it was the formidable 88mm guns and relentless air attacks of their adversaries that brought the French advance to a standstill.

None of this provided any comfort for Gort who was becoming increasingly conscious that his garrison at Arras and British units on Vimy Ridge, a few kilometres to the north-east, were becoming progressively more isolated in a narrow salient.

The troops in the Arras area – namely the Arras garrison, the 23rd Division and 36 Brigade from the 12th Division – had been grouped together as 'Petreforce' on 18 May under the command of Major General Roderic Petre. The following day, after the *Luftwaffe* had hit the town, Petre had established his headquarters in the maze of underground tunnels that had been used by British forces in 1917.

Making up the Arras garrison with a smattering of French troops were 1/Welsh Guards; 8/RNF; 150 of 9/West Yorkshires – many of whom were almost as old as their CO, the 56-year-old Lieutenant Colonel Richard Luxmore-Ball, a former Welsh Guards officer who had served in Arras in 1917; the 61st Chemical Warfare Company; a company of Auxiliary Military Pioneer Corps (AMPC) and a squadron of light tanks under Captain Geoffrey Cooke. Men of another Yorkshire-based battalion – 5/Green Howards of 150 Brigade, under the command of Lieutenant Colonel Charles Littleboy – 'trickled into Arras at about midnight' on 20 May and were deployed to guard the main approaches to Arras from the west. Command of the town garrison fell to 46-year-old Lieutenant Colonel Felix Copland-Griffith who, like Luxmore-Ball, had served with the Welsh Guards in the previous war.

On 20 May the garrison was strengthened by Major Alan Coleman and 257/Battery from the 65/Anti-Tank Regiment. Unlike those who were already *au fait* with German air attacks and had learned to take cover quickly, Coleman still had much to learn about urban bombing attacks:

'I noticed the whole of the large square, approximately the size of Piccadilly, seemed curiously deserted. Chancing to look upwards I soon saw the reason. An ugly looking packet of 12 dive bombers had approached unobserved [by me] *and the first three were just in the middle of their dive – their target being apparently Piccadilly. Normally the dive bomber gives very reasonable warning: you can see him circle his target with circumspection, then the leader gives a wicked little rock with his wings and leads the first three down with him in a good steep dive, making an awe*

inspiring whine with his engine, before releasing his bombs ... Normally, therefore, if you have a funk hole handy, you can conveniently wait till the machines are well into their dive before you pop as gracefully as you can under cover. In this case however, I had forgotten how deaf you are on a motorcycle and had ridden into trouble properly.'[22]

Escaping death by the skin of his teeth, Coleman remarked in his diary that from then on he did the 'most religious and continuous neck exercises' whenever he found himself on a motorcycle in daylight.

The order to evacuate was relayed to Coleman at a conference of commanding officers called by Petre at 11.00pm on 23 May. As Coleman wrote afterwards, it was news that suited him well. 'The idea of being left to history as the Heroic Defenders of Arras seemed good enough for the novels of Buchan, but its attractions to me at that particular time was largely theoretical.' Coleman's thoughts on the subject were most likely shared by the Welsh Guards who had born the brunt of German attacks on the town for several days. Typical of these indiscriminate assaults was one which 2 Company of the Welsh Guards repulsed on the Bapaume road. Lieutenant Rhidian Llewellyn and 5 Platoon remembered the attack began with a cow being driven up the road towards them:

'A single rifle shot despatched the cow before it could set off the mines. The platoon position was then attacked by six tanks. The battle raged for at least two hours. The road block was set alight and burnt furiously. The front section was blasted and burnt out of its position, as was the other section protecting platoon HQ. Both sections were withdrawn ... this left [Private] Austen Snead firing his anti-tank rifle exposed to the full onslaught of the attacking tanks' weapons, protected by no-one. He continued to fire for the next one and a half hours. The anti-tank rifle had little powers of penetration against armour, however, Austen's well aimed fire against these tanks persuaded them to disengage and withdraw, leaving a deafened anti-tank rifleman to lick his wounds and them to lick theirs.'[23]

Much to the fore in dealing with enemy incursions were the ten carriers of the Welsh Guards Carrier Platoon commanded by 28-year-old Lieutenant Hon Christopher 'Dickie' Furness. As the eldest son of Viscount Furness he was not only heir to the Furness Shipping Company and a considerable fortune but extremely well connected – in that his step mother, Thelma Furness, had been romantically linked with the Prince of Wales in the 1930s. His career with the Welsh Guards came to an abrupt end in 1935 when he was asked to resign his commission after an unfortunate affair with a brother officer's wife, a resignation that was reversed four years later when war was declared.

On the night of 23 May Furness with two carriers was searching for a downed *Luftwaffe* airman. After crossing St Catherine's Bridge in the north of the town he fired two bursts from his Bren gun in the hope of drawing fire from the fugitive. A split second later his carrier was struck by an anti-tank round wounding him and Guardsman Cyril Griffiths in the backside. The round was British and was fired from one of several 2-pounders in place on the road beyond the bridge. Lance Sergeant George Griffin described Furness standing up in his carrier and shouting: 'Who the hell fired that?' Although he makes no mention of it in his diary it looks very much as though Alan Coleman was the 'Anti-Tank Major' who rather indignantly replied that Furness's trigger happy behaviour was responsible, as the British gunners thought they were about to be attacked. Needless to say, after apologies all round Furness returned to Arras without the fugitive, leaving his disabled carrier behind.[24]

Furness was to be back in action only hours later when the evacuation began in the small hours of Friday morning with the Green Howards and RNF leaving first. The Welsh Guards companies travelled independently towards Douai but by the time Furness arrived at the road junction at St-Laurent-Blangy, the traffic was being directed to the right along D42 as the main road had been bombed. Passing under the railway bridge it became apparent that this road was also under fire and traffic was in the process of turning round. It was at this point that the light tanks – presumably from Cooke's detachment – went forward to deal with the enemy while the convoy turned around; joining them was Furness and three carriers.

Turning off to the left they climbed steadily towards the Douai road and having passed through a detachment of RNF, Furness, along with the light tanks, headed on towards the next ridge with two other carriers.[25] Sergeant George Griffin:

'On mounting the ridge we could see there was a German strong post on the crest. Mr Furness bore to the right so as to take the position in the flank. As we approached the top, Griffiths, my driver said 'I'm wounded.' I looked at him and he seemed so casual that I asked him if he would carry on, he said 'yes' but could only use his left arm. I had followed Mr Furness and on bearing round to the left behind the post, I saw one of the tanks with Mr Furness's carrier close beside it. Griffiths could hardly control the machine by this time, and it continued in a circle down the ridge and back again. I kept firing whenever we were facing the right way. We came round to the post a second time, and this time managed to stop close to Mr Furness's carrier. Griffiths was again hit, this time in the thigh. I saw Mr Furness stand up in his carrier grappling with a German over the side. Mr Furness shot him with his revolver, and he fell to the ground. Fire was very hot indeed by this time, pinging on the plates, it was suicide to stand up.'[26]

With Griffiths getting weaker by the moment he was unable to prevent his carrier crashing into the back of Furness's vehicle and stalling the engine. Eventually after several efforts the engine burst into life again:

'There was no sign of life either in the tank or in Mr Furness's carrier, bar the Germans squirming on the ground that he had shot, so we carried on round the back of the post. The windows were all misted over by this time, and it was difficult to see, but we managed to dodge their wire and some tank traps they had dug, and got back on the road at the bottom of the ridge.'[27]

It had been a costly episode but without it the Welsh Guards convoy would have been unable to escape Arras. Of the three carriers that went into action there were no survivors from Furness's vehicle – all were killed along with Guardsman David Williams. Four others were wounded and Lance Sergeant Hall was taken prisoner. Furness was awarded a posthumous VC which was announced after the war but apart from Cyril Griffiths who was Mentioned in Despatches none of the others involved appear to have been recommended for an award despite their apparent gallantry under fire.[28]

By 23 May German forces were across the River Scarpe and threatening to encircle the British in their besieged salient, cutting off the escape route to Douai. This may well have influenced Gort's decision to withdraw 25 miles to the north-east to the line of the rivers and canals that run from Gravelines, through Aire, Béthune and La Bassée, a line that became known as the Canal Line.

The BEF withdrawal from Arras served only to fester in the minds of the French, who declared the British had abandoned the Weygand Plan and were only intent upon saving themselves; an allegation which was palpably untrue. Figuring largely in Gort's mind must have been the breaching of the Belgian line at Courtrai leaving a dangerous gap on the BEF right flank. Twenty-four hours later the Germans were on the outskirts of Menin apparently meeting little opposition. Historian Charles More is quite sure that 'when Gort made his decision to call off the attack south and send the 5th and 50th Divisions to the Ypres-Comines front, he did so because of the information he was receiving about the Belgian collapse.' He is also of the opinion that Gort's decision was taken *before* and not *after* the discovery of German documents by a patrol of 1/7 Middlesex, which brought to light the intended German Sixth Army attack towards Ypres.[29] Accordingly, the two divisions earmarked for the Weygand Plan were immediately switched north to meet the crisis and Blanchard had little option but to formally cancel any further hopes of a joint offensive. On 26 May Secretary of State for War Anthony Eden formally ordered Gort to prepare plans for the evacuation of the BEF from mainland France.

Chapter Seven

The Hell that was Boulogne

22–25 May 1940

'There was little food and ammunition left and no more water, and after another hour of the greatest discomfort I decided my position was now quite hopeless and that a massacre would occur if I did not capitulate.'
> Major Jim Windsor-Lewis, 3 Company, 2nd Welsh Guards on surrendering his final position in the Gare Maritime at Boulogne.

Having taken Abbeville, elements of the 2nd Panzer Division reached the channel coast at Noyelles shortly before nightfall on 20 May and there, without instructions for the next move, they halted. The speed of Guderian's race for the sea had taken both the Allies and the *Wehrmacht* by surprise and it was not until the evening of 21 May that Guderian was ordered to move north and capture the channel ports. His immediate plan was for the 10th Panzer Division to move on Dunkirk via St Omer while the 2nd Panzers seized Boulogne and the 1st Panzers advanced on Calais. Then, perhaps with the Arras counter-stroke still playing on his mind, von Rundstedt held back the 10th Panzers and withdrew them from Guderian's command in a move that infuriated Guderian and delayed the attack on Dunkirk. Not to be outdone the wily German 'panzer leader', without waiting for orders from his immediate superior von Kleist, ordered his remaining two divisions north to take Boulogne and Calais. Although the 10th Panzers were restored to Guderian's command on 22 May and redirected to Calais, there would be a further Halt Order on 24 May (see Chapter 9) that would have further far-reaching repercussions.

In London, Churchill passed responsibility for the defence of the Channel ports to General Ironside, reasoning that Gort was preoccupied with maintaining the integrity of the BEF and thus had little time to deal with them. London based, Ironside had little first-hand intelligence as to exactly how many German units were operating in the Pas de Calais and was forced to rely on Lieutenant General Sir Douglas Brownrigg's inaccurate estimation of German forces. Had Brownrigg been correct in his assertion that only light enemy reconnaissance units were at large in the vicinity, the notion of inserting a blocking force into Boulogne and developing Calais as a supply base for the BEF would have been quite logical but as events turned out Brownrigg's information was dangerously wrong and his subsequent interference, which must have influenced Ironside's planning, resulted in the destruction of several of the finest British infantry regiments of the day.

The 2nd Panzer Division, under the command of 57-year-old General Rudolph Veiel, began their advance on Boulogne at dawn on 22 May. With the intention of encircling the town he divided his force into two combat groups: Combat Group von Prittwitz which advanced along the coast road via Etaples to attack west of the River Liane and Combat Group von Vaerst which advanced along the N1 towards Baincthun and the high ground of Mont Lambert. If Veiel thought his move north was going to be easy, however, he was mistaken as both columns came under fierce attack from RAF Fighter Command and French ground forces. At Neufchâtel, just south of the Forêt Domaine d'Hardelot, *Oberleutnant* Rudolph Behr's platoon of panzers ran into units of General Pierre Lanquetot's French 21st Division at 12.30pm:

'While I feverishly try to discover the positions of the anti-tank gun, I see a little cloud of dust and smoke rise up from the panzer ahead. That was a hit! Next moment the hatches are open, the panzer commander drags himself out and falls down to the rear and remains on the ground at the crossroads. The other two men of the crew dismount and run behind my [tank]. *In the next second my panzer is trembling from a hard metallic blow, the combat compartment is full of sparks as from a rocket during a firework display. The driver is slumped downwards, his head hangs forward. In the gloom and still dazed I perceive blood running over his face. There is nothing for it but to get out.'*[1]

Behr survived the encounter with the loss of two panzers but had run into the defence line between Samer and Neufchâtel where the French 21st Division had deployed most of its 75mm artillery and anti-tank batteries. It was a desperate struggle but by noon most of those guns and crews had been largely destroyed and as the remnants of Lanquetot's division withdrew to Boulogne.

Further north meanwhile, Brownrigg, who had moved his headquarters to Wimereux from the Imperial Hotel, was still trying to organize a defence with the mixture of units that had trickled into the port over the previous few days. Amongst these were Captain George Newbery's party of 70 officers and men of the 7/RWK and Major Tom Penlington and 74 officers and men from HQ Company, 5/Buffs, together with a number of men from the DLI whom he had picked up at Nucq. These men were joined later by the remnants of C Company, 5/Buffs, swelling their number to some 140 officers and men. More substantial was the 1,200 men of 5 Group AMPC, a large proportion of which were elderly reservists – many of them unarmed – who had retired from Doullens with their commanding officer, Lieutenant Colonel Donald Dean VC.

A Territorial officer, Dean had been awarded the VC in September 1918 serving as a lieutenant with the 8/RWK and, as one would expect from such

a man, had led his party in a remarkable journey overland by train and truck –
during which time they had had a brush with the 6th Panzer Division – to arrive
at Boulogne on 21 May. Dean's party were immediately set to work as labourers
on the docks and in guarding Brownrigg's rear headquarters BEF at Wimereaux.
On 22 May Newbery and the West Kents were detailed to hold two road blocks
at Huplandre, 3 miles out on the St Omer road which is where they came into
contact with the advanced units of Combat Group von Vaerst:

> *'At 3.00pm the refugee stream stopped and all was quiet and peaceful. Suddenly the
> enemy hurled an attack at the French who were out of sight across the stream to
> our right. Ten tanks were heard to advance – firing became incessant – something
> exploded and continued to send up a thick column of smoke – an aeroplane strafed
> and shots whistled across our front and into the farm. Tanks and artillery followed
> by infantry were then seen mounting the hill to our right.'[2]*

Newbery noted that the Welsh Guards had by this time taken up positions about
one mile behind him.

~

On the morning of 21 May, having just completed an arduous night exercise with
the 2/Irish Guards, Lieutenant Colonel Sir Alexander Stanier, commanding
2/Welsh Guards, was back at the tented camp at Old Dean Common near
Camberley. Tired from the ardours of military manoeuvres and hoping for a few
hours rest, he confessed to being somewhat dismayed at the arrival of a dispatch
rider with movement orders at 11.30am. Half an hour earlier, Lieutenant Colonel
Joseph Haydon had received an identical dispatch giving the 2/Irish Guards 4
hours in which to pack up and leave for Dover.

Not only did Haydon feel that the new orders 'could not have arrived at a
more inconvenient or tiresome moment' but this was the second occasion in less
than two weeks that he had been called upon to sail to the continent with a small
force of Irish and Welsh Guardsmen. On 13 May he and his men had landed at
the Hook of Holland to cover the evacuation of the Dutch Royal Family and had
only re-embarked by the skin of their teeth 48 hours later, leaving behind eleven
dead Guardsmen.[3]

Arriving at Dover, amidst the chaos of an air raid warning, Stanier and Haydon
were finally told by Brigadier Fox-Pitt, commanding 20 Guards Brigade, that
their destination was to be Boulogne and to get their men aboard the requisitioned
ships. The ensuing dockside confusion resulted in both battalions having to
proceed across the channel with a proportion of their men and equipment in
separate ships, which in the case of 1 Company and Captain Conolly McCausland
of the Irish Guards, meant they were only able to take up their defensive positions

thirty minutes before the first German attack commenced at 5.30pm the same evening.

Stanier disembarked at Boulogne at almost exactly the same spot as that which he had first set foot in France as a young subaltern in 1918. This time he was met by 'hundreds and hundreds of all kinds of troops standing on the quays' along with numerous wounded and civilian refugees all jostling for space aboard the newly arrived ships that were unloading the Guards Brigade. The majority of these men were non-combatants who were deemed to be making inroads into increasingly scarce resources and were now being evacuated on orders from Gort.

Even the most casual of observers will have little difficulty in noting that Boulogne is a town surrounded by high ground which, although bisected by the valley of the River Liane, immediately dictates the nature and location of

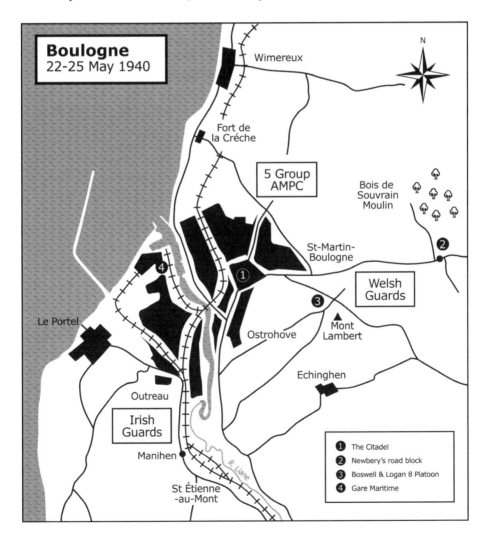

Boulogne
22-25 May 1940

N

Wimereux

Fort de
la Créche

5 Group
AMPC

Bois de
Souvrain
Moulin

St-Martin-
Boulogne

Welsh
Guards

Le Portel

Ostrohove

Mont
Lambert

Echinghen

Outreau

Irish
Guards

Manihen

R. Liane

St Étienne
-au-Mont

❶ The Citadel
❷ Newbery's road block
❸ Boswell & Logan 8 Platoon
❹ Gare Maritime

any defensive position. From the harbour the Rue de la Lampe climbs before turning into the Grand Rue and continuing its steep ascent to the walled Citadel or Haute Ville, 2½ miles beyond which are the heights of Mont Lambert at 950 feet above sea level. To the west of the river the ground is more undulating and incised with steep valleys. The question of which flank the two battalions would defend was decided by simple mathematics; with the Welsh Guards fielding over 250 more men than the 680 officers and men of the Irish Guards, the longer eastern perimeter was allocated to the Welsh.

Stanier was ordered to hold two sides of a 5-mile triangular perimeter with Major Hugh 'Cas' Jones-Mortimer and 2 Company holding a line from the River Liaine to Ostrohove and Major Jim Windsor-Lewis and 3 Company continuing the defensive line up to the crossroads near Mont Lambert. Captain Jack Higgon and 4 Company dug themselves in along the approximate line of the present day D341 as far as the church at St-Martin-Boulogne where they eventually linked with the right flank of Captain Cyril Herber-Percy's 1 Company after his late arrival. All of which left 3 Company on the apex of the triangle in the shadow of Mont Lambert and facing one of the main roads into the town from the extensive Forêt Domaniale de Boulogne. It was a critical position: if Mont Lambert fell to the Germans then Boulogne would unquestionably follow. Jim Windsor-Lewis would have been under no illusions as to its importance but with only three anti-tank guns at his disposal he and his men were going to be hard pressed to hold a sustained enemy attack.

Haydon was faced with defending a perimeter of over 2 miles. He initially positioned his three companies from the harbour breakwater north of Le Portel to the village of Manihen which sits above the Liane valley. Holding the left flank around the high ground just south of Outreau was Captain Murphy and 4 Company while to their right was Captain Madden's 2 Company holding Outreau. From Outreau to the sea was the responsibility of Captain Campbell Findlay and 3 Company. The late arrival of 1 Company and Captain Conolly McCausland completed Haydon's deployment and they were squeezed into position on the high ground leading up towards St-Étienne-au-Mont on the extreme left flank.

At around the same time as *Oberleutnant* Rudolph Behr had run into French anti-tank guns at Neufchâtel, scout vehicles of 2nd Panzer were seen on the ridge overlooking Outreau from the south and at 3.30pm Captain McCausland's company came under fire from the artillery of Combat Group von Prittwitz. Brigadier Fox-Pitt was still unsure of the exact location of the units of the French 21st Division, although if better communication between the various British units had existed he would have been aware of the contact made on the St Omer road by Newbery's men. Notwithstanding, he dispatched Lieutenant Peter Reynolds and a patrol to discover the whereabouts of the French to the south which apart from being fired upon north of Nesles, failed to see any French or enemy units. Hardly surprising as the surviving men of the French 21st Division were by now dispersed around the Boulogne perimeter and Lanquetot himself had taken up residence in the Citadel. However, Fox-Pitt did not have to wait long before the attack intensified. Colonel Haydon's account:

'At approximately 5.30pm, shelling recommenced on the left of the battalion's front and this shelling was followed by an attack which was accompanied by tanks, but which was not heavily pressed. The leading tank advancing up the road towards Outreau was engaged by an anti-tank gun commanded by 2/Lt [Anthony] Eardly-Wilmot. Seven direct hits were obtained and the tank came to an abrupt halt and never moved again ... Number 1 Company's advance platoon on the lower road near the river was to all intents and purposes isolated from the remainder of the company.'[4]

Forty-five minutes later, almost at the same time as a short air raid, a second platoon came under attack after which there was a lull until 10.00pm when 1 Company again took the weight of the enemy assault. This time the enemy overran two sections and destroyed two anti-tank guns in the process, an encounter from which few guardsmen managed to escape. Haydon quickly moved the Carrier Platoon into Outreau to block all roads and prevent any further penetration into the battalion's positions, his written account betraying his unease that the lower road into Boulogne running parallel to the river was now open to the enemy and that he had no reserve, let alone any heavy weapons, to support a counter-attack.

That afternoon the Welsh Guards also had their first sight of von Vaerst's Combat Group on Mont Lambert in the form of motorcycle units and some artillery which began to shell the light railway behind the Welsh lines. Soon afterwards tanks appeared, probing the 3 and 4 Company positions. Guardsmen Arthur Boswell and Alf Logan with 8 Platoon initially thought the large tank that appeared on the 3 Company front was French:

'Look Alf, I said, It must be one of those big French tanks – they were seen on cinema news-reels before the war – but it turned out to be a German tank! In a matter of seconds all Hell broke loose. The baptism of fire of the 20th Guards Brigade had begun in earnest. The tanks withdrew as the light failed and after some sporadic gunfire an uneasy calm fell across the line.'[5]

Apart from copious amounts of small arms ammunition (SAA) being expended, little more took place that evening but, as Stanier remarked later, all they had succeeded in doing was giving away their positions. The Guards still had a lot to learn about their adversaries.

In the early hours of 23 May 200 of Deane's pioneers were sent to reinforce the Welsh Guards' left flank running from St-Martin-Boulogne to the Casino on the northern edge of the dock. It was a force which also included Major Tom

Penlington and his 5/Buffs. When the expected dawn attack failed to materialize there was an uneasy lull until 7.30am, when the Germans fell on both the Welsh and Irish positions simultaneously. At the Mont Lambert crossroads it was Arthur Boswell's platoon that once again found itself at the forefront of the fighting. Having 'volunteered' to go for breakfast he and Alf Logan had just climbed out of their trench 'when a German machine gun opened fire. Alf and I slid back into the hole and Jack dropped flat just behind'. But it was only the prelude. Moments later Lieutenant Colonel Stanier, who was at 3 Company Headquarters, observed tanks heading down the road from Mont Lambert village:

> *'I saw the German tanks come bursting out of the village and start firing at the little anti-tank guns which were just in the hollow below me. They put one of two rather close to the farm where I was peering over the wall. They fired at the men holding the crossroads at Mont Lambert. They burst out of the village one behind the other and spread out. They were in threes; one would be in front and the other two would be looking out either side to protect it.'*[6]

Second Lieutenant Neil Perrins and 9 Platoon were next in line as 3 Company came under increasingly accurate shellfire. Dug in on the Boulogne side of the crossroads Perrins' platoon was under heavy machine-gun fire from a tank moving downhill towards 3 Company Headquarters where Corporal Joseph Bryan and three anti-tank guns from 20/Brigade Anti-Tank Company were positioned:

> *'Sergeant Green alerted us all to a tank that was coming down the same track as the other one, but it came a little closer to us. This was stopped – fired on by all three guns and it was stuck there. You could see using the telescopic sights of these old guns – you could see very clearly that one of the occupants had got out and was on the opposite side of the tank crawling on his hands and knees to keep out of the fire.'*[7]

But tanks were not the only problem facing the Welsh. The crossroads was continually under sniper fire from fifth columnists and Second Lieutenant Peter Hanbury's suspicions that 12 Platoon were under fire from the church at St-Martin-Boulogne were heightened when a round hit his trouser leg:

> *'I went up to the church to see if anyone was up the tower. I did not wish to upset the priest so took off my tin hat, which he thought strange, so I put it back on and started climbing the stairs. He dragged me down. Then I understood there was a fifth columnist or a parachutist up there ... I returned to my platoon and ordered Bartlett and another guardsman to neutralize his fire with two Bren guns. They slowly shot off the top of the tower and said a rifle had been dropped from the tower. Whether they had killed the opposition or wounded him I do not know but he stopped firing.'*[8]

As the attack grew in intensity the Anti-Tank Platoon under Second Lieutenant Hugh Hesketh 'Hexie' Hughes – in position at la Madeleine south of the Mont Lambert crossroads – had decided to withdraw after one of his guns had been knocked out and enemy tanks were now moving behind him. Reasoning he would soon be surrounded he gave orders to fall back across the road to the shelter of the Café Madeleine . He and half his platoon never made it. Another lesson had been learned – albeit at some cost – that moving from a good position of cover whilst under fire is inadvisable, even if the second position appears to be better.

Aware that the battle for the high ground was now lost, Stanier decided the moment had arrived for a withdrawal to form a new perimeter around the docks, a move that was not as straightforward as one would expect. As he later remarked, 'you must remember we had no maps to speak of – and men had to find their way as best they could.' But as 3 Company fell back Second Lieutenant Ralph Pilcher's 8 Platoon found itself cut off on the Mont Lambert crossroads. Arthur Boswell could see at least one enemy tank moving in their direction and several more were heard behind them. Pilcher gave orders for his men to make for a nearby wood one by one:

'I climbed out slowly and after glancing at the menacing tank to see if there was any movement, crawled very slowly towards the comparative safety of the nearby wood. I have never been so scared as I was then – I could feel the hair on the back of my neck curling! Further into the wood I joined Lieutenant Pilcher, Sergeant Pennington, Corporal Webb and others; about twelve in total.'[9]

Reports become confused at this point, illustrating perhaps the uncertainty that existed as the Welsh lines were penetrated. Hanbury writes that Captain Henry Coombe-Tennant appeared – having been sent by Captain Jack Higgon commanding 4 Company – and told him to move back to the light railway with his platoon to prevent the enemy from getting behind them. Sometime later Higgon met Hanbury again at 4 Company Headquarters, at La Madeleine crossroads and they had a hurried exchange:

'Hanbury appeared to give me his situation, bringing with him a few stragglers from 3 Company. Then Guardsman Potter, the battalion orderly arrived on a motorcycle, with a verbal message for us that we were to withdraw at once to the quay. I ordered Coombe-Tennant to take charge of the Company Headquarters and the wounded and directed him to evacuate them in a lorry which was near our position. In the meantime Hanbury was to take over 3 Company and remain in position until 11 Platoon had passed through them ... The enemy could see our movements and proceeded to shell and machine gun our route heavily and accurately, causing a number of casualties. I came back with 10 Platoon and when they had passed I told Hanbury he could move. Then he and I followed his men until we came to his own platoon [12 Platoon] *which had been acting as a rearguard under Heber-Percy.'*[10]

Sergeant Denys Cook was with 12 Platoon when the order was given to withdraw to the quay:

> *'The commander of another company* [possibly Captain Heber-Percy] *ordered me and my platoon to fall back toward the centre of the city, for by this time the street corner was a shambles. I found my company with our regimental headquarters in an area that in peacetime would have been a market or bus terminal. More roadblocks were erected at the foot of the hill and around the square near the wharf side.'*[11]

Windsor-Lewis and what was left of 3 Company withdrew to the Citadel sending a message to brigade headquarters letting them know his location. Later in the afternoon he was ordered to put up roadblocks in the town which was carried out with three sections of men who came under 'intense machine-gun and rifle fire' from the houses opposite. German infantry had managed to occupy a house on the left flank but 'were dealt with by the Bren gun fire' of one of the 3 Company sections. Windsor-Lewis was now established in a large white house at the junction of Rue du Mont St Adrien and Rue des Victoires.

To the west of the Liane the Irish Guards were under similar pressure as the attack opened against 4 Company dug in around the reservoir and high ground north of Manihen. Heavy shelling accompanied the assault, which initially focused on the forward platoon commanded by Lieutenant Peter Reynolds. Reynolds' platoon had, as Haydon noted at the time, already been 'rendered somewhat precarious by the destruction of 1 Company's forward platoon which had been in position immediately to its left'. It was hardly a fair contest and despite Lieutenant Simon Leveson and a section of his carrier platoon coming to their aid, German tanks soon overran the position and surrounded the hapless guardsmen. Orders to withdraw never reached Reynolds and Leveson who were killed defending their positions.

Reynolds was the third member of his family to be killed in action, his father, Major Douglas Reynolds was awarded the VC at Le Cateau in 1914 and was killed in 1916 and his brother-in-law, Lieutenant William Petersen, was killed in 1914 serving with the Life Guards at Zillebeke. Commanding another 4 Company platoon was Second Lieutenant Jack Leslie:

> *'There were bullets flashing all around us in our trenches and a lot of noise – people were shouting at the tops of their voices and the next thing we knew was a German sergeant appeared some yards away wielding a stick grenade shouting, 'Aus, Aus, Aus'. There was nothing for it but to get out of our trench. If we hadn't he would have blown us all to pieces.'*[12]

Leslie survived – and was taken prisoner along with Lieutenant Pat Butler and the survivors of 4 Company. When contacted in 2000 by historian Jon Cooksey, he claimed he could still 'smell' the exhaust fumes of the panzers' engines in his nostrils from the time he was marched past them into captivity sixty years earlier. From a company roll of 107 officers and men only 19 returned to England.

With 4 Company effectively destroyed and enemy units now pushing forward Haydon was left with no alternative but to shorten his perimeter by withdrawing into Outreau:

'Thus at this time the line ran from the post held by 1 Company in the village of Outreau itself, covering the road down the hill to the quay, and the road leading to Battalion Headquarters, through some fields which gave a field of fire of some 150 yards on its northern exits from Outreau, and thence to the original position held by 3 Company.'[13]

Leaving 21-year-old Second Lieutenant George 'Gipps' Romer's platoon in place at Outreau, Haydon's men withdrew under fire downhill to their new positions, Romer finally receiving orders to retire at 11.45am. There is little doubt that in holding his ground at Outreau, Romer had made it possible for the battalion to retire relatively intact. Haydon was full of praise for his platoon's stand:

'They had been in close contact with the enemy for nearly two hours at a range of not more than 30–50 yards. Throughout that time the posts had exchanged bursts of fire one with the other and all attempts to outflank 1 Company's position had each, in turn, been defeated. In my opinion, the holding of this post by 1 Company, which might easily have been somewhat demoralized by the very heavy losses which the company had suffered, reflects the greatest credit on Capt C R McCausland and 2/ Lt G Romer, and on the other ranks who held the post. I was very apprehensive as to whether they would be able to withdraw from such close contact without further heavy losses. The fact that they were able to, shows they must have made the fullest and most effective use of the ground.'[14]

At 1.00pm Haydon ordered a further retirement towards the docks, a move that was accompanied by severe shelling and several skirmishes with enemy tanks. It took a good hour to cover the final half mile down to the docks around the Bassin Napoléon where barricades were erected and the remaining men of the battalion ordered to take cover in the variety of sheds and warehouses that lined the dockside.

Meanwhile there had been a profusion of signals between Whitehall and Boulogne. The initial order for all fighting men to remain in Boulogne 'to the last man' had prompted Fox-Pitt to signal London with a rather terse request for air cover and heavy artillery, without which he said, Boulogne could not be held. His reply clearly had some effect as, with what must have been some relief to all concerned, the order was rescinded at 6.30pm and the evacuation ordered to go ahead. Unfortunately Lieutenant Colonel Stanier was unable to contact all his company commanders:

> *'At 6.00pm, orders came to withdraw into the railway yard and await destroyers who would come into the harbour. I sent an orderly to 3 Company but they could not be found. I had pointed out a white house to Major Windsor-Lewis and suggested that it might make a good Company Headquarters, I myself went to this white house, but there was no sign of Major Windsor-Lewis.'*[15]

With Number 1 Company already across the Pont Marguet and 2 and 4 Companies about to march across, Brigadier Fox-Pitt – who had installed his brigade headquarters in the nearby Hotel de la Paix – warned Stanier that regardless of the whereabouts of Major Windsor-Lewis and his men, the bridge was about to be destroyed. Fully aware that the destruction of the bridge 'wasn't a very pleasant decision to make' and would in effect isolate Windsor-Lewis and the men of Deane's AMPC detachment, the bridge was blown by naval demolition parties on the orders of Fox-Pitt.

~

The chances of carrying out a successful evacuation by sea of the 20 Brigade survivors and the waiting lines of 'useless mouths' appeared to defy the odds. German artillery was in command of the heights above Boulogne and a hail of gunfire was being directed at the harbour and its approaches. Added to that, German armour was forcing its way through the narrow streets of the town and making life extremely difficult, not only for the Guardsmen defending the dockside area, but also for the crews of the destroyers entering and leaving the harbour.

At 6.45pm the *Luftwaffe* appeared overhead in some strength, Haydon thought that there were over 100 machines in the air and about 10 of our own fighters; some of which could well have been Hurricanes of the Canadian 242 Squadron flying from Biggin Hill who reported five losses on 23 May. While the twin-engined Heinkel 111s bombed the town the most immediate danger was that posed by the Junkers 87s attacking the destroyers of the Dover Flotilla which were now returning to Boulogne to evacuate the troops they had delivered the previous day. HMS *Keith* and HMS *Vimy* were the first to enter the narrow harbour followed by HMS *Whitshed* and *Vimiera* who packed their decks with wounded and non-combatants and withdrew under a storm of fire. Next to arrive were HMS *Venomous* and HMS *Wild Swan* which entered the harbour and berthed either side of the Gare Maritime on the west side. Lieutenant Commander John McBeath berthed the *Venomous* on the eastern side of the Gare Maritime and ordered his gunnery officer to open fire with the ship's main armament on the German tanks and tracked vehicles that were now approaching the harbour.

Able Seaman Don Harris was on the bridge of HMS *Vimy* as they followed the *Keith* into the narrow harbour:

> '*I noticed our Captain, Lieutenant Commander Donald, train his binoculars on a hotel diagonally opposite but quite close to our ship. I heard another burst of firing from the snipers located in the hotel and then saw our captain struck down. He fell onto his back and as I leapt to his aid I saw a bullet had inflicted a frightful wound to the forehead, nose and eyes of his face. He was choking in his own blood so I moved him onto his side, and it was then I received his final order. It was 'Get the First Lieutenant onto the bridge urgently.' As I rose to my feet more shots from the hotel swept the bridge and the Sub Lieutenant fell directly in front of me. I glanced down and saw four bullet holes in line across his chest. He must have been dead before he hit the deck.*'[16]

The 21-year-old Sub Lieutenant Douglas Webster was dead and 35-year-old Lieutenant Commander Colin Donald died from his wounds at Dover later that day. Both men were victims of the open bridge structure which characterised the V and W Class destroyers of First World War vintage.

Although HMS *Keith* was a B Class Destroyer and commissioned in 1930 it still had an open bridge which is where Sub Lieutenant Graham Lumsden was when the air attacks began in earnest:

> '*One squadron of 30 Stukas proceeded to attack the 3 destroyers outside the harbour sinking a French* [L'Orage] *and damaging a British destroyer. The remaining 30 Stukas in single line wheeled to a point about 2,000 feet above us and then poured down in a single stream to attack the crowded quay and our two destroyers. The only opposition to this was scattered rifle fire mostly from soldiers ashore and the single barrelled two-pounder pom-poms in each destroyer. As the attack began, with immediate and terrible effect on the quay, the Captain ordered the bridge people below because the bridge was just above quay level and therefore exposed to splinters from bombs bursting there.*'[17]

Seconds later 47-year-old Captain David Simson was fatally hit by a German sniper and fell dead on the bridge. The next few rounds narrowly missed the coxswain but wounded Adrian Northey, the ship's first lieutenant, in the leg and hit the torpedo officer in the arm, resulting in a nervous Lumsden stepping up to manoeuvre the ship out to sea:

> '*The First Lieutenant, now our Captain, asked me if I could take the ship out. I had never commanded a ship going astern and certainly not down a narrow and curving channel peering through a small scuttle with bullets hitting people between me and the men who would carry out my orders.*'[18]

It was, in the opinion of Lieutenant David Verney, more like a 'Wild West shootout'! With no time to cast off, *Keith* broke her mooring ropes and as Lumsden successfully brought the ship out of harbour they passed another ship going into Boulogne.

The journey across the water to Dover was a short one and it wasn't long before HMS *Whitshed*, accompanied by the *Vimiera*, was again approaching Boulogne. The *Whitshed* was commanded by 39-year-old Commander Edward Conder, the eldest son of the Canon of Coventry Cathedral. After the death of Captain Simson, Conder assumed the mantle of Flotilla Commander and the senior naval officer at Boulogne. The *Whitshed's* guns had a considerable bite and were quickly brought to bear on targets in and around the harbour:

'A section of Irish Guards were engaging with rifle fire an enemy machine-gun post, established in a warehouse, as coolly and as methodically as if they had been on the practice ranges. "Tell the foremost guns to open fire," the Captain yelled. The guns swung round and with a crash two 4.7-inch HE shells tore into the building and blew it to the skies. Meanwhile the German infantry now passed ahead of the tanks and infiltrated closer and closer to the quays, the fine discipline of the Guards earned the open mouthed respect of all. Watching them in perfect order, moving exactly together as though on parade ground drill, it was difficult to realize this was the grim reality of battle.'[19]

Although *Whitshed* had taken off the surviving members of the brigade anti-tank platoon the main body of guardsmen were taken aboard HMS *Wild Swan* and *Venomous*. By 9.30pm Haydon and the Irish Guards were safely aboard *Wild Swan* and no doubt many of them were witness to the unfortunate HMS *Venetia* being hit amidships by one of the coastal guns that the Germans had managed to repair at the Fort de la Creche. Erupting in a sheet of flame the destroyer was in great danger of capsizing and blocking the narrow channel into the port. Haydon's account:

'The commander of the Venetia *however, completely saved the situation by going astern at full speed, firing with every gun that he could bring to bear, and altogether ignoring the fact that the quicker he steamed the quicker the flames spread. There is no doubt that the units on the quayside owe the officers and crew of the* Venetia *for their great courage and bold seamanship. The same debt is owed to the officers and crews of the remaining ships who remained alongside the quay embarking wounded and unwounded.'*[20]

The quick thinking of 34-year-old Lieutenant Commander Bernulf Mellor had saved the day but it was to be his last active service engagement as the wounds he received at Boulogne consigned him to a desk job for the remainder of the war.

At 9.30pm the vast majority of those guardsmen who had made it back to the quayside were steaming out of the harbour. At Dover the reality of just how many men had been left behind became clear to a distraught Stanier: not only had 3 Company not made it back to the ships but a substantial number from 2 and 4 Company were also missing. Some of those eventually turned up having boarded HMS *Windsor* at 11.00pm with little enemy interference.

Probably not of direct concern to Stanier was the large contingent of Lieutenant Colonel Deane's AMPC which had been left very much to its own devices to withdraw to the harbour. Making their way to the quayside and crossing the partially demolished Pont Marguet, Deane and his men were preparing to make a last stand along with a number of guardsmen and other stragglers when a ship was seen just offshore. Signalling frantically with a torch Deane and his men were overjoyed to watch HMS *Vimiera* slowly back into the harbour under the very noses of the Germans. In total silence Lieutenant Commander Bertram Hicks and his crew embarked 1,400 officers and men and slipped away in the small hours of 24 May without a shot being fired.

Realizing the remainder of the brigade had gone Jim Windsor-Lewis collected together those remaining stragglers who had not joined Captain Higgon's party – which had attempted in vain to break out towards Étaples – and made their way to the quayside by the Gare Maritime where they settled down to wait for the Navy to arrive. It was not long before their presence was detected:

'*The Germans then began to open fire upon us in the sheds and several men were wounded. I immediately began to retire my force to the station. This was quite easily effected as there was a covered way of approach afforded by a line of railway trucks. The fire from the German tanks was quite severe when we abandoned the sheds which shortly afterwards went up in flames. The Germans then began to fire incendiary bombs into the station and several of those lit up trucks which contained ammunition and inflammable material. I hastily prepared the station for defence by the erection of a sandbagged breastwork in front of the station and on the left flank overlooking the town and custom house.*'[21]

By midday on 24 May Windsor-Lewis and his men had completed their work and kept the Germans at bay for another 24 hours, defying all attempts to prise them from their positions despite the weight of fire being directed at them:

'*Firing from the German tanks, of whom 3 were in front of our position, continued all day, sometimes intense at other times mild, and after 11.00pm, dying down altogether. In the evening of 24 May, about 6.00pm, the Germans made an effort to land a boat on my right flank. Their party of infantry was a small one and we drove them back to the other side of the harbour with Bren and [anti-tank] rifle fire, inflicting losses on them.*'[22]

Still holding out hope of rescue or at least reinforcements the diminishing group held on through the night until the next day when it became obvious to Windsor-Lewis – by now wounded and walking with difficulty – that to continue would be pointless. Guardsmen Syd Prichard and Doug Davies had good cause to remember the surrender:

> *'Everybody was dirty and everybody did their stint. Lewis told us there was no hope – there was no way we were getting back. We were on this train* [stationary in the Gare Maritime], *just three of us firing, Windsor-Lewis was behind us with a load of sandbags and we did not know he had put the white flag up because we were firing after the white flag had gone up. I always say that Syd and I were among the last three blokes in action at Boulogne.'*[23]

During Windsor-Lewis' stand at the Gare Maritime General Lanquetot, with a mixed force of French soldiers and marines, had been holding out in the Citadel. There appears to have been little communication between Fox-Pitt and the French commander and no French troops had been seen on the perimeter defences, in fact it was not until the Guards fell back that the Citadel came under any enemy pressure. By the morning of 25 May the enemy assault had reduced the garrison to the confines of the fortified Calais Gate and permission was granted from the French command at Dunkirk for surrender.

The subsequent French complaint that the British had abandoned Boulogne without informing Lanquetot developed into a running sore that ultimately influenced the fate of British forces at Calais – but more of that in the next chapter. There is some truth in the French complaint that Fox-Pitt largely ignored the French presence and was only concerned with the welfare of 20 Brigade. Certainly, the rather cavalier manner in which Deane's AMPC men were treated in being left to their own devices during the retreat to the quayside, suggests a focused arrogance – understandable to a point – on the part of 20 Brigade Headquarters. Whether informing the French of the decision to evacuate Boulogne would have eased matters between the two governments is debatable but what it did was to add to the growing number of Frenchmen that considered the British were only concerned with their own welfare and lacked the determination to fight the common enemy.

The casualty return for the defence of Boulogne was a heavy one but even today a completely accurate return of who was wounded and taken prisoner is almost impossible to find. The Welsh Guards arrived back at Dover with 13 officers killed or missing and over 400 NCOs and other ranks killed or missing. The bulk of those men were from the three companies that were left behind, the majority of which went into captivity. The Irish Guards recorded 201 men killed, wounded or missing, a number that included 5 officers, however recent research had identified some 25 killed and 15 wounded leaving over 160 as prisoners of war. But whatever the number they, like the Welsh Guards, had lost almost a third of their strength. Number 4 Company had suffered the most, only 19 men answering their names on their return to England.[24] Amid the profusion of gallantry awards that followed over subsequent months were a DSO for Haydon, Stanier, Windsor-Lewis and McCausland and an MC for Heber-Percy.

Naval casualties from the ships carrying out the evacuation were approximately sixteen killed, nine of these coming from HMS *Venetia*. There is no complete record of the number wounded. Amongst the honours announced in the *London Gazette* of 27 August was Lieutenant Commander Clegg's award of the DSC for his command of the *Venetia* after it had been hit on 23 May. The gallantry of the captains of three other ships was also recognized with the award of the DSO to Commander Conder, HMS *Whitshed*, Lieutenant Commander Roger Hicks, HMS *Vimiera* and John McBeath, HMS *Venomous*.

Safely back at Dover Don Harris and the crew of HMS *Vimy* unloaded their human cargo and refuelled. The arrival of a new captain and fresh orders would no doubt send them back to sea again but in the meantime there was time to get some much needed sleep. It was only when the morning edition of the *Daily Mirror* appeared on the mess deck with the headline, 'The Hell That Was Boulogne' emblazoned across the front page, that Harris and his shipmates allowed themselves a wry smile of satisfaction for a job well done.

Chapter Eight

Calais – The Bitter Agony of Defeat

22–26 May 1940

'Two of my subalterns were shot dead by snipers outside my HQ, another of my officers was killed further up the street, and my second-in-command was mortally injured when a shell landed flush against my HQ.'

Major Jack Poole, commanding B Company,
2nd Battalion King's Royal Rifle Corps at Calais.

Twenty miles up the coast from Boulogne, the port of Calais had been an English possession for over 200 years prior to 1558, when Henry II of France finally conquered the last of the English territories taken during the Hundred Years War. In 1805 it was a staging area for Napoleon's troops during his planned invasion of the United Kingdom. Unlike Boulogne, Calais was not enclosed by semi-circle of rising ground to its direct hinterland making its defence an arguably easier task than that of Boulogne, particularly as it was blessed with numerous obstacles in the form of a network of canals and marshes, which gave defenders of the port an inherent advantage.

At the time of writing very few veterans of the Battle of Calais in 1940 are left and if they were able to cross the channel today they would recognize very little of the ground over which they fought. The expansion of the port as a major ferry and transport hub has seen development that has erased much, if not all, of the nineteenth century outer ramparts and bastions that once encased the town leaving only the canals to bear witness to one of the bloodiest battles of the 1940 Flanders campaign; one that shook this little town to its very foundations over four days in May 1940.

Late on 21 May Major Austin Brown commanding C Company, 1st Battalion Queen Victoria's Rifles, (QVR) was having supper at the Saracen's Head in Ashford when a phone call summoned him back to battalion headquarters. Orders had arrived for the battalion to proceed immediately to Dover leaving all vehicles in England and embark for what was described as 'an undisclosed destination'. Arriving at Dover by 7.30am on 22 May the light drizzle and accompanying mist failed to mask the boom of gunfire from across the water, leaving little to the imagination as to where the battalion was bound. Major

Theodore 'Tim' Timpson, the battalion's second-in-command, recalled the confusion on the quayside as the embarkation staff struggled to deal with the units that were arriving:

> *'A corporal on the RTO's staff handed* [me] *an envelope marked 'secret' and addressed to the Officer Commanding. This contained written orders from the War Office; they stated that a few German tanks had broken through towards the Channel ports and that 30 Infantry Brigade would disembark the next day either at Calais or at Dunkirk, according to the situation; the battalion was ordered to proceed to Calais and the CO to get in touch with the local commander or, if unable to do so, to take the necessary steps to secure the town.'*[1]

Having been informed ten days previously that the QVR were being transferred to the 1st London Division most of their vehicles had been handed over to units of the 1st Armoured Division, it now appeared from these new orders that the QVR were about to be reunited with 30 Brigade. Any pleasure that Lieutenant Colonel John Ellison-MacCartney may have gleaned from this news was immediately tempered by the alarming prospect of a Territorial Motor Cycle Reconnaissance Battalion embarking for active service without a single vehicle of any description and little, if any, training in infantry tactics. Rifleman Sam Kydd, serving in 11 Platoon with D Company, greeted their 'new' role with stoic resignation:

> *'We were of course a motorised battalion and had been trained as a mechanized reconnaissance unit with scout cars and motor cycle and sidecar combinations upon which a machine gun was to be mounted to search out and account for the enemy – in theory that was – and in practice in England. But not in France. All of a sudden we were now infantry and as infantry we marched.'*[2]

Infantry they may have been in theory but in reality the fire power that the battalion of 550 officers and men could generate was significantly below that of a conventional infantry battalion. Timpson was particularly concerned that none of his officers were armed at all and many of the men only possessed the service revolvers that had been standard issue to mechanized reconnaissance drivers.

Part of the problem faced by the embarkation staff at Dover was the influx of men from the 3rd Royal Tank Regiment (3/RTR) who were boarding the SS *Maid of Orleans*. Their troop train, which had arrived from Fordingbridge in the early hours of the morning, had been greeted by a furious Lieutenant Colonel Reginald Keller who had expected to be reunited with the regiment's tanks which were being loaded on the SS *City of Christchurch* at Southampton. Dealing with the irate Keller, who had assumed he was en-route to Cherbourg to join the 1st Armoured Division south of the Somme, was Major Henry Foote from SD 7 at the War Office:

'He was very angry and wanted to know what the hell was happening and where his tanks were. I explained the situation and gave him the last intelligence reports I had received before leaving London. I told him his tanks would arrive in Calais that morning. He pointed out that all his tank guns were in mineral jelly and it would take at least a day to clean and zero them.'[3]

Nevertheless, Keller was instructed to report to the senior British officer in Calais for further instructions. His mood was not improved by the fact that neither the name nor the location of this individual was provided.

The two ships taking the QVR and 3/RTR steamed out of Dover harbour at 11.00am to arrive at Calais two and a half hours later. As the *Maid of Orleans* tied up alongside the Gare Maritime the devastation that met the gaze of Major Bill Reeves, commanding B Squadron 3/RTR, was one that remained etched on his memory as he tried to reconcile the peace-time Calais with the scene that confronted him:

'The glass from the windows of the customs house and restaurant was strewn all over the quay-side and railway platforms. Black smoke was belching from most of the quay-side buildings and warehouses and the whole area was pretty much pock marked with bomb craters. We were told to get off the quay-side as quickly as possible as it was going to be bombed soon.'[4]

Reeves' tanks were by this time moving with the mass of the regiment round the Bassin des Chasses to the sand dunes where there was at least some cover from enemy aircraft.

If Keller had some difficulty locating the senior British officer in Calais it was nothing compared to the surprise on the face of Colonel Rupert Holland when the 46-year-old Keller arrived at his headquarters on the Boulevard Leon Gambetta brandishing the sealed orders he had been given at Dover. Although in daily contact with the War Office, Holland had been given no indication of the arrival of 3/RTR or, for that matter, the QVR and it was only when he read Ellison-MacCartney's orders that he realized that two battalions of 30 Brigade would more than likely be landing the next day. Furthermore, apart from rather lamely telling Keller his orders would come from GHQ at Hazebrouck, the only intelligence he could impart revolved around reports of light German armour in the area. At the time there were in fact three panzer divisions in the Pas de Calais.

Apparently incredulous that a motor cycle battalion had been sent to him without any of its transport, Holland sent the QVR to secure the six main roads leading into the town beyond the outer perimeter. With no transport, apart from what they could requisition on the spot, the QVR was to defend a wide frontage of 15 miles, which, for a lightly armed battalion without the benefit of any prior reconnaissance or heavy weaponry, was a ludicrous proposition at the best of times. Nevertheless, having established battalion headquarters at the Dunkirk Gate, Ellison-MacCartney returned to the quayside where the QVR had taken up defensive positions to pass on his orders to company commanders. Faced with the longest march along the D940 coast road to Sangatte, B Company, under the command of Captain George Bowring, requisitioned Oyez Farm as their headquarters and sent 5 Platoon and Second Lieutenant Dizer into Sangatte itself. Major Austin Brown and C Company were detailed to block the eastern roads to Dunkirk, Gravelines and Fort Vert while the road block on the Boulogne road was the preserve of Captain Tim Munby's Scout Platoon and the men of Second Lieutenant Nelson's 6 Platoon. D Company, which was possibly the least 'experienced' company, with a subaltern in command was sent to hold the roads to the south around Les Fontinettes. Appointed to command the company only days before leaving Ashford, Lieutenant Vic Jessop and his 26-year-old second-in-command, Second Lieutenant Anthony Jabez-Smith were very much aware that the road accident which had deprived them of their regular commanding officer two days earlier had removed the one officer who had any experience of warfare. This was soon to change.

∼

By the time Jabez-Smith and D Company were in position, the tanks and Dingo scout cars of 3/RTR were still being unloaded from the SS *Christchurch* which had finally docked at 4.00pm. As work progressed feverishly to unload 3/RTR's stores and equipment the tiresome figure of Lieutenant General Brownrigg arrived from Boulogne with orders for the regiment to move immediately to relieve 20 Guards Brigade. Unable to comply, Keller was at pains to point out to an agitated Brownrigg that it was going to be some time before his regiment was ready to move:

> *'Tanks are not put into ships by squadrons and are unloaded piecemeal. In consequence it was probable that squadrons would not get their tanks together. I was constantly asked how soon I could be ready and eventually, very reluctantly, said 1.00am on 23 May. Unloading went on during the night of 22/23 May, but very slowly and was considerably delayed.'*[5]

The delay was fortuitous. At roughly the same time Brownrigg was directing Keller to move to the aid of 20 Brigade, the 2nd Panzer Division was beginning its assault on the Boulogne garrison and the tanks of 1st Panzers were heading towards the Forêt de Boulogne; the very place Brownrigg was proposing Keller should direct his tanks towards! Fortunately these orders were superseded by a Major Bailey of the Ox and Bucks Light Infantry who arrived at 11.00pm from Gort's Headquarters with orders for 3/RTR to move immediately to secure the crossings over the Aa Canal at St Omer and Watten.

Since first arriving at Dover, Keller had been in receipt of three sets of orders in the space of some twelve hours and Bailey's verbal orders from GHQ – which would see 3/RTR moving southeast instead of southwest towards Boulogne – quite understandably aroused Keller's suspicions. As far as Keller was concerned he was still under Brownrigg's orders until Bailey's identity was vouched for by Holland himself. One cannot help but sympathise with the tank commander:

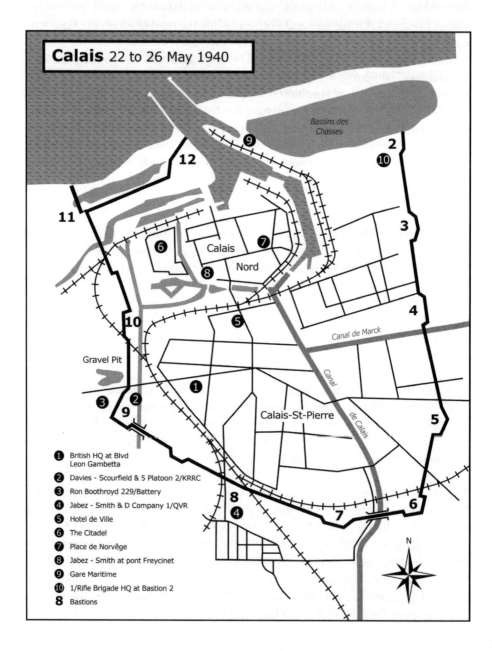

Calais 22 to 26 May 1940

Bassins des Chasses

Calais Nord

Canal de Marck

Canal de Calais

Gravel Pit

Calais-St-Pierre

N

❶ British HQ at Blvd Leon Gambetta
❷ Davies - Scourfield & 5 Platoon 2/KRRC
❸ Ron Boothroyd 229/Battery
❹ Jabez - Smith & D Company 1/QVR
❺ Hotel de Ville
❻ The Citadel
❼ Place de Norvêge
❽ Jabez - Smith at pont Freycinet
❾ Gare Maritime
❿ 1/Rifle Brigade HQ at Bastion 2
8 Bastions

torn between setting out for either Boulogne or St Omer it was only Bailey's insistence that GHQ orders had priority over all others which eventually won the day.

The task of unloading 3/RTR's armoured vehicles had not been helped by the loading schedule at Southampton. The twenty-seven Cruisers – the heaviest tanks – had been stowed in the bottom of the ship's hold with the twenty-one lighter Mark VI tanks and scout cars on the two levels above. Ammunition and spares had been distributed around the various holds without any regard to access and the whole cargo was capped by 7,000 gallons of petrol in four gallon 'flimsies' lashed to the deck. On arriving at Calais the job was not made any easier by the French dock workers disappearing shortly after the *Christchurch* had tied up. But, with the help of a section of RASC dock workers, each tank was slowly unloaded and filled with fuel while the main armament was cleansed by removing the mineral jelly which had been applied prior to travelling. Many, like Trooper Robert Watt, were more concerned with the leaking cans of petrol on the deck, expecting any minute an 'unfriendly enemy' to ignite the whole lot and blow them all to kingdom come! Given the huge task confronting the battalion it was hardly surprising that at 12.20am on 23 May 3/RTR was still not in a state of readiness.

Ultimately it was the urgency of the situation that pressed Keller into action. As soon as enough light tanks were unloaded Major Simpson, commanding A Squadron, was tasked with sending out a patrol towards St Omer. Second Lieutenant Mundy with 2 Troop got through to St Omer and reported the town to be in flames but devoid of Germans. Bailey, evidently dissatisfied with Mundy's report, urged Keller to try to reach St Omer again with his main force while he returned to GHQ with an escort of light tanks from A Squadron. Simpson's feelings regarding the use of his tanks as escort are not recorded but it is unlikely he was entirely happy about it:

> 'About 8.00am I received orders to send a light tank troop to escort Major Bailey to St Omer where he believed GHQ to be. I ordered 2/Lt Eastman with 3 Troop consisting of 3 light tanks to do this. About half an hour after they moved off I received a wireless message from 2/Lt Eastman to say they didn't know where Major Bailey had got to and asked me what to do. I told him if he could not find Major Bailey at once, to proceed on to St Omer and get in touch with GHQ.'[6]

Three miles south of Ardres on the N43 Eastman and his patrol ran into enemy forces and only one tank returned to Coquelles. Bailey, who had taken a wrong turning, managed to return after running into a German patrol near Les Cappes with his vehicle punctured by numerous bullet holes as a souvenir of his narrow escape.

By the time Bailey had made his way back to Calais the bulk of 3/RTR was formed up around Coquelles and Keller had established his headquarters at La

Beussingue Farm, which today is almost encircled by the channel tunnel terminal and the A16 Autoroute. On his return Bailey stressed the need for Keller to continue on to St Omer, a move that Keller admits was 'much against his better judgement' and a view shared by Major Bill Reeves who was now commanding B Squadron from a tank he was unfamiliar with:

> 'Owing to the urgency squadrons were formed of the tanks as they were unloaded, with the result that Squadron Commanders did not get their own tanks and in some cases not even their own crews, because the light tanks only had a crew of three, whereas the Cruisers had a crew of five. As squadrons were formed they moved off from the quayside to Coquelles where we arrived at approximately 11.00pm. There the CO gave out his orders. We were to proceed immediately to St Omer for the role of protecting GHQ.'[7]

3/RTR left Calais shortly after 2.00pm with a troop of light tanks from B Squadron pushing ahead as advance guard. Having passed through St Tricat the fleeting glimpse in the rain of enemy light tanks on the right flank was the first indication of an enemy column in the vicinity, a column that was finally spotted as Lieutenant Williams crested the rise which overlooked Guines. They had found the 1st Panzer Division en-route to Gravelines and there was little alternative but to engage them as best they could:

> 'It was not possible to gauge the exact strength of the enemy column, the CO decided to take up a position on the hill south of Guines and attack the column in the left flank. This would have been extremely sound tactics in normal circumstances but on this occasion all was against us. We had no supporting artillery, anti-tank guns, or infantry and our guns were far outranged by those of the enemy … It was very impressive to see the reaction of the German column on being attacked. They very rapidly dismounted from their vehicles and got their anti-tank guns into action, and soon shots were whizzing past our ears. My own tank was a Cruiser A9, which only had a smoke howitzer and one MG on it. This was not encouraging, as I could only watch other tanks fighting and not hit back myself.'[8]

Although it quickly became apparent the battalion was outgunned, in the seconds following the initial contact there was a concern that the 'enemy' tanks may actually be French. This thought may well have crossed the mind of Captain Barry O'Sullivan, who was second-in-command of B Squadron:

> 'On our mutual encounter, both forces appeared to hesitate for some seconds before opening fire. The German tanks were halted on the road and all in position behind trees. We were deployed on the fields and advancing towards them. From the start the enemy were able to concentrate superior fire power on us, as there appeared to

be only 3 or 4 of our Cruisers up, who would reply with any effect. We concentrated our machine guns on the lorries.'[9]

The poor visibility may have provided 3/RTR with a modicum of cover but the battle which ranged over the fields and tracks around Hames-Boucres was still very much a one-sided affair. The lesson that was being dished-out by the German panzers division was simple: that armour alone was unlikely to succeed in the face of an enemy who was able to deploy a combination of tanks, artillery and anti-tank weapons. It was a lesson many British tank units were slow to grasp in the early stages of the war with often fatal consequences: O'Sullivan's tank was amongst those to feel the full weight of the German fire:

'My tank was hit twice by 2-pounder shells which smashed part of the off-side suspension and track. We swung broadside to the enemy and managed to crawl down a bank into an extremely well camouflaged hull-down position. On examining the damage, I saw the suspension was damaged beyond repair, and the track was some seventy yards away.'[10]

O'Sullivan continued to engage the enemy for another ten minutes before the machine guns were put out of action by two further hits on the turret. With one of the crew wounded O'Sullivan managed to operate the third machine gun from the top of the turret until German troops who had moved up through the woods opened fire again with anti-tank guns from 600 yards range:

'I therefore dismounted the machine gun from the top of the tank and found a gap some fifteen yards away from which to deal with this threat. Whilst engaged in this and in getting the ammunition boxes out, with 4 members of the crew, Galbraith and Price were firing the machine gun …The two light tanks with me were by now knocked out and appeared deserted and the A13 Cruiser was on fire … There was no sign of the battalion reappearing and I judged by the shelling they had met heavy opposition behind the wood and had been forced to withdraw towards Calais.'[11]

They had indeed been forced to withdraw but Keller was determined to have another crack at the panzers, this time from the south. With his own tank damaged by a shell exploding against the turret and disabling the main armament, Keller ordered his tanks to retire under the cover of a smoke screen to a new position behind the railway line that ran southwest from Calais round Pihen-les-Guines:

'I rallied the battalion back behind the railway and had just ordered a squadron forward when a message from Calais was picked up saying a Brigadier Nicholson wanted to see me. I queried this but was told, as far as I could make out, that there

were new orders for me. The wireless was very indistinct and neither I nor my Adjutant could quite make out what was required.'[12]

Nicholson's ill-timed request had caught Keller in the midst of a tank battle and although Keller's account – which was written sometime after the battle – makes no mention of it, the story that echoed across the airwaves of the 3/RTR radio network was that Keller had replied with the words, 'Get off the air, I'm trying to fight a bloody battle'. Nevertheless, an order was an order and the surviving tanks of 3/RTR made their way back to Coquelles where the meeting between Keller and Nicholson took place at 8.00pm on 23 May.

∼

While the tank encounter between 3/RTR and the 1st Panzer Division was taking place during the afternoon of 23 May, the two Green Jacket battalions were disembarking at Calais. Both were regular battalions with a long pedigree whose parent regiments had been raised over 140 years previously. Both regiments had fought with distinction during the Napoleonic Wars and were arguably amongst the best trained rifle regiments in the British Army. Earmarked initially for the Norwegian campaign they were the only two mechanized infantry battalions the British Army possessed in 1940 and thus considered eminently suitable for securing Calais as a supply route for the beleaguered BEF.

The first to arrive was the 2/King's Royal Rifle Corps (2/KRRC) on board the SS *Royal Daffodil*. In command was 43-year-old Lieutenant Colonel Euan Miller who had served in the 4th Battalion in France with Jack Poole – now commanding B Company – in 1915. An experienced soldier, who had been awarded the MC in 1918, he was less than happy with the time it took to unload the battalion's vehicles and equipment from the SS *Kohistan* which finally nosed its way into the harbour at 4.00pm.

The 1/Rifle Brigade together with Brigadier Nicholson and the brigade staff arrived on the SS *Archangel* which docked shortly after the KRRC. In command of the Rifle Brigade was 44-year-old Lieutenant Colonel Chandos Hoskyns, a well respected officer who had been appointed in 1938 and, like Miller, had served in the previous war. The Rifle Brigade's vehicle ship, the SS *City of Canterbury*, the same ship that had brought the QVR from Dover the previous day, arrived an hour behind the *Kohistan* and did not berth until almost 5.00pm by which time the dock was being shelled by German artillery.

Nicholson had very little time in which to grasp the increasingly desperate nature of the picture that was now unfolding around him. Late in the afternoon, having made the return journey to see Holland at his Calais Headquarters, he briefed Miller and Hoskyns. Miller's recollection of that meeting, which he later relayed to his company commanders, bore little resemblance to the task they were expecting to carry out: that of securing the lines of communication between Calais and the BEF:

> 'The situation was that the QVR, who had landed yesterday, were blocking the main roads leading into the town. These blocks were generally a mile or two outside the town. 3/RTR Tanks had been sent off towards St Omer about midday on orders from GHQ and after some rather heavy losses near Guines were now astride the roads west of Coquelles and were in touch with the enemy. In and around the town were various AA and searchlight units and also troops from Boulogne. Most of these were disorganized and of little value. Germans with tanks and artillery were rapidly approaching the town and had begun to shell it. 30 Infantry Brigade could obviously not carry out its original role and the immediate problem was the defence of Calais itself.'[13]

It was now becoming obvious that the enemy was far stronger than originally expected. 3/RTR had already lost four light and three Cruiser tanks in the encounter at Hames-Boucres and although some crews like O'Sullivan's were trying to get back to the safety of British lines, the unit's introduction to mobile warfare had been hard. In a separate action at Les Attaques – some two hours before 3/RTR became engaged – the men of 1/Searchlight Battery had also clashed with the tanks of Kirchner's 1st Panzer Division. Arriving with three detachments from C Troop, Second Lieutenant Barr barricaded and held the crossroads for almost three hours before they were forced to surrender. Another detachment was in action at the Le Colombier crossroads just east of Orphanage Farm where the panzers were again held up for two hours before the survivors withdrew to the outer perimeter.

In Calais, Lieutenant Gris Davies-Scourfield – in command of 5 Platoon of B Company of the KRRC – noted the the precarious nature of the proposed defence as outlined during the short briefing given by his company commander, Major Jack Poole:

> 'Our battalion's immediate task was to secure the outer perimeter of Calais from the coast on the west to a point on the southern edge of town where the Rifle Brigade would continue to hold the line to the coast on the east side, a front of about 8 miles. The QVRs and 3rd Tanks would continue to hold their forward positions as long as possible: on withdrawing, the QVR companies would come under command of the battalion whose front they had been covering. The 2-pounder guns of 229 Anti-Tank Battery were to cover the main roads.'[14]

Nicholson opted to defend the seventy-year-old heart shaped, outer perimeter of Calais part of which, to the south of the town, roughly followed the line of the railway to Gravelines. This perimeter was interspersed by twelve bastions which had originally been an integral part of the outer earth rampart. While units of 30 Brigade would garrison the majority of the perimeter, the northernmost bastions and fortifications around the harbour would be manned largely by French naval reservists under *Capitaine* de Lambertye. The term 'bastion' was somewhat of a misnomer as many of these ageing redoubts – where they existed at all – now bore little resemblance to their original grandeur, as Lieutenant Davies-Scourfield found when deployed to Bastion 9 with 5 Platoon on the Coquelles road. He found himself defending 'a high semi-circular mound with blocks of stone and concrete round the crest of its circumference', which was all that remained after the embankment and bastion had been demolished to make way for the railway.

The 229/Battery anti-tank guns had arrived on the SS *Autocarrier* earlier in the afternoon of 23 May still carrying the vehicles of 12/Wireless Section which it had failed to unload two days earlier. According to Lieutenant Austin Evitts, the ship's captain had scuttled out of the harbour after being told he would have to wait until morning before power was restored to the dock cranes.[15] Now berthed alongside the Gare Maritime, there had only been room for eight of the twelve guns in the crowded hold. Disembarking with the men of the anti-tank battery was Gunner Ron Boothroyd, a territorial with eight year's service, who was soon employed with his mates digging a gun pit by 'the side of a country lane between two small hills'. Quite where Boothroyd's gun was is unclear but he may have been near Bastion 9 in front of the flooded gravel pit. Every gun, he wrote, went to a different spot outside the town about one mile apart. One of these guns was in position with D Company of the QVR at Les Fontinettes.

The QVR had passed a relatively peaceful night on 22 May with nothing particularly untoward taking place. Dawn the next day saw the platoons of D Company consolidating their road blocks on the approach roads to the town. The first brief contact with the enemy came at around 9.00am when two attempts by German light tanks were repulsed by the guns of a French detachment. There was little further excitement until later in the afternoon when two platoons of the KRRC and RB took up positions astride the St Omer Gate on the ramparts behind them. Jabez-Smith's account records that orders to retire to the area around Bastion 8 came soon after dawn on 24 May when D Company were ordered to reinforce the perimeter line held by the KRRC. From all accounts it was not a moment too soon. 'Immediately the men were in position, firing took place, the enemy being in houses and gardens in the neighbourhood we had just left.' After establishing company headquarters in a house behind the firing line, Jabez-Smith set off to visit the platoon positions:

> '*Bill* [Brewster, 11 Platoon] *was already in great trouble. He had, at the suggestion of the 60th* [the old regimental number of the KRRC] *platoon commander on his left, taken up a position with no protected line of withdrawal. There was an exposed railway embankment to cross to get to and from him and he was unable to get*

Carriers of the 2nd Battalion Essex Regiment advancing into Belgium on 11 May 1940. Refugees are seen moving in the opposite direction.

Lieutenant Richard Annand VC seen here on his marriage to Shirley Osborne in November 1940.

Captain Cyril Townsend who was wounded at St Venant and managed to return to England.

German armoured vehicles enter the outskirts of Calais on 26 May 1940

Defence of the River Dyle
15th/16th May 1940

Barnes A B	Pte	2DLI	Pearson J		2DLI
Brown WJ	Pte	2DLI	Pugmire JJ	Pte	2DLI
Cullen AE	Pte	2DLI	Shawcroft J	Pte	2DLI
Curtis W	Cpl	2DLI	Smart JW	Pte	2DLI
Cuthill J	Pte	2DLI	Smith WT	Pte	2DLI
Davison A	Pte	2DLI	Taylor W	Pte	1RBR
Ditchburn RW	WOII	2DLI	Thompson WH	Pte	2DLI
Flanaghan E		RWF	Walker K		2DLI
Foster P	Pte	2DLI	Warbey E	Pte	1RBR
Gibson R	Pte	2DLI	Waters REO	Pte	2DLI
Harper R	Pte	2DLI	White W	Pte	2DLI
Harrison H	Pte	2DLI	Wilson M	Cpl	2DLI
Hawkins E	Pte	2DLI	Wood J	Pte	2DLI
Higgins GF	Pte	2DLI	Wood W	Pte	2DLI
Lloyd J	Fus	1RWF	Young H	Pte	2DLI
Marshall R	Pte	2DLI	Unknown Soldier		
Ohalloran JJ	Pte	1RBR	Unknown Soldier		
Pullan J	Pte	2DLI			

The site of the bridge over the Dyle which was defended by
Lieutenant Richard Annand's platoon and resulted in his
award of the VC. *Inset:* The DLI Memorial on the bridge.

A British anti-tank crew at Louvain with their 25mm Hotchkiss gun. The gun fired a 2-pound solid shot which could penetrate the armour of German light tanks.

Lieutenant Colonel Herbert Lumsden who commanded the 12th Lancers in France and Flanders.

Lieutenant Michael Farr photographed in the dress uniform of the DLI.

The speed of the German armoured thrust through France took the Allies by surprise.

The Royal Welch Memorial at St Venant stands on the site of the bridge where Lieutenant Colonel Harrison was killed.

The British Commander-in-Chief, Lord Gort VC, inspecting troops.

The Matilda Mark II Tank.

John Hyde-Thompson, photographed before the Flanders campaign of 1940.

Mark Henniker photographed after the war in the uniform of a major general.

The gallant HMS *Keith* was one of the destroyers deployed to evacuate the Boulogne garrison. Coming under fire from German units ashore, Captain David Simson was killed on the bridge. She was sunk off Dunkirk on 1 June 1940.

A German anti-tank gun crew with their 3.7cm Pak 35/36 on the Menin–Ypres road. It was the rapid advance of the German Sixth Army after the capitulation of Belgium that first alerted Gort to the danger on his eastern flank.

Erwin Rommel commanded the 7th Panzer Division during the invasion of Belgium and France in 1940.

Brigadier Nigel Somerset, commanded 145 Brigade at Cassel.

The barn on the Chemin du Paradis where the men of the Royal Norfolks were murdered on 27 May 1940.

German troops in the main square at Cassel after the evacuation by 145 Brigade. The buildings behind the German motorcyclist show some of the damage inflicted on the town by the *Luftwaffe* bombardment.

The blockhouse at Peckel just north of Cassel on the D916 defended by Second Lieutenant Cresswell and 8 Platoon of 2/Gloucesters.

The pond on the Plaine au Bois where Captain James Lynn–Allen and Private Albert Evans sought refuge after escaping from the barn where their comrades were being murdered.

The monument on the D17 dedicated to the men who were murdered on the Plaine au Bois.

The bridge at Pont-à-Vendin on the Deûle Canal that Second Lieutenant Anthony Irvine watched being blown in 'a gentlemanly manner.'

This is thought to be the cottage occupied by Lieutenant Jimmy Langley on the banks of the Canal de la Basse Colme.

A contemporary photograph of the Foundation Warein Orphanage on the Rue de la Sous-Préfecture at Hazebrouck. Major Heyworth established the 1/Buckinghamshire Battalion HQ in this building before it was destroyed.

The Junkers 87b 'Stuka' was used extensively during the France and Flanders campaign. It was aircraft such as these which surprised Major Alan Coleman commanding 257/Battery in Arras.

Private Jim Laidler who fought with the 1/Tyneside Scottish at Ficheux.

Jimmy Langley and Angus McCorquodale: a caricature by Gdsm. Kingshott, C Company

A 1939 caricature of Jimmy Langley and Angus McCorquodale.

The château at West Cappel defended by 2 Company 1/Welsh Guards showing the moat bridge that sheltered both Gurney and Llewellyn from German tanks.

The headstones at Hondeghem Churchyard Cemetery marking the graves of Gunner Albert Adaway and Bombardier Jon Turner.

The *Mairie* at Ledringhem where Lieutenant Colonel Guy Buxton, commanding the 5/Gloucesters, established his battalion headquarters.

Captain Marcus Ervine-Andrews who won his Victoria Cross on 31 May near Hoymille.

WOII George Gristock died before his award of the Victoria Cross was announced.

The isolated communal cemetery at Mont-St-Eloi where five men of 208 Battery, 52/Anti-Tank Regiment are buried in the shadow of the ruined abbey.

British motorcycle combinations of the 4/Northumberland Fusiliers.

The Royal Sussex Memorial at Amiens.

Second Lieutenant Garrick Bowyer who fought with the 7/Royal Sussex at Amiens on 19 May.

The beach at Malo les Bains after the evacuation. The Dunkirk mole can be seen in the distance.

The Dunkirk Memorial commemorates more than 4,500 men who fell in the France and Flanders campaign of 1940.

across because the railway was under constant fire. Apparently Bill had reported to Vic [Jessop] that the position was untenable. He had already two dead and two wounded. Vic gave orders for him to withdraw behind the railway but the runner had been unable to get over [the railway].'[16]

Realizing Brewster's platoon desperately needed covering fire to escape their predicament Jabez-Smith resolved to see for himself the state of Brewster's men:

'*So I made a run for it, up over the embankment – a bullet whistled past my right ear – down the other side and I was soon with Bill. In a lock-up under the embankment were crowds of refugees. A dead soldier was lying up above in the open and could not yet be brought in. Another, wounded, had to be brought down behind the shelter.'*[17]

Running the gauntlet of enemy fire again Jabez-Smith safely negotiated the railway embankment 'with his heart in his mouth' and organized covering fire from the two platoons of the KRRC. Using the short breathing space this gave them, Brewster and his surviving men escaped the confines of the embankment without further casualties. The QVR – apart from Munby's men on the Boulogne road who had, by now withdrawn into Fort Nieulay – were now back on the perimeter, the battalion coming under the orders of the Green Jacket unit they were reinforcing..

At Bastion 9, Davies-Scourfield and 5 Platoon were being pressurised by an increasing level of fire as the German attack gradually gathered momentum during the morning. From his vantage point he was able to see an enemy armoured attack begin to move forward:

'*I watched fascinated and I'm sure the eyes of all of us were on them, as what seemed to be a squadron of medium tanks slowly deployed into two long lines … I wondered how we would stop them if they kept rolling forward, which was probably what they intended to do. In fact they eventually descended into dead ground where we could not see them, by-passed Fort Nieulay and supported an infantry advance against Wally's [Findlayson] two sections south of the road and against the gap between us and C Company on our right: here enemy infantry succeeded in getting into a cemetery but were quickly driven out.'*[18]

Support soon clattered up in the form of three light tanks from 3/RTR, under the command of 21-year-old Second Lieutenant Tresham Gregg. Gregg's opinion of Bastion 9 as a laughable defensive position against tanks proved to be alarmingly prophetic and was one that Davies-Scourfield remembered throughout his subsequent captivity. But there was little time to consider Gregg's opinion as German infantry and tanks advanced on their position in strength:

'Martin Willan's [8 Platoon] *was severely pressed, but after a prolonged and at times desperate fight, repulsed the enemy and destroyed two of his light tanks, but only after two counter-attacks had restored their original positions. Meanwhile Wally Findlayson and his two sections were forced to abandon their forward posts and come back to join us in the redoubt. This cleared the way for the enemy to come forwards into the houses and gardens immediately facing us, and a lot of bullets started whizzing past our ears or chipping the concrete blocks.'*[19]

It looked very much as though Nicholson's fears of a breach in the outer perimeter was becoming a reality.

~

On the Rifle Brigade sector Lieutenant Colonel Hoskyns had established his headquarters at Bastion 2 near the Bassin des Chasses de l'Est and was still fuming over the loss of half his battalion's fighting vehicles. Incredibly the *City of Canterbury* had closed down the hatches at 7.30am on 24 May and sailed full of wounded before the RB could complete their unloading. His subsequent concerns over the battalion's severe deficiency of equipment –which left them 50 per cent short of weapons and ammunition – may well have been further fuelled by the intelligence brought back by 22-year-old Second Lieutenant Tony Rolt.

During the evening of 23 May Rolt's Scout Platoon was sent out from Calais ahead of a ration column which was waiting to leave for Dunkirk and escorted by 40-year-old Major Arthur 'Boy' Hamilton-Russell and four Rifle Brigade platoons. As darkness fell, Rolt's patrol reached Fort Vert on the D119 where they discovered from the locals that German tanks had been seen in the area. It was while pondering his next move that a dispatch rider (DR) arrived with orders for the platoon to return to Calais. Rolt, fearing the DR may be a Fifth Columnist, was suspicious and asked for written confirmation while he moved his vehicles into an all-round defence position to wait for the ration column to pass. It failed to arrive. With the darkness came the full realization that the myriad of bonfires they could see all around them were in fact the fires lit by the tank crews and units of the 1st Panzer Division and it was only with great dexterity that they managed to slip away undetected early the next morning.

While Rolt's patrol was contemplating the strength of the German panzer units which appeared to completely surround them, another episode was unfolding along the Gravelines road. Having met Lieutenant Colonel Keller at 11.00pm on 23 May at the Pont St Pierre, Brigadier Nicholson asked that a patrol be sent out towards Marck with the intention of getting through to Gravelines and making contact with 69 Brigade. Bill Reeves left Calais with three light tanks and a heavier Cruiser later that evening:

'Sergeant [Jim] Cornwell was commanding the point tank of my troop, followed by Peter Williams, the troop commander, with his reserve tank in rear of him. I followed close behind ready to give covering fire with my 2-pounder should we encounter anything … Nothing happened for the first two miles as we drove out of Calais to the clear air of the open country [and] our spirits began to rise. They soon dropped off again though when we saw in front of us an ominous black looking mass in the middle of the road.'[20]

The 'black looking mass' was a road block made up of abandoned vehicles that had been towed across the road. Reeves, determined to get through to Gravelines if at all possible, gave the order to continue through the gap that had been left between the vehicles. All four of Reeves' tanks managed to squeeze through. But as Reeves later wrote, there were three road blocks which fortunately were not defended or even manned as check-points:

'No sooner had we got through than we realized that whatever happened there was no turning back, for the enemy was present in large numbers on either side of the road … we pushed on rapidly and in another few hundred yards we were among German troops who were sitting and walking about, they did not seem to be in the least perturbed at seeing us, and I soon realized that they thought we were their own tanks.'[21]

Passing German troops who waved at them, they pressed on to Pont Pollard in Marck where the road crosses the canal. Here the vigilant Cornwell in the lead tank spotted a 'daisy chain' of eight tank mines wired together. If a tank ran over one, the whole lot would explode together:

'I called up Bill Reeves and he used his 2-pounder but no luck. The noise we made roused the enemy and things were getting a bit hectic so I asked him to give me covering fire while I had a look … Luckily the tow rope on the front of the tank was handy and I got Davis (the driver) to come up close and I hooked the rope over the [mines].'[22]

Davis reversed the tank and cleared the bridge of its deadly payload, but their troubles were not over. A short distance further on another tank obstacle brought two of the light tanks to a standstill. Coils of anti-tank wire, designed to wind itself around a tank's sprockets, had been laid across the road and it took several more heart-pounding minutes to remove this with wire cutters. That done Reeves and his tanks were clear of the enemy and arrived at Gravelines at 2.00am on 24 May.

There are conflicting accounts concerning the radio message that was reported to have been sent from Reeves to Keller. Reeves is adamant that his radio was not working and no warning was sent back to Calais but in one of the three reports of the Calais action written by Keller he mentions a garbled message from Reeves containing the words 'Gravelines' and 'canal'. If this is correct then Nicholson may very well have taken this to mean the route was clear of the enemy and consequently ordered the ration convoy to proceed.

Hamilton-Russell got away some time after 4.00am on 24 May along the D248 – over a mile south of Rolt's route – with five tanks from C Squadron 3/RTR leading. About 2 miles outside Calais amongst the 'suburban ribbon development and allotments' they found the road blocked at le Beau Marais with the same road blocks that Reeves had passed earlier. This time the brazen approach used by the B Squadron tanks was clearly not going to work and the convoy stuttered to a halt under a hail of enemy fire. Despite Lieutenant John Surtees pinning down German riflemen with his carrier platoon and Lieutenant Edward Bird's platoon attempting to outflank them, the enemy were too strong. With increasing casualties from mortar fire and with every chance of being surrounded, Hamilton-Russell received orders to withdraw with two dead and several wounded.

Dawn on Friday 24 May began with a hail of heavy mortar fire on the 30 Brigade positions along the outer perimeter. *Generalleutnant* Ferdinand Schaal's 10th Panzer Division had now surrounded the town and two battalions of IR 86 were intent on capturing the old town of Calais Nord and the Citadel, while a further two battalions from IR 69 had the harbour and Gare Maritime as their objective. The IR 69 attack on the Rifle Brigade did not really materialize until later in the afternoon as their first task was to relieve the units of the 1st Panzer Division allowing them to continue towards Dunkirk.

By late afternoon the situation along the perimeter had become critical and hour by hour it was becoming obvious that it could not be held much longer. Enemy attacks along the KRRC front were so severe that on several occasions Hoskyns was asked by Miller for assistance from his reserve platoon to plug gaps in the line. At 4.00pm Tony Rolt was ordered to take his mortar section and 11 Platoon to put down mortar fire on the Rue Gambetta. Here he learned from the QVR that enemy tanks had already penetrated the KRRC perimeter and were at large in Calais-St-Pierre. As the day drew to a close Nicholson would have drawn some consolation from the assessment of his defence recorded in the 10th Panzer Division war diary which noted that British resistance from 'scarcely perceptible positions' was strong enough to prevent anything more than local successes along the perimeter. The diary also noted that 'a good half' of their tanks and a third of their personnel, equipment and vehicles had been lost.

However, on the debit side, the French garrison at Fort Nieulay in the west had surrendered along with Captain Tim Munby's detachment of QVR who had taken refuge there. The surviving units of the QVR had all withdrawn from their positions and, ceasing to operate as a separate battalion, had been distributed between the two Green Jacket battalions. Six of the eight guns of 229/Anti-Tank

Battery had been destroyed including Ron Boothroyd's, his detachment needing no persuasion to climb aboard the truck and make 'like lightning for Calais'.

Although the outer perimeter was now under considerable pressure, Nicholson's decision to order the brigade to fall back at dusk onto a shorter line along the Canal de Marck was given further impetus by the encouraging signal he had received earlier informing him that the evacuation of 30 Brigade had been agreed 'in principle'. It would begin at 7.00am the next morning, a decision heartily welcomed by Lieutenant Colonel Miller of the KRRC:

> '[Nicholson] *ordered companies to hang on where they were until after dark and organised a line of posts across the centre of the town to prevent any further penetration by the enemy from the southwest. These posts consisted of two platoons of the Rifle Brigade sent up to help, some parties of A and B Companies and the Cruiser tank, which was left on the main crossroads on Rue Gambetta, and one searchlight platoon which blocked the road by the station behind the right of B Company.*'[23]

It was a short lived reprieve. At 11.30pm that evening the imposing figure of Admiral James Somerville arrived at Nicholson's headquarters with a brusque message from the War Office. Somerville, who had crossed the channel in HMS *Wolfhound* to explore the possibility of using dismounted naval guns as anti-tank weapons, reported that Nicholson received the message with a stoical calm. Its contents were blunt and to the point:

> '*In spite of the policy of evacuation given you this morning, fact that British forces in your area now under Fagalde who has ordered no, repeat no, evacuation means you must comply for the sake of Allied solidarity. Your role is therefore to hold on, harbour being for the present of no importance.*'[24]

Commanding the French XVI Corps, General Robert Fagalde had been appointed by Weygand on 24 May to command the troops in the three Channel ports and had at once issued orders forbidding evacuation from Calais. It is probable that had Churchill not been personally 'stung' by Reynard's complaint that the British had abandoned Arras, Fagalde's almost resentful order would have been ignored. As it was Churchill was of the opinion that British honour was at stake and 30 Brigade was to be sacrificed to appease the French and bolster the alliance.

Giving little credence to the notion that the British 48th Division had been ordered to fight its way through to Calais – although orders had indeed been given to 145 Brigade to move there – Nicholson decided to make Schall's tanks and infantry fight for every inch of the disputed port and so moved his headquarters to the Gare Maritime. The British withdrawal to Calais Nord was marked by the failure of the French to destroy the three main bridges, making the security of 30 Brigade far more difficult for 40-year-old Major 'Puffin' Owen, second-in-command of the KRRC, who had been given responsibility for holding the bridges.

At dawn on 25 May Second Lieutenant Jabez-Smith and D Company of the QVR were established behind the canal close to the barricaded Pont Freycinet alongside D Company of the KRRC. Since leaving Les Fontinettes they had lost some twenty men either killed or wounded including Lieutenant Rae Snowden who had been hit in the eye the day before. Though the day had begun with the usual mortar bombardment, which continued intermittently throughout the morning, Lance Corporal Richard Illingworth was more concerned with the escalating level of machine-gun fire that was being directed at them from across the canal. German forces were a matter of yards away:

> *'Heavy machine-gun fire started from the direction of the bridge over the canal near 13 Platoon. As many of D as was possible returned fire: this was difficult as our line was at right-angles to the bridge. The Boche fire was all too accurate; as I was going along the road to battalion HQ I could feel the whiz of bullets. One rifleman (I forget who) was killed as I was talking to him.'[25]*

With every bridge blocked by abandoned vehicles and practically every house along the perimeter turned into a defensive position, the men of 30 Brigade were certainly in no mood to give up their ground. Completely overlooked from the clock tower of the Hotel de Ville they were at the mercy of German snipers making any movement around the bridges particularly difficult. Anthony Jabez-Smith admitted to being more than a little rattled by spasmodic bullets that whistled past him like mosquitoes, noting at one point that he thought they were coming from behind him!

After the German swastika was raised over the Hotel de Ville the captured Calais mayor, a Jewish shopkeeper named Andre Gershell, was escorted to the Citadel with a demand from his German captors for Nicholson's surrender. Lieutenant Austin Evitts was present when Gershell arrived:

> *'It was in the courtyard of the quadrangle where the Brigadier received him and the message was an ultimatum. If he had not surrendered in 24 hours, the Germans had said, Calais would be bombed and shelled and razed to the ground, and the Mayor was making a special plea, he said, to save the town from further destruction and loss of life.'[26]*

Evitts tells us that Nicholson's answer was decidedly brusque and was spoken loud enough for all those in the vicinity to hear. 'Tell the Germans', he said, 'that if they want Calais they will have to fight for it.' This reply, which has passed into Green Jacket legend, was hardly what the 51-year-old Schaal was expecting.

In what seemed like a fit of pique the British refusal was met by a ferocious bombardment which rained down on the British positions in a blizzard of high explosive. Near Pont Freycinet Rifleman Sam Kydd was taking cover with the men of 11 Platoon and remembered the 'shattering crack of mortar fire ... one direct hit wiped out a pocket of our chaps and a rain of shrapnel incapacitated several near me'.

At 2.15pm, while still under this ferocious attack, Nicholson received a message from Anthony Eden, the Secretary of State for War, which Lance Corporal Jordan dutifully recorded in the wireless log before handing it to Lieutenant Evitts:

> *'Defence of Calais to utmost is of vital importance to our country and BEF as showing our continued co-operation with France. The eyes of the whole Empire are upon the defence of Calais and we are confident you and your gallant Regiments will perform an exploit worthy of any in the annals of British History.'*[27]

Then, abruptly the German barrage stopped. Tightening their grip on their weapons the riflemen of 30 Brigade waited for the next onslaught. But instead of infantry and tanks it came in the form of a flag of truce carried by a blindfolded 69th Panzer Grenadier officer called Hofmann, flanked by a French captain and a Belgian soldier. Once again surrender was demanded and once again Nicholson refused: 'The answer is no as it is the British Army's duty to fight as it is the German's.' Hofmann was sent back alone with Nicholson's reply in his hand.

The inner perimeter was finally pierced after a German radio message was intercepted indicating an assault on the southwest defences was being planned. Whether Nicholson's decision to tackle this threat with a counter attack was an error of judgement is debatable, but the subsequent order for the Rifle Brigade to release all its carriers to join the attack may well have been imprudent in the circumstances as Major Allen was at pains to point out:

> *'All reserves had become involved from the previous day with the exception of Headquarters and two platoons of C Company. I Company relied particularly on their three carriers and Corporal Blackman's mortar section of Tony Rolt's carrier platoon to cover bridges on their extended front, and both these and A Company's bridges were in imminent danger of being forced.'*[28]

With Nicholson out of radio contact, the objections voiced by Hoskyns were overruled by Holland who insisted the attack went ahead. Even though the attack was cancelled at the last minute, several vehicles were already committed and it was too late to prevent the enemy from entering Calais Nord.

By 3.00pm enemy units had succeeded in breaking through the Rifle Brigade positions in two places and after working their way through the narrow streets established themselves behind the platoons holding the southern perimeter line. In the street fighting that followed 21-year-old Second Lieutenant David Sladen was killed during a counter-attack and Major John Taylor commanding A Company was severely wounded. Also amongst those killed during this desperate encounter were Second Lieutenant George Thomas and 36-year-old PSM Ivan Williams who lost his life on almost the same spot as Second Lieutenant Adrian Van der Weyer.

As the Rifle Brigade fell back, the left flank of the KRRC became exposed; a situation not helped by the canal bridges in their sector remaining intact which handed the advantage to the superior strength of the enemy. But what really added to the already high casualty rate was the heavy and increasingly accurate mortar fire, directed from the vantage point of the Hotel de Ville clock tower. It engulfed the Citadel in sheets of flame during which two tanks were knocked out on the bridges and Major Owen of the KRRC was killed; news which Davies-Scourfield found 'quite devastating'.

But there was worse to come. At 3.30pm a shell exploded in the Rifle Brigade HQ Company positions wounding Company Quarter Master Sergeant Clifton and the unfortunate John Taylor for a second time. As the smoke cleared it became obvious that Hoskyns had also been hit, and although at the time he put on a brave face his wounds were so severe that he died in England after being evacuated.[29] Taylor survived but never regained his fitness for further active service.

With command of the Rifle Brigade now in the hands of Major Alexander Allan and each company reduced to fighting its own battle, they withdrew street by street towards the harbour. Soldiers fight for their mates and rely on their training and experience to see them through adversity. These men were no different. They gave ground reluctantly, counter-attacked when they could and continued their resolve to make their enemy fight for every inch of the battered streets. Fortunately the enemy assaults died away at dusk giving the Royal Navy the opportunity to bring in more ammunition and evacuate some of the wounded. Amongst these men was Second Lieutenant Gregg of 3/RTR who had been badly wounded by mortar fire, Major John Taylor and Chandos Hoskyns.

Sunday 26 May opened with the usual artillery bombardment but the expected dawn attack by IR 69 failed to materialize. At 9.30am the air was filled with the sound of enemy aircraft. Lieutenant Davis-Scourfield was in the Place de Norvège with B Company KRRC when the air attack began:

'No-one who experienced the attack that morning is ever likely to forget it. A hundred aircraft attacked the Citadel and old town in waves. They dived in threes, with a prolonged scream, dropping one high explosive and three or four incendiary bombs. Each of this series of attacks lasted twenty-five minutes. The first effects on the defence were paralyzing but, as others had experienced with Stukas, the damage was moral rather than physical ... As the Stuka attack died away our contemplation was quickly disrupted, for down the street came running

and clattering some 15 men headed by Richard Warre (D Company Scout Platoon Commander) and his Corporal Birt: they flooded into the house and cellar, Richard reporting that our forward positions had been shelled out and the enemy had forced the line of the canal.[30]

Whether it was common knowledge that there was to be no evacuation was of little importance to the surviving men of 30 Brigade and even to the most optimistic it must have been obvious that they were now engaged in a battle that would only conclude in death or captivity. Some such as Major Austin Brown of the QVR still held out some hope for a final evacuation:

'At dawn we moved down to the quay. We had hoped we would be evacuated, but there were no ships to be seen and the prospects seemed very gloomy. Some wounded were taken off later in a pinnace during the bombing. We were ordered to continue the defence and positions were taken up around the Gare Maritime.[31]

If any ships were to be seen they would have been those responding to Nicholson's request for a naval bombardment which had been asked for in the last message sent from the Gare Maritime from Calais garrison. Sadly the bombardment only materialized later that evening by which time it was too late.

By midday the British line had been pushed back to a final perimeter around the harbour, a withdrawal that had cost all three battalions further casualties. Major Allan's account makes for difficult reading as he describes the last hours of the Rifle Brigade:

'Much more could be written of the fighting on this last day: the tough resistance put up on the right by Tony Rolt's scout platoon, PSM Easen's platoon of B Company (he later died of wounds) and others; of Arthur Hamilton-Russell, mortally wounded in an attempt to gain observation from the most exposed point near him, after as hard a four days fighting and work as ever a soldier did; of Tony Rolt's final gallant effort, almost alone, to seize a possible point of vantage … of the hours of steady and accurate shooting put in by Peter Brush's command where Rifleman [Frederick] Gurr got badly wounded in the leg he was to lose, Sergeant Welsh shot through the jaw, Rifleman Murphy, who had found and got into working order a Lewis gun; David Fellowes of C Company, with a large hole in his head … Of those who died, although the deeds of some are not known in full, it would be impossible to write too much.[32]

Shortly before 4.30pm Nicholson realized the fight for Calais was over. Austin Evitts recalled the gloom and despair that descended on the small group ensconced in the Citadel. 'I looked across at the Brigadier. The bitter agony of defeat lay unmistakably written on his face. Now he was about to suffer the humiliation of surrender.' Moments later Nicholson surrendered the Calais garrison. Major Austin Brown remembered the Germans shouting for them to surrender as they were surrounded and the look of anguish on the face of Lieutenant Colonel Ellison-MacCartney's face as he ordered them to put their weapons down. But even if Nicholson had wanted to, he could not have surrendered his entire brigade as communications had long since broken down. Split into small groups they were inevitably hunted down and either killed or captured when their ammunition ran out.

~

No doubt watched by Austin Brown and the surviving QVRs of C Company, Major Hamilton-Russell was spirited away with several other wounded by a naval vessel that had managed to berth long enough to embark the most seriously injured. Sadly he died of his wounds later that afternoon, but for many others their final resting place would be where they fell. While the number of wounded will never be known, the exact number of those killed in action or who later died of their wounds still remains imprecise. The CWGC database lists 192 men of the three 30 Brigade infantry battalions killed in action or died later of wounds, it is thought another 100 were lost from 3/RTR and the various Royal Artillery units that fought in the battle.[33]

Over 200 men were evacuated before the town fell and another 47 were taken off the eastern breakwater by HMS *Gulzar* during the night of 26 May; added to this number should be the 200 wounded that were taken off by the Royal Navy during the course of the battle. Lieutenant Colonel Keller escaped with Major Simpson and reached Gravelines by walking along the beach and both were evacuated from Dunkirk. Barry O'Sullivan was eventually captured and taken prisoner along with some 2,400 men of all ranks who surrendered with Nicholson.

Of those who evaded capture and returned to England the adventures of Lance Corporal Richard Illingworth, Major Denis Talbot – Nicholson's brigade major – Lieutenant William Millet and Captain Alick Williams – the KRRC Adjutant – took them south to the River Authie from where they crossed the channel by boat with a party of French soldiers and were picked up by HMS *Vesper* on 17 June. Another officer who put to sea was Second Lieutenant Lucas who had commanded 8 Platoon in C Company of the QVR. Escaping from the long line of prisoners as they were marched down the St Omer road he managed to find a rowing boat near Cap Gris Nez, which he then steered for Dover, 'rowing like a Brighton boatman on a Saturday afternoon'. He was picked up by the Navy half a mile off the British coast.

In 1945 when the full story of the fight for Calais had been told, the September issue of the *London Gazette* published the full list of gallantry awards. Amongst the profusion of names was Lieutenant Colonel Miller who was awarded the DSO along with Major Alexander Allan. Gris Davis-Scourfield, Tony Rolt, William Millet and Geoffrey Bowring each received the MC while Rifleman Frederick Gurr was awarded the MM. Disappointingly both Lieutenant Colonels Hoskyns and Ellison MacCartney were only mentioned in despatches as was the gallant Arthur Hamilton-Russell.

The political fallout which followed the capture of Calais has been the subject of controversy amongst historians ever since. Churchill always maintained it played an essential part in the escape of the BEF from Dunkirk but others, such as Heinz Guderian and Basil Liddell Hart, took the opposite stance. However, the facts of the matter are quite clear. Nicholson's 30 Brigade held the 10th Panzer Division up for three days and inflicted a severe mauling of its infantry and armoured vehicles thus diverting much of Guderian's heavy artillery from pounding Dunkirk – his key objective. If one also considers the delay on the 2nd Panzer Division imposed by 20 Brigade at Boulogne, then the feat of arms accomplished by two under-strength infantry brigades and a regiment of tanks was considerable.

The notion that the Germans considered Calais and Boulogne a threat to their advance on Dunkirk is supported by Captain Barry O'Sullivan's statement after his escape from captivity in 1941. Under interrogation on 22 May his German captors were most anxious to learn more about the 'large and powerful tank which they heard we had kept very secret' and was said to have landed with the whole of the 1st Armoured Division at Calais. O'Sullivan saw no reason to dissuade his interrogators of their belief in a 'supertank' and was left with the distinct impression that the enemy 'would not consider moving in the direction of the BEF with this threat to their left flank in being'.[34]

Of greater significance is the fact that between 22 and 26 May Boulogne and Calais were not simply by-passed as Arras had been, but were the objects of costly and time consuming assaults by two panzer divisions that could very well have been directed straight to Dunkirk. What's more, the infamous Halt Order (see Chapter 9) was not applied to Boulogne and Calais, leaving one to speculate whether the two channel ports were indeed regarded as a continuing threat to the flanks of the German attack.

Without doubt a large proportion of the Calais garrison could have been evacuated on the night of 25 May, as had happened at Boulogne two days earlier. The Royal Navy may well have been able to evacuate the surviving units of 30 Brigade, whose continued presence in Calais served only to add to the already soaring casualty figures. As it was, most of the surviving Calais garrison spent the remaining years of the war in prison camps which, for men like Major Jack Poole of the KRRC – who went into 'the bag' near Abbeville – would be their second period of captivity in twenty-three years.

Chapter Nine

The Canal Line

20–28 May 1940

'We advanced in a line through a field on the right. We were met with a fearsome hail of gunfire. We threw ourselves flat on the ground. One of us reached for our machine gun, aimed and gently squeezed the trigger and fired; then he fell to the ground. The group leader jumped up to take the gun but just as he took aim he too was gunned down.'

Infanterist Hofmann coming under fire from B Company, 1/RWF in Robecq on 26 May 1940.

We must now return to the point where we left the BEF withdrawing from Arras and the danger to the British right flank created by the collapse of Belgian forces on the Lys. Lord Gort believed that the German threat was severe enough to move two divisions north from Arras to prevent the BEF's only avenue of escape from being closed. The threat that the BEF might not only be outflanked but completely encircled had undoubtedly been anticipated well in advance and from 20 May Gort had been moving forces to defend the line of the rivers and canals which run through Gravelines, Aire, Béthune, La Bassée and beyond.

The so-called Canal Line followed the old line of fortified towns which Marlborough had found so necessary to capture in 1710. In 1940 – as they are today – these towns were linked together by an unbroken line of canalised rivers and canals forming a natural barrier to the armoured units of the German Army Group A who were intent on assaulting the rear of the BEF while Gort was facing the pressure of Army Group B from the east. On 20 May 'Polforce' had been assembled, under the command of Major General Curtis, to defend the sector between St Omer and Pont Maudit; a development which may have put men on the ground but could hardly be considered to be a coherent fighting force. 137 Brigade, for example, consisted of 2/5 West Yorkshires, men returning from leave known as the 'Don' Details and some engineers. Further south, however, Polforce was bolstered by the three battalions of 25 Brigade from the 50th Division and a battery from 98/Field Regiment. To the west, 'Usherforce', under the command of Lieutenant Colonel Charles Usher, was given the defence of the Canal Line from Gravelines to a point 3 miles south near St-Pierre-Brouck.

On 22 May Major Charles Cubitt and his 25-pounders of 392 (Surrey) Battery arrived on the canal with orders to cover the bridging points along the 15-mile sector between St Momelin and Wittes. There were seven bridges to be covered – at St Momelin, St Omer, Arques, Renescure, Wardreques, Blaringhem and Wittes – and that night one gun was deployed to cover each of them. 'Everything went smoothly', wrote Cubitt, with one exception: 'the second gun of E Troop, destined for the crossing at St Omer, was stopped as it passed through Hazebrouck' by a staff officer and ordered to defend GHQ which was in the town. Unfortunately another one of E Troops guns was under repair and so the crossing at St Omer was left without artillery, leaving one to speculate on the outcome had 3/RTR – which was still unloading at Calais – been able to arrive in time. However, the 392/Battery gun which had been redeployed was positioned in a garden on the western outskirts of Hazebrouck to cover the road from St Omer and came into action against an enemy column from the 8th Panzer Division advancing up the St Omer road at 2.00pm on 24 May:

> '*The first shot disabled one of the leading vehicles. The enemy halted and withdrew, but not without sustaining several more hits from the gun. After about a quarter of an hour the second round of the engagement was opened by the enemy who brought up eleven medium or heavy tanks to attack the gun. As the tanks manoeuvred the gun opened fire. One tank was put out of action by a direct hit and it is probable that at least two others were badly damaged. But the odds were too heavy. Three direct hits were then scored on the gun. The first shell disabled the layer, and his place was at once taken by Sergeant Mordin who was performing the duties of Troop Sergeant Major. The second shot wounded Mordin in the eye, but he carried on until the third shell killed L/Sgt Woolven and badly injured the remaining crew.*'[1]

At that moment the reserve ammunition limber turned up and was destroyed by another direct hit from an enemy tank. With no serviceable gun, Sergeant James Mordin ordered the remaining crew to retire.

Back on the canal the first attacks were launched at 8.30am on 23 May and continued throughout the day, pushing the men of 137 Brigade back to a new line running between Robecq and Calonne. The 392/Battery guns were spaced out along a wide front each gun and its crew fighting its own, independent action. There was some confusion at Arques when the bridge was destroyed at 4.30pm and the gun crew withdrew with the sappers. Ordered back to Arques by Major Cubitt they arrived to find Germans already in the village and came into action near the crossroads about a mile east of the canal. Here they fired nineteen rounds at the advancing enemy before Major Andrew Horsbrugh-Porter arrived with a troop of 12/Lancers and gave covering fire to enable the gun to be limbered up and withdrawn.

The bridge at Blaringhem was defended by a contingent of French infantry, two searchlight detachments and some Royal Army Ordnance Corps (RAOC) personnel. The first attack began at 8.30am and Lance Sergeant Love, commanding the gun, scored direct hits on one tank and two other armoured vehicles. Two hours later a second heavier attack followed, during which the French and British detachments withdrew leaving the 392/Battery gun in position shooting at enemy targets over open sights under the direction of Second Lieutenant Kenneth Payne:

> '*In this manner no less than 130 rounds were fired into the advancing enemy and when the German infantry were within hand-grenade range, the order was given to withdraw. Under the very noses of the enemy the gun was limbered up and might well have got away had not an unlucky shell from a German tank severed the engine-connector as the party pulled out of the position. The gun was lost.*'[2]

Kenneth Payne's award of the MC was announced along with Sergeant Mordin's DCM in December 1940.

But despite these actions the Germans had got across the canal at St Omer and Wittes and although there was no general advance, the leading troops of the 6th and 8th Panzer Divisions consolidated their hold on the east bank of the canal. At 11.00am on 24 May some thirty enemy tanks from the 8th Panzer Division moved off in the direction of Lynde – heading for Hazebrouck – and it was this column that Sergeant Mordin engaged with his 25-pounder later that day. With GHQ packing up and hurriedly evacuating the town, the defence of Hazebrouck was about to begin – an encounter dealt with in the next chapter.

Further east along the canal the three battalions of 25 Brigade had been in place since 21 May and were defending the sector running from Béthune to Pont-à-Vendin, a distance of just over 15 miles. The 1/Royal Irish Fusiliers, under the command of Lieutenant Colonel Guy Gough, were assigned a frontage of just over 6 miles, a sector that Gough quickly recognised was far from ideal. Apart from the difficulties imposed by the ground itself, his initial reconnaissance revealed hundreds of barges which, in places, were packed so tightly together that one could almost cross the canal without getting wet. His worry, that their presence would neutralize the effect of the canal as an obstacle, was shared by the 1/7 Queen's on his left who had been allocated a 6,000 yard sector running from Givenchy to Salome. Over the next day or so these barges were systematically destroyed, a task that Gough admits was heartbreaking, as 'we were destroying the homes, the stock-in-trade and the household goods of the Bargees'.

As expected, the 7th Panzer Division's assaults were focused on the bridging points along the canal and although several of these had been destroyed by 22 May, a further four road bridges and a footbridge were not destroyed until forty-eight hours later, possibly prompted by enemy attempts to rush the road bridge at Béthune on the B Company front. 'They were stopped short in their tracks', wrote Gough, 'with very heavy casualties by withering fire from 11 Platoon.' The bridge was blown during the second assault. The lessons learned during the retreat of the Fifth Army in March 1918 had still not been fully absorbed by the British Army of 1940 which was having to come to terms with the fact that, unless bridges were totally destroyed and blown to oblivion, enemy infantry were generally able to cross over the wreckage unless the structure remained under fire.

D Company had three road bridges in its sector of canal which ran east from the junction at les Champs Boucquet. In charge was 24-year-old Captain John Horsfall, who despite his age and relative inexperience, was to demonstrate a skill and tenacity on the canal that would earn him the MC. The first real test came soon after the enemy attack on the Béthune bridge when the two forward platoons were located by the enemy:

'[PSM] *Sidney Kirkpatrick's positions* [18 Platoon] *gradually became untenable as the enemy pinpointed them, and they were gradually shot to bits. He was hit himself about midday, but although incapacitated he held on until nightfall, saying nothing in the meantime. Connolly had already been killed and his number 2 wounded. Kirkpatrick had taken over the Bren and was still in action with it, with the assistance of Fusilier Wilson, when the run of luck ended for both of them. As the blast from the Spandau came through the place their gun was wrecked, Wilson lay dead and Sidney had a bullet through the shoulder with another that ripped down the side of his leg and had stripped off his gaiter buckles.'*[3]*

In the space of an hour 18 Platoon had lost eight men and had been reduced to only one working Bren gun.

On 25 May the battle intensified as enemy artillery units were brought into play. Horsfall admits that had the enemy been allowed to form any sort of front along the opposite bank of the canal, they would have swept across the water in strength. From the very beginning the Irish marksmen held the upper hand over their German counterparts by dispersing any attempts to cross the narrow stretch of water that divided the two sides:

'*Having learned nothing yesterday our assailants were still periodically trying to cross the main street* [of Beuvry] *and other open ground in small groups. Mostly out of view of 17* [Platoon], *18's men were still able to fire straight down it and engaged them every time they tried it. After a while a sizeable detachment tried rushing across together, and most of them went down under the storm of fire which greeted them the instant they broke cover – though I doubt all of them were hit.'*[4]

In the early hours of the 26th the 1/8 Lancashire Fusiliers, described by Gough as a 'stout-hearted but inexperienced battalion', began their relief of the battalion and, through no fault of their own, were thrown into an already deteriorating situation. Moving forward under severe shellfire the Irish Fusiliers disengaged and headed north towards la Croix Rouge.

At Pont-à-Vendin on the Deûle Canal – 10 miles to the southeast – Lieutenant Anthony Irwin and the 2/Essex were holding a 4½ mile sector from Salome to Estevelles. Irwin and 11 Platoon were at Pont-à-Vendin where the road bridge was blown on 24 May, an event which Irwin described as a source of great relief to all concerned: 'Once the bridge had gone up the constant flow of refugees would have to go elsewhere to cross the canal.' In the meantime they had the problem of barges to contend with but, as the canal was somewhat deeper than it was around Béthune, simply towing them midstream and sinking them appeared to do the trick. Apart from the occasional skirmish with German advanced units and bombing raids from twin-engined Dorniers, enemy activity on C Company's sector didn't, according to Irwin, 'begin to get interesting' until 24 May:

> *'Suddenly there was a burst of fire from my left-hand section. I raced down to see what was happening, and was just in time to see a Hun motorcycle combination go head-over-heels into the canal, with its crew of three all dead. Another was turning in the road when a shot from the anti-tank rifle knocked the engine out and into the lap of the man sitting in the sidecar. The other two leapt off and ran into the wood, dragging their pal with them. A third vehicle stopped in the corner and got a machine gun into action against us in double quick time. A long burst of bullets hit the wall by my head, and I got down quick. Then came the shot of the century. It was our anti-tank man again. With one shot he hit the gunner and knocked his head clean off his shoulders.'*[5]

From across the canal they could hear the Germans 'crashing about in the wood' and put in a long burst of Bren gun fire to encourage them to run faster. On the road lay the wrecked motorcycles and a machine gun:

> *'I shouted for volunteers and Barnes and Fox, two old soldiers with pretty grubby crime sheets and hearts of lions, ran up. We hopped into a small boat and rowed across the canal. We had a quick look into the wood but the Hun seemed to have fled. Fox then ran for the machine gun and I got some maps out of the motorcycle and a couple of boxes of ammunition; we rowed back like hell with the booty.'*[6]

No sooner had they scrambled up the side of the canal when a German tank appeared on the far side and began blazing away at Irwin's platoon. 'Bullets at the rate of a thousand a minute plopped, skidded and screamed at our feet. Stewart behind the anti-tank rifle was shooting like a man possessed.' The tank

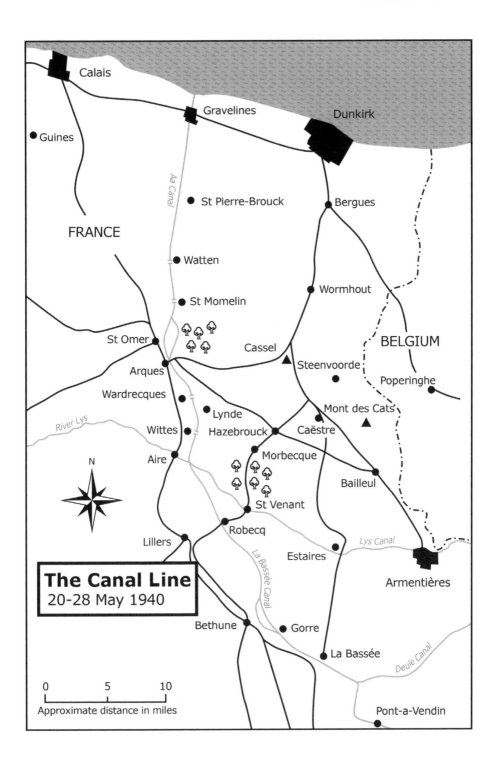

Calais

Gravelines

Dunkirk

Guines

Aa Canal

St Pierre-Brouck

Bergues

FRANCE

Watten

St Momelin

Wormhout

BELGIUM

St Omer

Cassel

Steenvoorde

Arques

Poperinghe

Wardrecques

Mont des Cats

Lynde

River Lys

Wittes

Hazebrouck

Caëstre

Aire

Morbecque

Bailleul

St Venant

N

Robecq

Lys Canal

Lillers

Estaires

Armentières

The Canal Line
20-28 May 1940

La Bassée Canal

Bethune

Gorre

La Bassée

Deule Canal

0   5   10
Approximate distance in miles

Pont-a-Vendin

then retired only to reappear pushing an anti-tank gun into position which opened fire at the very same moment as Stewart – the German gunner missed his target, smashing the brickwork behind Irvine, but Stewart's round went 'straight through the shield, hit the gunner and threw him spread-eagled onto the top of the tank'. Twenty rounds were put into the tank which according to Irvine 'looked like a colander by the time we had finished'.

When Irwin's MC was announced in October 1940 the regiment made much of the fact that not only was the young subaltern commanding the same platoon as his father had 25 years earlier, but also that the decoration was the first to be awarded to the Essex Regiment. Many more were to follow over the next five years. Anthony Irwin's father was 48-year-old Brigadier Noel Irwin, then commanding the 2nd Division, who by way of coincidence, had also been the first officer in the regiment to receive the MC in the previous conflict.

The Essex were relieved on 25 May by 2/5 Leicestershire, a Territorial battalion that had arrived in France during April 1940 with 139 Brigade for labouring and construction work. Now with Polforce, desperation had forced the transformation of Lieutenant Colonel Ken Ruddle's men from a labour battalion to a front line fighting force in the space of less than a fortnight! Faced by units of the German 12th Infantry Division the outcome was inevitable, and over the next 36 hours the Leicesters bravely defended their sector of canal before being overwhelmed, the survivors breaking out toward Dunkirk leaving their dead behind.

∽

As was becoming apparent, German forces along the Canal Line were consolidating and in some areas, such as St Omer, were enlarging their bridgeheads. The reason why there was no determined assault on the BEF positions is explained by the Halt Order of 24 May. Although its architect was von Rundstedt, German armour was halted on the Canal Line by a directive signed by Adolf Hitler. Von Rundstedt's application of the brakes on the panzer columns was almost certainly necessary as far as rest and refit was concerned but, more importantly, it prevented the complete defeat of the BEF by reducing what could have been an overall strategic victory into a more localized tactical victory. While German High Command certainly underestimated the Royal Navy's capability to evacuate the BEF, the Halt Order was perhaps the result of a lack of cohesion and the internal struggles that existed between Hitler and his generals. But whatever the reasons behind the order it was a mistake and, as events turned out, proved to be a very costly one.

Yet, despite the Halt Order remaining in force until 3.30pm on Sunday 26 May, there were at least two enemy incursions authorized on 24 May. Guderian sanctioned Sepp Dietrich's SS *Leibstandarte Adolf Hitler* Regiment to cross the canal at Watten to take the high ground to the east and he probably knew of the SS *Verfügungs* Division's incursion between Thiennes and Robecq in the Polforce sector. Whether the orders for the *Verfügungs* assault were issued before the Halt Order is open to conjecture but the French units which had been holding the canal came under a furious attack early that morning. German infantry accompanied by motorcycles and armoured cars engaged the French 401/Pioneers Regiment and the sappers of 315/Bridging Regiment from the 5th Motorised Division. Short of ammunition the French units withdrew, leaving a gap in the line which the Germans were quick to exploit. Three battalions of the SS *Germania* Regiment were ordered across the canal at Robecq, Busnes and Guarbecque to move on St Venant, a small town which lay two miles north on the canalised River Lys – often referred to as the Bourne Canal in regimental histories.

Having thrown temporary bridges over the canal the 15/Motorcycle Company commanded by *Hauptsturmführer* Mulhenkamp set out for Robecq, whilst other detachments of the SS headed westwards towards St Venant. Horst Kallmeyer and 7 *Kompanie* of the SS *Germania* Regiment most likely crossed the canal over the ruined l'Epinette bridge:

'Our group is the lead company and advances forward making our way across the damaged bridge across the canal, which in places was below the water line. On the other side we advance forward. We receive gun fire. The groups go behind houses to take cover. I am selected as a battlefield observer and get the field glasses of Lengemann. At a fork in the road I lie down in a ditch and observe. We wait for other companies and anti-tank guns to move up to the canal. On the street about 800–1000m on the left, enemy motorized columns withdraw. From the first houses in Saint Venant in front of our position we received some gun fire. [We] fire back. Finally, as we advance further, the gun fire continues, some wounded of our anti-tank are brought back by motorbike. When we finally enter the first houses in Saint Venant we find that the Tommies have gone but left their baggage and ammunition behind.'[7]

At 12.30am the remaining troops in Robecq – including the 2/5 West Yorkshires who we first met briefly in Chapter 4 – had withdrawn towards Calonne-sur-la-Lys via the Bois du Pacaut. In St Venant 9 *Compagnie* of the French 401/Pioneer Regiment were surrounded on the edge of the village and almost completely wiped out.

There is an alarming entry in Kallmeyer's diary which betrays an underlying brutality then prevalent amongst some SS soldiers:

'We advanced on the left along Saint Venant. A slightly wounded Tommy stands up in his trench with his arms in the air. The horror and the fear are reflected in his face. Unfortunately [two men] over reacted and hit the Tommy in the face with a grenade.'[8]

Although difficult to pinpoint, this act of barbarism could well have taken place at St Venant where B Company of the 6/King's Own Royal Regiment ambushed Kallmeyer's company before withdrawing to Merville, but wherever it took place, it was symptopmatic of the utter disregard for the welfare of prisoners that was to surface again over the coming days.

The loss of St Venant and Robecq now involved the 2nd Division and it is worth noting that the withdrawal of the SS *Verfügungs* back to the canal was not driven by the Halt Order but by the 1/Royal Welch Fusiliers from 6 Brigade. Their task – to recapture the four bridges over the canal near Robecq – was a tall order for any battalion to undertake, but for a severely under-strength unit with little or no fire support it was all but impossible. The first attempt to take the bridges was made on the evening of 24 May. C Company was detailed to take the l'Epinette Bridge and B Company the two bridges at Robecq. Lieutenant Robin Boyle and D Company took the direct route to the Blackfriars Bridge on the present day D937 down the Calonne – Robecq Road. Leading the way was 16 Platoon with 17 and 18 Platoons checking the buildings on either side of the road for signs of the enemy. Just before Robecq the company was ambushed and in the ensuing fire fight the 24-year-old Boyle was killed before the survivors managed to disengage and withdraw.

As darkness fell 43-year-old Lieutenant Colonel Herbert 'Harry' Harrison had no clear idea of exactly where all his companies were and without maps or information concerning the strength of enemy forces, any further attempts to reach the canal seemed inadvisable. Withdrawing his companies around St Floris for the night, Harrison suspended operations until dawn on 25 May. Continuing the advance early the next morning St Venant was cleared by A and C Companies but they were subsequently held up just south of the hospital on the D916 where they dug in. Captain James Johnson and B Company fought their way into Robecq but heavy machine-gun fire prevented them from reaching the bridge. Intent on holding on to their positions, Johnson began fortifying the village, discovering too late that the enemy had worked round behind him and surrounded the company. Whether they expected to be relieved or not there was little the Fusiliers could do that evening apart from strengthen their defensive positions around the brewery at the intersection of the Calonne and St Venant roads. Johnson was wounded that evening and command devolved to Second Lieutenant Michael Edwards.

Apparently unaware of the situation in which the Royal Welch had become embroiled, Brigadier Dennis Furlong, commanding 6 Brigade, ordered the 1/Royal Berkshires to seize the bridges over the Aire at Guarbecque on 24 May to protect the western side of the corridor to Dunkirk, a task they were told would be relatively straightforward. Lieutenant Colonel Geoffrey Bull's suspicions that all was not as it appeared were first raised by an artillery barrage which greeted his battalion's exit from St Venant and then by heavy machine-gun fire as it advanced towards Guarbecque on the D186. Without artillery support and unsure of the strength of enemy forces ahead of him, Bull sensibly withdrew the battalion around Bas Hamel placing C Company in reserve across the canal at Haverskerque.

Captain Cyril Townsend's diary for Saturday 25 May 1940 tells us the 2/DLI left Calonne in companies and marched by separate routes to occupy the line of the railway that ran through St Venant. Regardless of which company a soldier had fought with on the Dyle, the surviving men of the Durhams were by now marching in four amalgamated companies, a situation that was not improved by the temporary loss of two companies a week earlier near Overyssche. The war diary does not record a further reorganization but it is likely there was some further redistribution of men on the mistaken assumption the two missing companies had been overwhelmed by the enemy. All of which may account for Lieutenant Michael Farr writing in his diary, 'To say we were a bewildered bunch of men would be to put it lightly.'

Meanwhile Harrison had established his headquarters near the railway station at St Venant and leaving Captain Willes, the battalion Intelligence Officer, to collect and redirect men to their new positions, he set off with his adjutant to establish contact with Lieutenant Colonel Simpson. The Welch line ran along the road running south of the railway from the level crossing to the crossroads at the eastern end of the embankment and covered the bridge over the canal where they were in touch with the Durhams. Simpson, concerned at the gap between the Berkshires and the town, deployed D Company with Lieutenant John Gregson on the right flank and the remaining three companies along the railway line between the Robecq and Les Amuzoires road. Establishing his headquarters in the Taverne farmhouse near the canal, he managed to place the battalion transport under cover in one of the barns. The left flank, like that on the right, appeared to be wide open and it was this flank that would ultimately seal the fate of many of those at St Venant.

The brigade was supported by the ever faithful 44/Battery from 13/Anti-Tank Regiment and 226/Battery from 57/Anti-Tank Regiment who had been detached from the 44th Division, together with a battery of guns from 99 (Buckinghamshire Yeomanry) Field Regiment. Still with the brigade was Captain George Frampton and the machine guns of C Company, 2/Manchesters, that had fought with them on the Dyle and Escaut.

As night fell on St Venant the surrounded Welshmen at Robecq could only listen to the movement of enemy forces crossing the canal and await the onslaught that would come the next morning. It began at 7.30am with a barrage of artillery and mortar fire which preceded the 1/IR 3 attack along the Eclème road. *Infanterist* Hofmann and his company were waiting to advance once the guns had ceased firing:

'At 7.30am exactly our artillery began firing on Robecq. Houses burst into flames as they were hit; the grey skies above were traced with red light. However our artillery had little effect and nothing moved in the area; even after 300 rounds the nervous silence hung over the rooftops ... We approached the village, our commander leading the way. We had just passed the first houses and we still had not heard a single shot. The road seemed deserted and with each step we took the silence seemed to deepen. The crossroads loomed in front of us; there was the cemetery. It was at this moment that a heavy weight of fire rained down from the surrounding houses.'[9]

Slowly B Company were driven back into a continually contracting perimeter but with flat ground all around there was little chance of a break-out succeeding in daylight. Edwards split the remaining men of the company into small groups and ordered them to attempt to get back under cover of darkness. But it was not to be. The regimental historian concludes his description of B Company's stand with the words 'At 11.00am B Company, as a company, ceased to exist.' Edwards was taken prisoner along with the majority of the survivors while Johnson, with a bullet wound in the neck and back, was taken to the former English hospital at Camiers from where he eventually made a successful escape over the Pyrenees to Spain.

Quite why Brigadier Furlong deployed 6 Brigade south of the Lys Canal at St Venant is anyone's guess but it proved to be an error which contributed significantly to the destruction of the two battalions there. It was a decision made even more questionable by his refusal to grant Harrison's request to withdraw north of the canal on 26 May. His award of the DSO for his command of 6 Brigade specifically mentions the 48 hours of the St Venant defence, 'not withstanding the very heavy casualties they suffered'. Furlong was killed on the Yorkshire coast on 5 September 1940 whilst inspecting a mine field.

The German assault on 6 Brigade began at around 7.00am on 27 May under the overall command of *Oberst* Ulrich Kleemann who moved across the La Bassée Canal with three battalions of infantry, a battery of guns from FAR 75 and elements of the SS *Germania* Regiment. Kleemann's infantry assault was announced by a heavy artillery bombardment which, noted a delighted Michael Farr, did not prevent the combined fire of the Welch and Durham riflemen mowing [them] 'down like ninepins'. His euphoria was short-lived: the heavy growl of tanks of the 3rd Panzer Division could be heard behind the infantry swaying the battle in the Germans' favour. It was the beginning of the end. Cyril Townsend's diary again:

'Heavy mortar fire and possibly artillery fire was put down on our company positions. The church spire was hit and movement in the village was difficult and dangerous. The enemy was moving across our front to the left. About 15 tanks could be seen from battalion HQ. Our artillery opened fire but later ceased firing.'[10]

D Company – with its headquarters at the junction of the Ruelle Berthelotte and Rue d'Aire – was on the western edge of St Venant positioned just south of the Rue d'Aire with the Guarbecque Canal to their front. Having been joined by Sergeant Martin McLane and some of his men from the Mortar Platoon they were on the extreme right flank of the battalion with no contact between themselves and the Royal Berkshires. The previous day enemy artillery fire had claimed the life of 24-year-old John Gregson who was hit with 'a bowl-sized piece of shrapnel' which lodged in the base of his spine, leaving command of the company to CSM Norman Metcalf.

The events of 27 May on the D Company front are largely confined to those few accounts that have survived the ravages of time. Once the tanks moved in the company was heavily engaged but without heavy weapons their struggle against armoured vehicles became futile. Inevitably, as their resistance collapsed, the fighting became fractured with small groups of men defending their own piece of ground. Private Dusty Miller, who was still with his mate George Blackburn, was in front of a privet hedge near a farm. 'We could hear shots going through the hedge, like the sound of bees; we were pinned down and couldn't do anything'.[11]

In St Venant the story was much the same. The Royal Welch lost heavily as their much depleted companies came up against enemy armour. A Company, which had already been reduced to two platoons, was soon overwhelmed after being completely surrounded. Twenty–nine-year-old Captain Edward Parker-Jervis commanding C Company, was killed defending a house which had been surrounded and D Company, under Second Lieutenant Kemp, could only muster fifteen men after they retired towards the canal in the face of several German tanks with PSM Jenkins being pushed along in a wheelbarrow.

Nevertheless, with 6 Brigade contesting every inch of ground, enemy units were finding the British defence hard to overcome. Men of 8 *Kompanie* II/IR 3 found the advance up the Busnes road to be painfully slow as they moved from house to house, losing *Leutnant* Wallenburg as they reached the railway line. Also taking heavy casualties was 7 *Kompanie* which reached the water tower by the station under a hail of fire:

'Leutnant *von Bismark was fatally wounded in this attempt. He was quickly taken to a field hospital but was dead on arrival. The company engaged the enemy in the town and a street battle raged, fought across the ruins and debris of burning houses … During this time Major Zimmermann set up his battalion HQ in the hospital and 6* Kompanie *managed to reach the town, in so doing they suffered casualties at the hands of a few isolated machine gunners.'*[12]

Forced back onto the Lys Canal, a runner arrived at at Simpson's DLI headquarters at Taverne's Farm with a message from Lieutenant Colonel Harrison who had by this time moved his Royal Welch HQ to the communal cemetery. Cyril Townsend, not knowing exactly where his CO was, made the perilous journey along the canal bank where Harrison told him of his intention to hold the canal bridge to enable the survivors to get across:

> *'I crawled back to see Colonel Harrison. He said the position was untenable and that he was taking what men he could to form a bridgehead. I was to bring back any men I could. I sent Lyster-Todd and some men back at once and crawled forward to find CSM Birkitt and Private Worthy, the C Company runner. By this time armoured cars had almost reached the café and although I waved to the men inside, I realized they could no more come out than I could go to them across open space.'*[13]

The bridge over the canal was the only exit available but for Simpson and the men at the Durhams' headquarters it was a bridge too far. Harrison's move to the canal crossing was in response to Brigadier Furlong's orders to retire, but there is some discussion as to what time Furlong actually arrived. The account in *Y Ddraig Gogh* says 9.15am, Townsend's diary declared Furlong arrived at 11.00am with orders for the brigade to retire but Michael Farr was quite sure that no orders for retirement arrived at the Durhams' headquarters at Taverne's Farm. He may of course have been too occupied with the severity of the fighting to notice the arrival of anything other than German armour:

> *'I saw the position getting more and more serious. The Boche had infiltrated around the left flank, snipers had crossed the canal and the bastards were shooting our soldiers in the back. Meanwhile huge and ugly tanks were bearing down upon us. Our one and only anti-tank gun was destroyed. The men were driven to the edge of the river bank; they had nowhere to go but backwards into the water.'*[14]

The Durhams' last stand by the canal was made at the barn, which by now was under fire and in flames with Simpson defiantly firing his pistol at German tanks which were advancing up the Les Amuzoires road. Enemy units had also got in behind them after advancing up the undefended left flank. Surrounded, the British threw down their weapons and surrendered.

After Cyril Townsend had left the RWF Headquarters, Captain Walter Clough-Taylor was instructed by Harrison to form a defensive flank by the bridge, but first they had to run the gauntlet of enemy fire to get there:

> *'I saw many men stagger and fall as they ran. Martin, my trusty servant, had his arm blown off. Then it was my turn. I summoned courage, waited for a burst of fire and dashed forward. I was only a yard or so on to the bridge when I was hit in the leg, I recoiled and staggered crazily back to the culvert. As I stood thinking wildly how I was going to get across alive, I noticed there were girders rising to about a foot in height in the centre, above the roadway ... I got up and was at once hit again in the arm and hip, I staggered on to the shelter of some houses.'*[15]

Clough-Taylor was taken prisoner but fortunately a few of the Durhams did manage to get across the bridge with Townsend who was shot through the face as he reached the other side. He remembered a Welshman putting a field dressing on the wound before he managed to walk away under more machine-gun fire. He describes the final moments at the bridge:

> *'When Colonel Harrison saw that no one else could get across the bridge owing to the close proximity of the leading tanks, which by this time were only 150 yards away, he ordered the Royal Engineers to blow [it] unfortunately there were none available. The situation then became impossible as there were perhaps twenty men holding the bridge with only one Bren gun and no anti-tank rifle against at least five tanks. The leading tank came across the bridge and wiped out most of the men holding it.'*[16]

The leading German tank hesitated before crossing the bridge and bringing its fire to bear on the cottages ahead. Harrison was killed 'in the last flurry of fighting while attempting to delay the crossing' and those that could began making their way north towards Haverskerque where 6 Brigade Headquarters was situated.

The surviving men of D Company were also heading for the Lys Canal. Dusty Miller remembers there were tanks approaching when he heard the order from Martin McLane to make for the canal:

> *'We started running across a field, I did not know there was a canal there, I don't think any of the other lads knew there was a canal … As we were running, George was behind me and I heard him shout 'Jim, Jim', so I stopped and George was lying on his back, he had been hit in the legs I think, I ran back towards him and I saw a young officer running towards me and he shouted 'keep going, keep going' and I had to leave George.'*[17]

The sacrifice of the two 6 Brigade battalions at St Venant was an almost inevitable conclusion from the moment they took up position along the railway line. The Berkshires, although attacked at dawn on 27 May, did manage 'a discreet battalion withdrawal, under heavy fire' to new positions behind the Lys Canal but there are still over twenty identified men buried locally. That evening only 212 officers and men answered their names at roll call. The casualty list for the St Venant defenders was significantly greater as the CWGC cemeteries in the area bear witness. In the St Venant Communal Cemetery there are over 120 identified men who were killed in the action including Captain Edward Parker-Jervis. Lieutenant Colonel Harrison and a further ten men lie in the Haverskerque Churchyard and the Robecq Communal Cemetery contains the Fusiliers of B and D Company. This number does not take into account the unidentified dead – whose names appear on the Dunkirk Memorial – the wounded and those taken prisoner.

Yet, there is a darker side to the casualty lists that first came to light when the dead at St Venant were reinterred from the mass grave they had originally been buried in. Post mortem files indicated that in a number of cases there were impact blows to the skull which could only have been inflicted at close range. The testimony from the local population and from survivors, point to units of the SS *Germania* Regiment being responsible for the shooting and bayoneting of British prisoners to the west of the town after they had surrendered. In the subsequent inquiry the Judge Advocate's Office initially found that six prisoners had been executed in this manner and although the perpetrators were identified as SS soldiers from the *Germania* Regiment their names remain unknown. In addition there is also a body of evidence that suggests other war crimes against wounded and captured British soldiers in the vicinity did take place, although to date no confirmation has surfaced in the public domain. There may still be MI19 documents which are still classified and unavailable for public scrutiny and until these files – if they exist – are examined, the full story of the St Venant murders will remain untold.[18]

~

Along with the 1/8 Lancashire Fusiliers and the 2/Norfolks, the 1/Royal Scots were withdrawn from the Escaut at midnight on 22 May and ordered to relieve the 25 Brigade units along the La Bassée Canal. The Norfolks were now under the command of their third commanding officer, 37-year-old Major Lisle Ryder, who had taken charge after his predecessor had been wounded on the Escaut. Lisle Ryder was the brother of Robert Dudley Ryder who, as a Commander RN, led the raid on St Nazaire in 1942 resulting in his award of the VC. Even before the battalion arrived on the canal to take up their allotted sector between the Bois Pacault and the bridge at Béthune, two companies of Norfolks had inadvertently deployed to a subsidiary loop in the canal, leaving a large gap on the left flank and no doubt increasing Ryder's unease.

Although the wayward companies were back in place twenty-four hours later the Pioneer Section from HQ Company had been pushed into the gap by Ryder and told to make every round count. Private Ernie Farrow and his mates found that by using rifle fire instead of the more 'ammunition hungry' Bren gun they were able to conserve on ammunition and bluff the Germans into thinking 'there was a great company of us there'. To Farrow's amazement they managed to hold off the German assault until B and D Companies finally turned up. That evening Ryder withdrew his headquarters to Druries Farm on the Chemin de Paradis about 500 yards west of the Paradis crossroads where Farrow and the surviving pioneers rejoined. The scene that confronted him was shocking:

> '*I ran into this cow shed and was amazed to see all my comrades lying about, some of them had lost a foot, some an arm, they were laying about everywhere, being*

tended by the bandsmen who were all first aid men. The first thing I wanted was a cigarette, I wanted a fag. I was dying! I'd never smoked a lot but this time to save my nerves I found someone who had some fags, and I just smoked my head off.'[19]

Overnight on 26 May German forces, including the SS *Totenkopf* Division, moved up the south bank of the La Bassée Canal in preparation for an assault on British forces the next morning. Temporary pontoon bridges were quickly put across the water to enable armoured vehicles to cross. Advancing with the 2nd SS Battalion, Herbert Brunnegger and 3 *Kompanie* crossed the ruins of the bridge at Pont Supplie where he came across his first wounded British soldier:

'*His face is distinctive and brown but the proximity of death is making his skin go pale. He is standing up and leaning against a wall made of earth. In his eyes there is an indescribably hopeless expression while the whole time bright spurts of blood are coming out of a wound at the base of his neck. In vain his hands try to press on a vein in order to try and keep the life in his body. He cannot be saved.*'[20]

The fierce fighting around Le Cornet Malo – which was held by the Norfolks – slowed the SS advance considerably although Private Arthur Brough, who was with the B Company Mortar Platoon, considered it was getting a bit hectic:

'*Lots of tanks and heavy gunfire. We were putting as much stuff down the mortar as we could. We were trying to repulse them but we knew it wasn't a lot of good because there were so many there … The mortar must have been red hot, anything we could get hold of we were putting down the mortar until it got so bad that we even resorted to rifles.*'[21]

There were only three of the platoon left standing when Brough and his mates resorted to firing their rifles at the approaching enemy which they continued to do until the arrival of enemy tanks, at which point he confesses they 'just ran for it'.

The actual detail of the fighting remains obscure but we do know from the various war diaries that with the aid of several counter-attacks and with assistance from the Royal Scots, a fragile equilibrium was restored by nightfall with the Germans in occupation of Riez du Vinage and the Bois Pacault. But there had been heavy casualties on both sides and only about sixty men of A and B Companies of the Norfolks remained capable of fighting leaving Lieutenant Murray-Brown wondering just how long they would be able to 'hold the position to the last man and the last round'. It was, he thought, getting a little desperate.

The attack continued at 3.00am the next morning with German forces emerging from the shelter of the Bois Pacault. Brunnegger and his *Kompanie* moved slowly towards Le Cornet Malo:

'The attack is renewed. A weak sun is rising out of the ground mist. A signpost points to Le Cornet Malo. Mortars and sub-machine guns move into position on the edge of the wood and fire at recognizable targets in a village a couple of hundred metres in front of us. While they do this our soldiers move forward on both sides of the path … Onwards! A surprise as bursts of machine-gun fire hit a section as it moves out of a cutting. The bursts toss them into a tangle of bodies. One stands up and sways past me to the rear – he has a finger stuck into a hole in his stomach.'[22]

If Brunnegger thought for a moment that the fight for Le Cornet Malo would be relatively easy, his confidence was to be rudely shattered by the dogged defence of the Norfolks and C Company of the Royal Scots:

'The English defend themselves with incredible bravery … we are completely pinned to the ground in front of the enemy who are totally invisible and whose ability commands our admiration. We have to adapt ourselves completely to the enemy's tactics. We work ourselves forward by creeping, crawling and slithering along. The enemy retreat skilfully without showing themselves.'[23]

However, overwhelmed by the sheer number of German soldiers and their supporting artillery, and with the village in flames, the survivors were slowly pushed back on Paradis.

A Company of the Royal Scots, having now moved east, was in position three-quarters of a mile south east of le Cornet Malo astride the present day D945 Merville road when they beat off a strong German force heading north from the canal. During the fighting Major Butcher was badly wounded but continued to be carried around on the broad back of CSM Johnstone until the arrival of Harold Money who sent him up to the RAP in Paradis. In the subsequent fighting both of the remaining subalterns were either killed or captured leaving Johnstone to maintain their hold on the farm buildings they had by now fortified:

'The Jocks did their best to turn the place into a strongpoint, blocking windows with tables and chairs and piling grain bags filled with earth in the gateway. Here they were prepared to make a last stand. Everyone realized that there must be no relinquishing a position from which they could deny the enemy passage up this important road.'[24]

The Scots headquarters at Paradis was in a farm complex on the Rue de Derrière with the RAP nearby, along the same road but closer to the village, was Major Watson's D Company Headquarters. Realizing a strong attack up the Merville road was forthcoming, Money pulled the remains of Captain Mackinnon and B Company – which up until this point, had been deployed along the Rue de Cerisiers – back into the village. Further south A Company had beaten off several enemy attacks before Captain Nick Hallet of the Norfolks arrived from the direction of le Cornet Malo and ordered Johnstone to withdraw but it was too late. Caught trying to escape along a ditch, the surviving men surrendered and Johnstone – accused of 'gouging out the eyes of dead German soldiers with his jack-knife' – was led into a field along with his companions to be shot. 'By a piece of good luck a staff officer in this division happened to come along in a car. He spoke to me in English and it was he who saved us from being shot.'[25]

At Paradis, Harold Money was wounded and sent off to the La Gorge dressing-station which was the very spot he had been taken to in May 1915 after he had been wounded in the First World War. The end of the battalion's stand arrived with a ferocious German attack which shattered the buildings of the village. Lance Corporal James Howe was in the Royal Scots' RAP at Paradis when SS troops first appeared:

'We were with the Royal Norfolks; they had one end of the village and we had the other … We were about fifty yards from the centre of the village. We were in this house tending our wounded in the RAP, with the medical officer and the padre with about six of us attendants, and maybe twenty wounded … the first thing I saw was a hand preparing to throw a hand grenade through the window of our aid post. This hand grenade came in, blew up and we all dived into the corner. Of course the building caught fire so we had no option but to get out as quickly as we could.'[26]

In a horrifying episode witnessed by Howe, a German NCO announced his intention to shoot the wounded Scots. Challenged by Padre McLean and the Medical Officer, the NCO attempted to justify himself by saying the British had been using dum-dum bullets. It was only the intervention of those present that prevented the murder of wounded men. Whether or not any of the remaining Royal Scots were executed after they had surrendered is still open to conjecture but there are reports in the various Paradis War Crimes files of men with similar wounds to the back of their heads being discovered in mass graves and another detailing evidence from a local Frenchwoman of the apparent execution of seventeen Royal Scots found hiding in a hayloft. We will probably never know the truth of exactly what occurred on that afternoon in May 1940.[27]

At Druries Farm the perimeter defences were slowly being taken out by enemy machine-gun sections. Signaller Robert Brown was in the farmhouse when Major Ryder gave the men the option of surrendering or trying to escape. By sheer luck Brown and two others made the decision to leave the building by a door leading onto the road:

'The smoke from the burning house was going that way so we thought we'd keep in the smoke as extra cover in the hopes of getting away. We went in a ditch at the side of the road and in the ditch was the adjutant [Captain Charles Long], *lying on the*

ground wounded and the medical officer was there. We attempted to go out of the ditch and cross the road but as we did so the German patrols were coming up from the village of Paradis and we couldn't get over.'[28]

Druries Farm represented the boundary between the Norfolks and the Royal Scots and the location of the farm on Chemin du Paradis goes some way to explaining the tragic events that followed Ryder's surrender of HQ Company. The farm was attacked by Brunnegger's 2nd Battalion and Brown's decision to leave by the door facing the road undoubtedly saved his life as he was taken prisoner by another unit moving up from the village. Ryder and the remaining men left through the stable door leading to the fields at the rear of the farm. Their fate was now in the hands of of *Hauptsturmführer* Fritz Knoechlein's men.

What happened next as Ryder and the men of Headquarters Company were marched up the road to Louis Creton's farm will always rank as one of the most appalling atrocities committed during the 1940 campaign in France. Signaller Albert Pooley was one of the men who had surrendered with Ryder:

'There were a hundred of us prisoners marching in column of threes. We turned off the dusty French road through a gateway and into a meadow beside the buildings of a farm. I saw, with one of the nastiest feelings I've ever had in my life, two heavy machine guns inside the meadow. They were manned and pointing at the head of our column.'[29]

Herbert Brunnegger was at the farm when he saw the column of prisoners by the barn:

'Many of them reach out in despair towards me with pictures of their families … As I look more closely I notice two heavy machine guns which have been set up in front of them. Whilst I look on, surprised that two valuable machine guns should be used to guard prisoners, a dreadful thought occurs to me. I turn to the nearest machine-gun post and ask what is going on here. 'They are to be shot!' is the embarrassed answer.'[30]

Brunnegger's account goes on to say that he understood the orders for the prisoners to be shot had been given by Knoechlein. It is difficult to say exactly what we would do in Brunnegger's place, as it was he writes that he chose to leave the scene in order not to witness the murder of prisoners, but he must have heard the cries of the Norfolks as they were cut down by the barn wall. Albert Pooley wrote afterwards that he felt an icy hand grip his stomach as the guns opened fire on them:

'For a few seconds the cries and shrieks of our stricken men drowned the crackling of the guns. Men fell like grass before a scythe. The invisible blade came nearer and then swept through me. I felt a searing pain in my left leg and wrist and pitched forward in a red world of tearing agony ... but even as I fell forward into a heap of dying men the thought stabbed my brain, 'If I ever get out of here the swine who did this will pay for it.'[31]

Pooley did have his revenge and Knoechlein was brought to trial in 1948 where his defence claimed the British had used soft-nosed dum-dum bullets and had misused a white flag of truce, all of which were denied by the prosecution team. But some of the most damming evidence was given by Albert Pooley and the other survivor of the massacre, William O'Callaghan, all of which resulted in Knoechlein's conviction and sentencing – death by hanging – which was carried out in January 1949.

The Royal Scots' D Company made their last stand at a farm north of Paradis where Major Watson was killed and James Bruce – now in command – held out long enough to allow him and a handful of men to escape. Sadly they were captured near the Merville airfield 24 hours later.

The dead of the Paradis massacre were exhumed from their mass grave in 1942 and moved to the Paradis War Cemetery where they now lie with the other casualties from 4 Brigade who were killed in that desperate engagement. Both battalions were practically annihilated, only five officers and ninety men of the Royal Scots and three officers and sixty-nine other ranks from the Norfolks eventually making it home via Dunkirk

~

North of the Lys Canal lay the expansive Forêt de Nieppe which was the direction in which Private Dusty Miller and Sergeant Martin McLane were running after enemy tanks had overwhelmed D Company of the 2/DLI at St Venant. The shots that felled George Blackburn south of the Lys Canal had, unbeknown to Miller, also wounded him in the shoulder and having been told to wait for an ambulance in a nearby barn he found himself completely alone:

'I came out of the barn and I did not know where I was, what I should do, where I should go so I just kept walking. I must have been walking northwest because I got into a forest ... There was a battalion standing there behind trees with their bayonets fixed and I said what regiment are you and a young lad said "The West Kents, 4th Battalion".'[32]

If Miller is correct then he was walking in the direction of Morbecque when he was picked up by a truck belonging to an artillery unit which was subsequently hit by Stukas. 'The driver must have been hit and the truck tipped over and I got flung out.' The next thing he was aware of were German soldiers all around him; the truck had gone as had the artillery unit:

> '*I don't know what the Germans thought of me sitting there with a sleeve off and no equipment. Then this German, he was yelling at me, he was a big paratrooper, I was scared, I was really frightened, he pulled me up and he was shouting at me, I was looking all over the place and as I turned he hit me, I don't know what he hit me with and down I went … the soldier had hit me pretty hard, he had mashed my face up, he had knocked some teeth out and knocked half my eyebrow off.*'[33]

Miller had more than likely been hit with a stick grenade being used as a club, an attack that bore a remarkable resemblance to the one described by Horst Kallmeyer at St Venant three days earlier. His reference to 'a big paratrooper' may have been influenced by the camouflaged smocks and helmet covers in use by SS troops as there were certainly no parachute troops in the area at the time. What is even more interesting is that according to Kallmeyer's diary, units of the SS *Germania* Regiment were in the Morbecque area on 27 May, leaving one to wonder if the violent attack on Miller was carried out by the same unit.

Despite Dusty Miller's confused state, his reference to the 4/RWK was correct as on 26 May the 4 and 5/RWK had moved to the western edge of the Forêt de Nieppe where D Company at Morbecque came under attack from German tanks. At dawn the next morning the 4/RWK were somewhere along the line running from Croix Mairesse to the Canal de la Nieppe which is where Miller ran into them that afternoon. Corporal Bertie Bell, who was serving in B Company, 4/RWK, remembers being sent to Morbecque to engage three tanks:

> '*After some fighting B Company was forced to fall back to the position on the [Hazebrouck] canal held by the battalion. From this position, after fighting involving heavy casualties, the battalion retired. Later a new position was formed along a forest path running north and south near the east end of the forest. A small group of five men and a corporal, commanded by me, was on the left or southern end of this new position.*'[34]

From all accounts it seems that the RWKs inflicted heavy casualties on the SS units opposing them, which may go some way to explain the treatment inflicted on Bell's section. Finding themselves cut off from the battalion, Bell's men came under fire again when Privates Henry Daniels and Fred Carter were wounded. Fortunately they found a barn where they sought shelter for the night. Early the next morning they were discovered by German troops and marched off into the forest:

> '*I had heard tales of prisoners being shot in Norway and feared the worst, especially as almost immediately we came upon a section of about six German soldiers lying*

down parallel to our line of march and facing in our direction with rifles laid out in front of them as though in readiness for action … When we had proceeded a few steps further the officer who was marching on the left of the parade with drawn revolver gave an order whereupon the rear gunner opened fire without warning and shot down my comrades. I was on the alert and threw myself down unwounded immediately I heard the first shot. I lay perfectly still and held my breath. A few seconds later there were three revolver shots. I then heard the Germans walk away. Remaining in my position for some five minutes more, I got up and looked at my comrades. I saw that one revolver shot had been fired at Private Shilling and blown half his head off. The other two shots appeared to have been aimed at Private Daniels who was shot in both eyes. He was lying on his back with his face to the sky. They were all beyond human aid. I had to move away quickly on account of returning Germans.'[35]

Evidence given by Bell in 1943 after his escape across the Pyrenees to Gibraltar pointed firmly to the SS *Der Fuhrer* Regiment being responsible for the murders, which is supported to an extent by the movements of the 3rd Panzer Division. There is differing opinion on the movements of the SS *Verfügungs* Division on 27/28 May, nevertheless, what is certain is the *Der Fuhrer* Regiment, together with *Germania* and *Deutschland,* crossed the La Bassée Canal on 27 May. *Deutschland* and, very possibly *Der Fuhrer,* were part of the right hand column of the 3rd Panzer Division under the command of *Generalleutnant* Horst Stumpff. *Germania* we know was further west and *Deutschland* was across to the east around Bailleul, leaving *Der Fuhrer* operating in the Merville area and the eastern side of the Forêt de Nieppe.

While the West Kents were fighting in the Forêt de Nieppe the 2/Dorsets were under orders to cover the movement of 5 Brigade by holding Festubert. The battalion had taken over a three mile sector along canal line on 25 May running from Gorre to Pont Fixe at Cuinchy and were very conscious that they were now fighting over the same ground the 1st Battalion had fought on during October 1914 twenty-six years previously. The battalion was commanded by Lieutenant Colonel Eric Stephenson, a remarkable individual who, at 48-years-of-age, had already been decorated with the MC and two bars for his gallantry with the regiment in the Great War. He was about to excel once again.

The 27 May opened with a heavy enemy assault on the Dorsets and the 1/8 Lancashire Fusiliers on the battalion's right flank. Later in the morning Stephenson realized the situation was becoming desperate when a handful of Lancashire Fusiliers arrived with news that the battalion had been overrun. Reports had also come in that 1/Cameron Highlanders had been almost completely wiped out and that the 7/Worcesters on their left 'were none too happy'. With the enemy enveloping the Dorsets' right flank and the Argylls' machine-gun section destroyed to a man, Stephenson was more than a little relieved to receive orders to withdraw to Festubert where the 1st Battalion had been billeted on 16/17 October 1914.

With a textbook display of professional soldiering the Dorsets disengaged and withdrew under fire to establish their new perimeter around the village; with them were the remnants of D Company, 7/Worcesters. Stephenson's plan was to hold Festubert by defending the four major approach roads: D Company to the north straddling the D116; B Company to the southwest holding the D72; A Company defending the southern approaches from the canal and C Company the eastern end of the D72 and approaches from Violaines. Controlling the battle from battalion headquarters at the crossroads in the centre of the village, Stephenson barely had time to get his men into position before the first attack began at 4.45pm. Infantry supported by six armoured vehicles assaulted the C Company sector but were driven off with the loss of one light tank. Regrouping, the enemy then switched their attack to B Company with nine tanks which, from all accounts, proved to be a 'hectic action' as the tanks were driven off again by the remaining 25mm anti-tank guns, Boys rifles and Bren guns. As the enemy withdrew towards Gorre they left eight of the Dorsets' carriers burning and one destroyed anti-tank gun.

With dusk approaching the B Echelon transport attempted to break out to the north but ran headlong into a German armoured column, the few surviving vehicles managing to return to the perimeter. Time was now running out for the Dorsets as D Company came under attack from six armoured vehicles, one firing straight down the Rue des Cailloux. Major Bob Goff, already wounded from a previous attack, continued to lead the company as they withdrew into an orchard 'with both sides firing point blank at each other until the Boche decided to pull out'. The final attack came shortly after 7.00pm which, although repulsed, convinced Stephenson the time to break out had arrived.

A lesser individual may well have considered surrendering the battalion at this point but far from beaten and determined to outmanoeuvre his enemy, Stephenson took the decision to lead his surviving men across country to Estaires – a march of about 10 miles. At 9.30pm 15 officers and 230 other ranks – all that was left of the battalion – and a collection of other men from various regiments, assembled south of the village. With Stephenson in the lead and Major Tom Molloy as his assistant navigator, the battalion moved south of the village across the fields before heading northwest to cross the D72. On three occasions they encountered the enemy but each time fortune was on their side and they escaped unscathed. At 2.30am they found themselves on the banks of the canalised River Lawe, a water obstacle they had to cross twice as their route took them unwittingly across a large bend. Tired, wet but triumphant, they arrived at Estaires at 5.00am on 28 May. It had been another impressive chapter in the long history of the regiment and one that was rewarded by Stephenson's DSO which was announced in October 1940.

Chapter Ten

Hazebrouck and Cassel

24–29 May 1940

'Often the enemy came near to gaining a foothold, as when a party of them infiltrated through the woods almost into the heart of our sector and were only checked by the prompt action of CSM Bailey who collected a small party of clerks, signallers, cooks, anyone he could find, loaded them with as many grenades as they could carry and led them in a hectic bombing counter-attack which utterly routed the enemy.'

Lieutenant Michael Duncan, 4/Ox and Bucks, at Cassel on 28 May 1940.

We last heard of 145 Brigade on 17 May at Hal, covering the retreat of the 2nd Division. It was a day that the Territorials of the 1/Buckinghamshire Battalion of the Ox and Bucks Light Infantry remembered vividly as their commanding officer, 46-year-old Lieutenant Colonel Alexander Burnett-Brown, collapsed from exhaustion and command was handed down to Major Brian Heyworth. A Cambridge graduate, Heyworth moved from Manchester in 1936 after his appointment as a barrister in the Treasury Solicitor's Department in London, a move that took him to Beaconsfield and a transfer to the Ox and Bucks Light Infantry Depot at Newbury.

On 24 May 145 Brigade, under the command of Brigadier Nigel Somerset, were in billets at Nomain, southeast of Lille and had been warned that their move to Calais was imminent. Captain Hugh Saunders commanding D Company of 1/Bucks was delighted by this news declaring that a 'restful task such as the strengthening of the garrison of Calais' would be most welcome after 'the buffeting of the last ten days'. Completely unaware of what was unfolding at Calais, Heyworth's battalion spent all day waiting for orders, which finally arrived at 9.30pm along with the transport. Few of the slumbering men of 145 Brigade would have had any idea that the destination on the route card had been changed from Calais to Cassel or that at Bailleul, the Buckinghamshires' destination had changed again to Hazebrouck. The fast moving pace of events now focused the minds of the British commanders on keeping the corridor to Dunkirk open and 145 Brigade was about to play its part.

Somerset's orders on 24 May were refreshingly straightforward: Hazebrouck, Cassel, Wormhout and Bergues were now part of the outer perimeter around Dunkirk and were to be held at all costs and 145 Brigade was to move immediately to secure Hazebrouck and Cassel. An element of fate dictated the move of the Buckinghamshires to Hazebrouck, one which rested on the movement order which placed the battalion at the rear of the brigade column that left Nomain. As the convoy travelled up the D933 it was a simple matter to divert Heyworth's men to Hazebrouck while the remainder of the brigade continued to Cassel.

Hazebrouck had been a hive of activity since Gort and Pownall had arrived on the afternoon of 22 May with the intention of moving their command post and reuniting GHQ in the town – a move that was swiftly reversed when news of the enemy incursions on the Canal Line dictated a rapid relocation, leaving a handful of staff to follow on. Saunders tells us that on arrival in the town the battalion was greeted by a Captain Alistair Campbell who was commanding the Hazebrouck garrison:

> '*Campbell explained that GHQ troops, supplemented by various small detachments of troops lost from their units, at present occupied the town and owing to a penetration by enemy AFVs* [armoured fighting vehicles] *in an easterly direction over the canal running through St Omer it had been decided that Hazebrouck was to be held at all costs.*'[1]

The action involving Sergeant James Mordin and the 392/Battery gun had taken place the day before and, although enemy tanks had reluctantly withdrawn in compliance with Hitler's Halt Order, the town had been severely bombed on several occasions resulting in the majority of the inhabitants leaving. Thus it was a largely deserted town that greeted Heyworth's initial reconnaissance – apart from the *Luftwaffe* who regularly machine-gunned the streets. Realizing the town was too large an area to defend Heyworth – hoping the railway lines would form an anti-tank barrier – deployed his companies to hold the town south of the Calais-Bailleul railway and west of the railway line running south to Isbergues; an entirely sensible decision but even then there were several undefended gaps between company positions which ultimately allowed German units to infiltrate between them.

Heyworth had some difficulty in establishing with any accuracy exactly how many troops he was to command. Extracting an approximate list from Campbell along with a map of the town, he appeared to have inherited a contingent of leave men from the 6/York and Lancaster Regiment, a collection of orderlies, signallers and drivers from the former GHQ and a platoon of 4/Cheshires with four Vickers guns. The guns of 223/Battery were added to by one platoon from 145/Brigade Anti-Tank Company armed with 25mm Hotchkiss guns under Sergeant Ken Trussell and a composite battery of 98/Field Regiment based at

Le Souverain farm southeast of the town. It is unlikely that Heyworth could have held out at Hazebrouck as long as he did without the support of 98/Field Regiment which, early on in the battle, established an observation post in the Hazebrouck church tower to direct the battery's fire.

Heyworth established his battalion headquarters in the centre of town in the Foundation Warein Orphanage on the Rue de la Sous-Préfecture. A Company and Captain Dick Stevens were placed in reserve and occupied the former GHQ building across the road. As groups of stragglers drifted into town Heyworth directed them to A Company which by nightfall on the 26th had been reinforced by nearly 200 men. The three remaining Buckinghamshire companies were distributed around the perimeter with B Company on the right, C Company astride the D916 and D Company covering the western approaches.

Lieutenant Trevor Gibbens, the medical officer attached to the battalion, found the orphanage cellar a convenient location in which to set up the RAP and spent most of 26 May collecting medical supplies from any doctors' houses he could find in the town. Fortunately ambulances were still able to come and go without enemy interference as were individuals from other units seeking medical treatment. One of these was a gunner officer from 98/Field Regiment:

'A Jeep came roaring up the road and stopped. An officer beside the driver got out and said in the most conversational tone "I seem to have got one in the elbow, doc". I cut off his sleeve and realized that his elbow joint had been completely shot away, with a gap of an inch or two between the bones. The radial artery and tissues in the limb were intact, so I put a long wire splint on the whole arm and sent him off in one of the last ambulances.'[2]

The individual in question was Captain Lord Cowdray who had been hit northeast of Steenbecque by a burst of machine-gun fire which had also killed Gunner Ronald Scoates who was driving the vehicle and wounded one of the two signallers in the back. Cowdray later had his arm amputated but was successfully evacuated from Dunkirk thanks to Gibbens.

The battle for Hazebrouck began on a wet and misty Monday 27 May when tanks from the 8th Panzer Division overran the 2/Royal Sussex positions south of the town. One of the first units in action was D Company which was overwhelmed by tanks from *Oberst* Neumann-Silkow's *Panzer Kampfgruppe* in the Bois des Huit Rues. Shortly after this the battle opened in Hugh Saunders' sector when his attention was drawn to a German vehicle near the level crossing on the western edge of his sector. Calling in artillery support from a nearby 25-pounder of 223/Battery – which missed its target, allowing a German reconnaissance group to escape – it wasn't long before the tanks arrived:

'We had not been back in our Company HQ for more than a quarter of an hour before three light tanks appeared and swooped down on the 25-pounder, smashing the gun and wounding all its crew save one. The crew retreated through one of 17 Platoon's outposts, hotly pursued by two tanks which fired a salvo straight into the weapon pits, before they turned and made their way off.'³

Saunders was relieved to discover there were no casualties from 17 Platoon but the ease with which enemy tanks had penetrated the perimeter left no one in any doubt of what was to come. At 10.00am Saunders received a message from Second Lieutenant Tom Garside commanding 18 Platoon that a large force of enemy armoured vehicles was approaching from the direction of St Omer, a message confirmed ten minutes later by the observation post on the Wallon-Cappel road. Saunders had a distinct feeling they were 'for it':

'While we were waiting, for some obscure and still incomprehensible reason, the battalion water truck arrived to fill up eight water bottles which I had reported were empty. The arrival was unhappily the signal for the commencement of the attack and, hardly had [the truck] stopped outside the gate than an enemy tank rushed up from the area of Les Cinq Rues and, with a carefully aimed shot, hit the water cart straight in the [water] tank … The [German] tank in question was one of three that were circling round 17 Platoon's position, harassing them as much as possible and trying to unnerve the defenders. They were hotly engaged by 17 Platoon's anti-tank rifles, and after one of them was hit, they withdrew.'⁴

The Bucks were certainly 'for it'. By 11.00am all three companies were engaged as enemy tanks probed their defences and German artillery and mortars bombarded their positions, making life very difficult for Lieutenant John Palmer in his observation post in the church tower and eventually forcing him to beat a hasty retreat.

But this was only the beginning. Half an hour later a runner from 16 Platoon announced that infantry were being brought up along the St Omer road in strength and although they had already been engaged by Corporal Wade and his section from 17 Platoon, and temporarily scattered by the battalion's single 3-inch mortar, D Company's supremacy over the enemy was short lived. Within minutes a steady machine-gun fire made it almost impossible for anyone to lift their heads. But, as Saunders reflected later, it looked as if the attack was developing on the C Company front. It was. While D Company were coming under heavy fire, 30-year-old Captain Rupert Barry and his platoons of C Company were fending off an attack by five enemy tanks with their Boys rifles. It was a desperate fight and despite putting most of the tanks out of action, 14 Platoon was overrun and another – possibly Lieutenant Geoffrey Rowe's 13 Platoon – was cut off and surrounded by the afternoon. Responding to Barry's SOS, Heyworth ordered A

Company to establish a fresh line in the buildings behind C Company in order for Barry and his men to withdraw. Very few of A Company reached the new line and Barry – one of only two regular officers in the battalion – was captured later that evening.

On the eastern edge of the perimeter, Lieutenant Clive Le Neve Foster's 11 Platoon of B Company did not have to wait long before it too became engaged by German infantry advancing down the railway line. Beating off the initial attack the company held their ground under enemy machine-gun fire and occasional sniping which appeared to be directed from buildings to the north of the railway. Foster remembered that later that day an anti-tank officer arrived at their positions with news that the Germans were in the north of the town and asking for help in retrieving an anti-tank gun which was 'on the wrong side' of the railway line:

'*There was very heavy machine-gun fire down the railway and six sets of rails to get it over. I took the sergeant major and about 8 others for the job and we ran over and all crossed safely. We got hold of the gun and it was a heavy affair to move. We then drove a 15cwt lorry over and after some difficulty hitched it up and got safely back again. I can well remember watching the machine-gun tracer bullets streaking down the line.*'[5]

Back across the railway line Foster found the company had withdrawn and large numbers of German infantry were approaching the town. Quite where the company had gone is not clear but the company commander, Captain John Kaye, was amongst those who made it back to England. Saunders and his men were also conscious that enemy forces were pouring into the town and they were powerless to stop them:

'*By about 7.00pm the enemy were well inside the town and we could hear the sound of firing in the streets. In several places fires had broken out from incendiary shells and clouds of smoke filled the air, but Battalion HQ was still intact. I decided to make contact, if I possibly could, and Pte Page volunteered to make his way to Battalion HQ. He had only, however, to put his foot outside the gap in the wall which we used as a door to bring a veritable hail of tracer bullets down on him. After several attempts we realized it was hopeless to get out of the building by daylight, as all our lines of departure were covered by machine guns.*'[6]

At battalion headquarters the 27-year-old Gibbens was struggling desperately with the wounded as the upper floors of the orphanage were being bombarded by mortars and tank shells. From below floor level they could hear the crack and rumble of masonry as battle raged above:

'*Bit by bit the wounded were brought down … There was clearly not going to be much opportunity to get the wounded away for some days … I did the rounds in quiet moments, gave plenty of morphia and sips of water ... one man was brought down with his abdomen completely opened up and his bowels pouring out. There seemed to be nothing to do but put wet, warm packs on him and fill him up with morphia. He died quietly the next day.'[7]*

Unbeknown to Gibbens, enemy forces were closing on battalion headquarters from three sides, having cut off and surrounded the rifle companies whose resistance had been reduced to platoon-sized pockets. By the time darkness had descended over a burning Hazebrouck the battalion had been practically destroyed. It appears that in the confusion of battle, withdrawal orders were not received by the men in isolated company positions and those that did receive them were given no point of reference to withdraw to.

At 8.30pm the Germans completely broke through the D and C Company positions and pushed on towards the centre of town. Saunders took it upon himself to order the surviving men of his company to get way, feeling that in the circumstances Major Heyworth would have acted in a similar fashion. Foster, who was cut off from B Company, lay up behind the railway embankment with two others until dark when all three managed to evade capture and get to Dunkirk. As to how many of the battalion escaped captivity is uncertain but Ian Watson is of the opinion that up to half of the battalion may have escaped, particularly those from the outlying rifle companies.[8]

It was a different story for the men still holding out at battalion headquarters. Private Perkins, one of the D Company runners, was one of a number of men who had drifted back to the orphanage where he was ordered to take up a defensive position:

'At two points in the building were Bren guns covering two streets and one more covering the big yard at the back of the building ... Myself along with the other HQ personnel took up our positions with our rifles at every available window there was ... for the first hour or two it was more or less a sniper's job, as I had quite a few crack shots at motor cyclists who kept crossing quite frequently at the top [of the road]. The building was now getting in a bad way, one part of it had already collapsed, as at this stage we were handicapped by our anti-tank rifles having been put out of action so it was left to our Bren guns to try and stop the tanks. It was hopeless and heartbreaking for the Bren gunners, their bullets just bounced off, but undaunted they kept on.'[9]

The war diary, which was completed by Saunders shortly after he had returned to England, describes the fighting coming to an end around 9.30pm on 27 May. Certainly by nightfall all contact had been lost with the rifle companies and battalion headquarters was surrounded. In a final effort to make contact with any troops still holding on Heyworth sent out two patrols: one to find the B Echelon transport and the other to B Company. Second Lieutenant Martin Preston got as far as the town square before he was killed while Second Lieutenant David Stebbings, the Intelligence Officer, finding the B Company positions deserted, managed to return with the news. Only then was it fully realized at battalion headquarters that 'it and HQ Company were the only parts of the battalion available and capable of fighting another day'.

As soon as it was light on 28 May enemy mortars ranged in on the convent hitting an unloaded ammunition lorry which added to the noise of battle by a series of continuous explosions for almost two hours. At 1.00pm a number of tanks came past the front of the building firing at almost point blank range at the beleaguered garrison which replied with rifle, anti-tank rifle and Bren gun fire, the intensity of which was reduced somewhat by the GHQ troops' unfamiliarity with the workings of the Lee Enfield rifle! That the end was near must have been obvious to all concerned but still they held on.

The *Ox and Bucks War Chronicle* gives the time of Major Heyworth's death as 4.30pm. He was crossing the Rue de la Sous-Préfecture to the former GHQ Headquarters when he was hit by a sniper's bullet. It was an imperfect end to a gallant individual's short life. There is some evidence to suggest Heyworth and his second-in-command, Major Elliott Viney disagreed about surrendering, Heyworth being determined to defend the building to the last man as he had been ordered. But with Heyworth's death command devolved to Viney who soon afterwards evacuated the building with the hundred or so men who were still able to fight, taking up position in the small, walled orphanage garden. It was around this time that the adjutant, 32-year-old Captain James Ritchie was killed attempting to leave the building by another entrance. Trevor Gibbens' account provides a glimpse of the final minutes before the building collapsed:

> 'The school was virtually being razed to the ground it seemed. The noise of falling floors got louder. I remember hearing that the part of a house which is last to collapse is the doorways. I think it is certainly true. Anyway I stood in the doorway between cellars three and four. Number four led to the stairs to the front door. Soon after the roof came in, covering all the fifty or so wounded on stretchers on the floor with rubble. I imagined they would all be killed and as I walked to the doorway, I remember a voice under the rubble saying "get off my face".'[10]

Trapped and with virtually no ammunition, Viney's men waited patiently in the orphanage garden, determined to make their break for freedom under the cover of darkness. It never happened. Spotted by a German patrol Viney had little choice but to surrender the remaining garrison. The defence of Hazebrouck was over.

～

A little over 5 miles to the northwest of Hazebrouck is the small and ancient town of Cassel, built on top of a significant hill which rises nearly 600 feet and dominates the surrounding countryside. Before May 1940 it was probably more associated with Frederick Duke of York who is supposed to have marched his ten thousand men up and down the hill during the Flanders campaign of 1793. During the 1914–18 war the town had remained firmly behind Allied lines and hosted the headquarters of General Ferdinand Foch; but recent German bombing and marauding tanks spotted in the area now undermined any historical security the town may have enjoyed.

With its unique view across the flat Flanders plain, the town sits on a vital road junction with Dunkirk 25 miles immediately to the north and Lille to the south-east. Half a mile to the east of Cassel is the wooded Mont des Récollets standing some 60 feet lower. It was a place that Corporal Moore and B Squadron of the East Riding Yeomanry remembered as cold, wet and continually under fire. With Ledringhem about 4 miles to the north-west and Bavinchove to the south-west, Cassel had become one of the lynchpins protecting the western face of the Dunkirk Corridor.

The trucks carrying Lieutenant Michael Duncan and the men of A Company, 4/Ox and Bucks from Lille had lost their way five times during the night, an experience which Duncan found somewhat unnerving as he 'had no idea where the enemy were and any deviation from the route might well land us amongst them'. Duncan's opinion was undoubtedly shared by Major Maurice Gilmore, commanding 2/Gloucesters, who observed, with his usual clipped tone that 'the battalion reached Cassel after a journey of some vicissitude in the early morning of Saturday, 25 May'.

From the moment 145 Brigade was redirected to Cassel it was referred to as 'SomerForce' by GHQ. Whether or not Brigadier Somerset approved of this term is not recorded but as the various units headed towards the hilltop town Somerset was very much aware he was now commanding a mixed force of regular soldiers from the 2/Gloucesters under Gilmore's command, and Territorials in the shape of the 4/Ox and Bucks, a battalion which had only recently welcomed Lieutenant Colonel Geoffrey Kennedy as their new commanding officer. The two infantry battalions were supported by two troops from 5/Royal Horse Artillery (RHA), the 367/Battery guns from 140/Field Regiment, two batteries of 53 (Worcestershire Yeomany) Anti-Tank Regiment and some machine gunners from the 4/Cheshires. There were also a smattering of Royal Engineers from 226/Field Company, Royal Signals and RAMC personnel which Second Lieutenant Tom Carmichael of the East Riding Yeomanry rather dismissively called 'the odds and sods.'

The East Riding Yeomanry (ERY) had been in France since February 1940, moving into Belgium on 14 May with the 1/Fife and Forfar Yeomanry which made up the 1/Armoured Light Reconnaissance Brigade. Arriving at Cassel on

24 May, the regiment was equipped with Mark VIb light tanks and carriers and made a welcome addition to Brigadier Somerset's 145 Brigade. Sharing the ERY's occupation of Mont de Récollets were the two RHA troops of 18-pounders – D Troop taking the west side and B Troop the east – and the Welsh Guards who had recently been defending Arras.

Captain Eric Jones, the Gloucesters' adjutant, recalls driving up the hill towards the town with Major Gilmore and meeting Kennedy of 4/Ox and Bucks about halfway up: 'The two COs discussed the situation and as brigade HQ had not yet arrived, decided, by mutual agreement, to divide Cassel for defence.' This gentleman's agreement divided the defence of Cassel into two halves with the Ox and Bucks holding the eastern half of the perimeter and the Gloucesters the western half. Keeping A Company in reserve, Gilmore established battalion headquarters in what is now the Banque du Nord on the southern edge of the Place du Général Vandamme deploying B Company under Captain Bill Wilson facing north and west and linking up with C Company of the Ox and Bucks Two of Wilson's platoons occupied the houses on the north side of the road on the edge of town immediately before the 'S' bends on the D 52 and faced open country with 10 Platoon and 27-year-old Second Lieutenant George Weightman occupying the isolated farm – called Weightman's Farm in Eric Jones' account – 400 yards down the hill to the north.[11] D Company and the Mortar Platoon under Captain Anthony Cholmondeley were in the centre facing west overlooking a wooded area sandwiched between the present day D11 and the D933 with their headquarters in a huge pigeon loft in the grounds of a large house. C Company and Captain Esmond Lynn-Allen faced south and southwest and linked up with A Company of the Ox and Bucks.

Lieutenant Colonel Kennedy took over the large red brick Gendarmerie on the Rue des Berques as his battalion headquarters, a building he shared with Lieutenant Colonel Douglas Thompson who commanded the 1/ERY. Kennedy kept B Company in reserve and deployed D Company to cover the Steenvoorde road from Mont de Récollets while A and C Companies took up position along the eastern perimeter. The anti-tank defence was coordinated by 33-year-old Major Ronnie Cartland of 53/Anti-Tank Regiment who sited all his 2-pounders to cover the main approaches.

The Reverend David Wild probably took the same approach road into Cassel as Eric Jones and Major Gilmore had which he described as a long climb following a series of zig-zags up the steep face of the hill. Where the road takes a sharp right-angled bend by the cemetery he was stopped short by the carnage that lay before him:

> *'Some Belgian horse-drawn artillery had taken a direct hit at this point, and all over the road were the remains of wagons, guns, horses and men. A hundred yards farther up the street was a burnt out six-wheeled petrol lorry, and several of the houses, including Haig's old GHQ, were just empty shells.'*[12]

Returning later, Wild buried the bodies of the dead in the cemetery and had the horses dragged away, noting that thereafter all the troops in the town referred to the corner as Dead Horse Corner.

To Michael Duncan it was obvious that if the Germans attacked between the various fortified points along the corridor there was little to stop them, the only hope was that the enemy would be delayed by strongly fortified and tank-proof localities. The defence of Cassel was a much better prospect than that of Hazebrouck and to that end the troops settled down to digging and fortifying the town in their allotted company areas. However, it was almost inevitable that these initial dispositions were to change in what Gilmore called 'tactical rearrangements':

> 'The first of these alterations was the sending out of 8 Platoon under 2/Lt R W Cresswell to occupy a partially completed blockhouse about two and a half miles out of Cassel on the road to Dunkirk. The second was the sending out of the rest of A Company to occupy the village of Zuytpeene, on the railway line west of the town. [D Company] of the 4/Ox and Bucks was similarly sent out to occupy Bavinchove, also on the railway, south by a mile or two, of Zuytpeene. These three forward positions were to break up any enemy onslaught before reaching the main position.'[13]

As D Company moved out to Bavinchove their place was taken up by B Squadron ERY, who, like the infantry, were digging new positions until well after dark. 'Tempers were not improved' by this additional digging, remarked Duncan, nor were they soothed by the slice of fried meat loaf and cup of tea which masqueraded under the name of dinner.

Second Lieutenant Roy Cresswell and 8 Platoon moved north to the blockhouse during the evening of 26 May to find the structure still incomplete and occupied by refugees who he says were persuaded to leave. Early the next morning the platoon worked hard to block up the entrances and remove the builder's hut and scaffolding before the enemy attack that Cresswell was expecting later that day:

> 'At 6.00pm the Germans were seen advancing in open order across the western skyline. The side entrance was immediately shut and a heavy fire brought to bear on the advancing enemy, upon which several casualties must have been inflicted at a range of 600 yards. Between 7.00pm and 8.00pm a furious attack was launched against us, which was beaten off, the only lasting effect being that one nearby haystack was fired by tracer. This proved to be advantageous to us, since it burnt all night, and the light this caused made the work of the look-outs slightly easier. In the attack the Germans used a type of shell which was about 2-inches long and which burst inside the blockhouse. Part of one of these hit L/Cpl Ruddy, who was severely wounded in the head and throat.'[14]

Tuesday May 28 was relatively quiet for Cresswell and his men, no enemy attacks took place although mechanized columns were seen moving east of Cassell, leading to much speculation as to what was happening to the battalion in the hill. Everything changed the next morning, a day which Cresswell described as 'one of the worst days we had experienced in the blockhouse.' It began at about 9.00am with the appearance of Captain Derick Lorraine, a wounded British artillery officer, who was seen hobbling on a crutch shouting 'wounded British officer here'. Already a POW, Lorraine had been turned out of an ambulance by his captors. Forced to approach the blockhouse at gunpoint, Lorraine made every effort to indicate there were Germans on the roof attempting to start a fire with petrol in the well of the unfinished turret housing. Cresswell remembered that he responded immediately and that Lorraine replied 'do not reply' in a lower voice:

> *'When he reached the east side he looked down at a dead German and said out loud, "There are many English and Germans like that round here." At the same time he looked up at the roof of the blockhouse, an action which seemed to indicate German presence on the roof. With that he hobbled out of sight.'*[15]

Lorraine's silent gesturing was not lost on Creswell. As smoke filled the blockhouse the defending Gloucesters donned gas masks while they struggled to put out the fire, Cresswell remarking that they had failed again to drive them out but in the process had improved the warmth inside the blockhouse.

Their battle came to an end on 30 May, heavy weapons were brought up and their continued resistance seemed futile, particularly as nothing had been heard from Cassel. They had held the blockhouse for three days keeping the smoke from the fire at bay by the use of an old quilt damped with water from the blockhouse well and demonstrated a grit and determination worthy of their famous cap badge. As Cresswell and his platoon were being marched away the fire continued to burn for the next week as a constant reminder of a tenacious defence.

At Zuytpeene Major Bill Percy-Hardman and A Company came under attack at 8.00am on 27 May from a strong force of tanks and infantry which surrounded the garrison and cut off all communication with Cassel. Fighting continued all day with individual sections gradually withdrawing on to company headquarters situated in the centre of the village. Orders to withdraw were sent from Cassel at 12.15pm but the dispatch rider returned having failed to get through to them. Sent out again he returned a second time only to find his way blocked again by enemy forces. However, at 7.00pm Privates Tickner and Bennet arrived at battalion headquarters in what was described by Jones as 'an exhausted and hysterical state' having left Percy-Hardman some three and a half hours earlier:

> *'They had volunteered to bring a message to Bn HQ after previous runners had been killed. When they left the company, it was surrounded and under heavy mortar fire.*

There had been many casualties. The last thing they had seen was a mortar shell land upon the house in which company HQ was situated (in the cellar). They had passed through the enemy line along a drain and by ditches and had great difficulty in entering our own lines. Both were convinced that Major Percy-Hardman was killed.'[16]

In actual fact Percy-Hardman was still very much alive but his company had been reduced to a handful of survivors and one Bren gun which allowed them to fight off one final attack before they surrendered. Both Percy-Hardman and Cresswell were later awarded the MC.

One mile east of Zuytpeene D Company of the 4/Ox and Bucks were coming under attack at Bavinchove. Commanded by Captain Charles Clutsom, they had been sent to hold the east side of the village but it wasn't until early on 27 May that they came into contact with the enemy. From their vantage point above the Rue des Ramparts at Cassel, Michael Duncan and Captain Lord 'Pat' Rathcreedan were able to watch the approach of an armoured column:

'As Pat, the Company Commander, and I stood watching for signs of the enemy we saw, winding out along the road from St Omer to Bavinchove, a long column of enemy tanks preceded by motor cyclists and armoured cars and followed by infantry in half tracks ... suddenly the head of the column broke, as if splintered, with pieces flying in every direction as they came under fire from the defenders of Bavinchove. For a while there was a lull, as if orders were being given and then, methodically, inexorably, the encircling movement began.'[17]

Second Lieutenant David Wallis, an officer attached to the Brigade Anti-Tank Company, does not say if he was present at Bavinchove but does confirm that D Company were attacked by motorcycle troops, troops in lorries and about six light tanks:

'The front section of D Company were attacked first on its flanks, the enemy stalking it. Grenades were thrown by both sides. At about 9.30am when the section withdrew across the line to its rear platoon, it found the enemy were on its right flank and pushing round behind the whole company. At this time the wounded were sent back in the transport and narrowly escaped capture. The rest of the company withdrew across the fields.'[18]

With the battle around Cassel beginning in earnest the gun crews found no shortage of targets and, as was the case at Hazebrouck, it is doubtful the garrison could have held out for so long without the fifteen 2-pounders of the Worcestershire Yeomanry and the 18-pounders of 367/Battery. There were however, limitations. Captain Eric Jones recalled his frustration at being told the 18-pounders were unable to elevate sufficiently to hit targets below the hill, he also remarks that companies 'repeatedly asked for artillery support and even though targets were pinpointed on the map, the gunners were either not available or could not give any support'.

Nevertheless, the gunners inflicted heavy losses on enemy armour. Bombardier Harry Munn's anti-tank gun was overlooking the D11 Gravelines road when he spotted twenty-four tanks heading towards him. Opening fire through a gap in the woods below, his crew were alarmed to see their shells bouncing off the lead tank:

'By now the tank was less than 100 yards from our position and we still could not penetrate its armour. The only thing I could think of was that the wheels that propelled the tank tracks were unprotected and so I shouted to Frank 'Hit the bastard in the tracks, Frank.' The gun muzzle dipped slightly and just as the tank moved we fired hitting the track propulsion wheels and the tank halted abruptly swinging to one side. Still full of fight they turned their gun in our direction and fired again hitting the bank in front of the gun. Our next shell must have disabled the turret as they opened the escape hatch and ran for their lives back towards their lines. George Prosser our Troop Sergeant had left his Troop HQ when he saw we were about to engage the tanks and laid down by the gun taking pot shots with his rifle. He hit the last German to leave the tank, who fell down by the side of his tank. The other two tanks that came through with the one we had just stopped were on the right and left of our position. I decided to engage the one on the left as it was close to the outskirts of the town and firing mortars at a target in our lines. It was a perfect target silhouetted against a small hillock. I gave the necessary commands – direction – range – and a zero lead fire. Frank pressed the firing pedal and this time the shell penetrated the armour, exploded inside the tank and blew it into small pieces as its own ammunition went up. There were no survivors. The third tank had not moved from the point where we had first sighted it and its turret moved slowly round searching for our gun. I re-laid the gun on the new target, gave the order 'Fire!' Bill Vaux had already loaded and Frank followed the tank traversing left and right as it searched for our position. Frank talked to himself as he followed the target, 'Keep still you bastard' and as the tank paused for a second he fired, completely destroying this one as we had the previous one.'[19]

The Worcester gunners would account for some forty AFVs before the town was finally evacuated. On the Mont des Récollets the guns of B Troop RHA accounted for a number of tanks as well as responding to K Battery's request in Hondeghem for supporting fire – an action we will look at more closely later. B Troop on the eastern side of the hill disabled at least two tanks before losing two guns to a *Luftwaffe* attack.

On the western edge of the town the Gloucesters' D Company line was penetrated by an enemy tank on the first day of the battle and although destroyed, must have rung some alarm bells with the company commander, Anthony Cholmondley:

'A very tricky situation arose when an enemy tank succeeded in getting into the grounds of the company [headquarters]. *An attempt by a party from B Company, consisting of Captain Wilson, 2/Lt Fane, CSM Robinson and Private Palmer, to assist D Company by a flanking stalk, was nullified by a direct mortar bomb hit on their Boys rifle. Eventually the tank was set on fire by one of the anti-tank guns.'*[20]

Private Palmer had actually hit the tank with one round from the Boys rifle before the mortar bomb exploded destroying the gun and wounding him in the back. Tragically the mortar round was from the Gloucesters' own mortar platoon, which, although it discouraged any further activity from the German tank, left a shocked Lieutenant Julian Fane attempting to get a shell dressing on the hole in Palmer's back before the medics arrived.

If the ground attack was not enough the constant bombardment from enemy artillery and aircraft caused mounting casualties which, in Michael Duncan's opinion, made life quite difficult at times. However, what was noticed on the Ox and Bucks A Company front was the reluctance of German infantry to press home their attacks where their supporting armour failed to make headway. It had not gone unnoticed elsewhere along the perimeter and as the day wore on tank attacks were becoming perceptibly more cautious, often firing from hull-down positions in an attempt to get the infantry forward.[21] That evening the scattered remains of enemy tanks were visible for all to see and as dusk settled over Cassel the evening rain at least helped extinguish some of the fires that were still burning furiously.

Yet, for all the enforced jollity which no doubt did much for morale, the end was inexorably creeping up on the Cassel defenders. The Reverend David Wild was a little perturbed when German infantry managed to direct machine-gun fire onto Dead Horse Corner. 'Bit by bit they seemed to be working themselves closer to the town' noted Wild, forcing him to climb the grassy slope above the communal cemetery to make his way to the Gendarmerie. In the B Company sector pressure was increasing around 10 Platoon at Weightman's Farm which, by 10.30pm on 29 May, was completely cut off. The previous day Captain Bill Wilson had been at the farm when several tanks approached the position, they were beaten off with anti-tank rounds but infantry were seen to be gathering about 400 yards away.

The farm had already received two direct hits from enemy shellfire and there had been several casualties, added to which came the disconcerting news that tanks were again reported crossing the road towards the farm. Shortly after

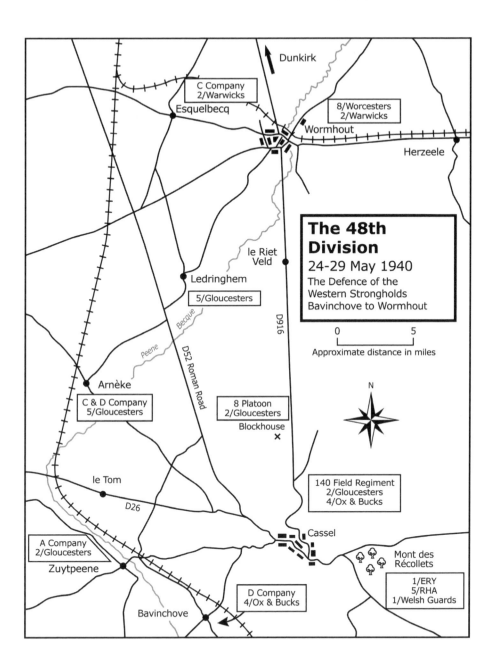

The 48th Division
24-29 May 1940
The Defence of the Western Strongholds Bavinchove to Wormhout

Approximate distance in miles

this news arrived at the Gloucesters' headquarters that a direct hit on the farm had killed George Weightman and left the survivors in disarray. With Corporal Christopher Waite and his section of 10 Platoon still grimly holding the position, the remainder were collected up by Bill Wilson:

> *'Pulling the rather shaken 10 platoon together, I started to lead them back to their position. We had just got into the tiny yard at the back of HQ when a shell landed in the kitchen doorway. L/Cpl Badnell, one of my signallers was killed outright, dreadfully mutilated. About 10 others were badly injured. Private Phelps next to me had both legs blown off, save for tiny threads of muscle. I was for the third time amazingly lucky, receiving only a small piece of shrapnel in the thigh.'[22]*

Later in the day the farm was abandoned with Wilson placing the survivors further up the hill in what had been the Cheshires' machine-gun positions.

The attacks appeared to be focused initially on B and D Companies of the Gloucesters and during one of these a mortar shell hit an 18-pounder gun positioned near the B Company Headquarters, killing 21-year-old Second Lieutenant Gerald French, the battalion Intelligence Officer, who was on his way to liaise with the gunners. Later in the morning the attacks spread round the perimeter seeking a weak spot but none were successful in penetrating the defences at any point.

During the morning when the battle was at its height a badly shaken despatch rider arrived with orders to withdraw, an order which should have arrived the previous day. Apparently Captain John Vaughan serving with the 8/Worcesters had spoken to the DR ten miles to the north-east at Bambecque early on the 29 May, Vaughan says the DR was asking the way to Cassel after having got lost during the night. Whether this was because the DR was trying to avoid enemy patrols is unclear but Vaughan gave the man directions, which explains why the order did not reach Somerset until after 8.30am.

With Cassel surrounded the lateness of the message had effectively landed the whole garrison 'in the bag'. Michael Duncan's grim assessment of the situation did not hide his irritation:

> *'It was already too late. Even had it been possible to break off the battle, which it was not, no attempt could be made to leave during the hours of daylight, and, by nightfall, all the enemy tank units had been heavily reinforced with infantry so that the chances of even getting out of Cassel were small whilst those of reaching Dunkirk were hardly worth a consideration.'[23]*

Nevertheless, orders for the withdrawal were circulated and zero hour set for 9.30pm. The garrison assembled between Cassel and the Mont de Récollets and moved off towards Dunkirk in single file, the last unit to leave the stricken town being the ERY who had destroyed all their vehicles save the carriers. It is a matter of record now that the rearguard actions fought by the ERY were largely responsible for keeping a large German force occupied while 145 Brigade attempted to reach the coast. In June it was apparent that only 7 officers and 230 men of the regiment had got home, a large proportion of which were from the B

Echelon detachment commanded by Second Lieutenant Edmund Scott who had left Cassel on 28 May.

The break-out was remarkably successful but, as one might expect, there were casualties. 24-year-old Second Lieutenant John Clerke Brown, commanding the Ox and Bucks Carrier Platoon clashed early on with enemy tanks and died of wounds a week later and Major James Graham, commanding C Company, was killed leading a bayonet charge at Winnezeele – the 38-year-old Graham was a former international athlete and cricketer. Captain Michael Fleming, whose father was killed in 1917 serving with the Oxfordshire Hussars, was mortally wounded near Watou and, like Clerke Brown, died of wounds in captivity. Amongst the many who were taken prisoner was Michael Duncan of whom we will hear more in Chapter 15.

The Dunkirk perimeter line was over ten miles to the north and by dawn few, if any, parties were more than halfway there. It was not long before most of the men were either caught in the open or rounded up after being surrounded by German units. Small groups did manage to evade capture and make it back to England but the majority were destined to spend the next five years in German POW camps.[24]

Chapter Eleven

Hondeghem and Cäestre

25–28 May 1940

'We had no tanks or aircraft to support us, as there were only a few in France. Often the Germans would have one small plane above us guiding and giving range to their artillery. On one occasion Colonel Whistler sent back a message request: "Give me a Hurricane for half an hour" but there were none to give.'

Private Bert Bleach, 4th Battalion Royal Sussex.

Brigadier Nigel Somerset's Somerforce command also extended to Hondeghem, a small village a little over 3 miles southeast of Cassel. The story of the stand at Hondeghem, now firmly enshrined in RHA legend, began on 24 May when 5/RHA moved from the Forêt de Nieppe and was stopped on its way to Cassel with orders to deploy one troop to the village. Accordingly, the four 18-pounders of F Troop, under the command of Captain Brian Teacher, were detached from K Battery to hold the village along with seventy-five men and an officer from the 2/Searchlight Regiment armed with twelve Bren guns and half a dozen anti-tank rifles. Joining them was the battery commander, Major Robert Rawdon Hoare and a small HQ under Battery Sergeant Major (BSM) Reginald Millard.

Rawdon Hoare deployed two guns – I and J Subsections – covering the southern outskirts of the village on the Rue de Staple and the remaining pair – K and L Subsections – in the square around the church. Headquarters was set up close to the church while the remaining troops were set to work blocking roads and preparing defensive positions. Their first brush with enemy tanks came early on 26 May 1940 when Second Lieutenant Mortimer Lanyon was sent out with one gun to support a reconnaissance troop of 1/Fife and Forfar Yeomanry. Lanyon positioned his gun 3 miles west of Cassel by a farm at le Tom on the D26 where he was informed enemy units were digging anti-tank positions in a copse about one and a half miles to the south-east:

'I was about to shell the copse … when two hostile tanks appeared near it. I opened fire and they disappeared into it. I shelled the copse, and waited, and later my No.1 reported that he could see tanks coming down a hedge. At the same time a third

tank, which we could not see, opened fire on us from a different area. I engaged the two tanks at 2,000 yards and both were put out of action. The third tank escaped in another direction.[1]

Lanyon had very possibly met the advance units of the 6th Panzer Division as le Tom was directly in the path of Johann von Ravenstein's combat group which was heading towards Cassel from Arques. His local action was just the precursor of the events that unfolded at Hondeghem the next morning when *Hauptmann* Löwe arrived with 65/Panzer Battalion.

Löwe's orders were to advance to l'Hazewinde and Poperinghe and crush any resistance he might find en-route. Travelling from Staple he reached the roadblock on the D161 at about 8.15am on 27 May where the leading tanks were fired on by the J Subsection Gun and possibly by the I Subsection Gun which was 700 yards further east on the Rue de Staple. Troop Sergeant Major (TSM) Ralph Opie was at the J Gun position when he observed the German column break across to the fields on their right, moments later the gun came under infantry attack which was initially dealt with by the defenders in nearby buildings. Still under attack from enemy armoured vehicles, the J Gun took a direct hit, killing one of the gun crew and wounding 33-year-old Gunner Reginald Manning in the head and chest and TSM Opie in the head.[2]

Opie remembered the roadblock was 80 yards further down the road and after the first tank was put out of action he and the surviving members of the gun crew struggled to keep the gun firing before they were overwhelmed and taken prisoner. Manning was sent back to the German casualty clearing station at St Omer where he died of his wounds. There is little detail as to what took place around the I Gun and we can only assume that it was put out of action in a similar fashion before Löwe and his battle group continued their advance along the D161 leaving the remaining two RHA guns in the village for the next wave of German troops to deal with.

The news of the demise of the guns on the main road would have travelled back to the village very quickly and if the sounds of battle had not already alerted Rawdon Hoare to the presence of the enemy, the arrival of IR 4 would have left him in no doubt. The German report of the battle in the village was recorded by *Leutnant* Kelletat whose account leaves us in no doubt of the determination that the surviving men of F Troop demonstrated in their defence of the village. Kelletat and his men arrived just as the D Troop guns opened fire on the village from their positions on the Mont de Récollets, their targets being relayed from the observation post in the church tower:

'At around 10.00am our vehicles turned off just ahead of the village onto the byway leading to Hondeghem. As we dismounted, heavy artillery fire rained down on our vehicles from the direction of Cassel ...There was shooting from just about every

direction as we entered the village … I remained with my platoon on the left of the road and advanced a bit further through houses and over hedgerows. Then we ran straight into enemy machine-gun and rifle fire lashing through the hedgerows. We could not see the enemy, but he seemed to have his emplacements everywhere. At any rate an advance towards the centre of the village was out of the question.'³

Kelletat may well have been advancing up the Rue St Pierre towards the L Gun which was firing over open sights down the road. In attempting to cross the road he was slightly wounded by a shell which hit a building just behind him. Hoping to outflank the gun he moved forward again only to be 'lashed by a sheaf of machine guns fire through the hedgerow'.

The L Gun had been manhandled from its original position in the north western corner of the square and was now firing from the southwest corner at the advancing German units who were attempting to make headway. One of the first targets was the battery cookhouse which had been occupied by the Germans who were busy firing a machine gun from the upper story. One round sealed the fate of the cookhouse and the remains of the machine gun is now a prized possession of the battery. Enemy machine-gun fire was now coming from all quarters and the gun crews were constantly changing position:

'Both K and L Guns were now hotly engaged, firing at the point blank range of one hundred yards using Fuse 1. So close were the Germans that the gun crews were being bombed with hand grenades, but casualties remained small, only one man having been killed and two wounded. Both guns were in very exposed positions but they maintained a fast rate of accurate fire and every round took effect.'⁴

It is likely that Captain Jimmy Haggas, commanding B Squadron of the Fife and Forfar Yeomanry, arrived in the village in response to the request for reinforcements although he was under the impression that he was to report to the brigadier! Haggas' account does not allude to any reaction that Major Rawdon Hoare may have felt about this instant promotion but it must have raised a few smiles at the time:

'On arrival at Hondeghem we found it occupied by a troop of RHA under Major Hawdon Hoare. Two guns were in action but the other section had been previously knocked out … I formed a line of men with Bren guns and advanced up some streets in order to clear the village, but found they had withdrawn leaving some dead. I later took out a patrol and sighted a strong force of Germans about 1,000 yards away. This force was composed of heavy tanks and motorised infantry. Two large tanks were also moving down a lane some 300 yards away. Meanwhile the shelling of the village increased.'⁵

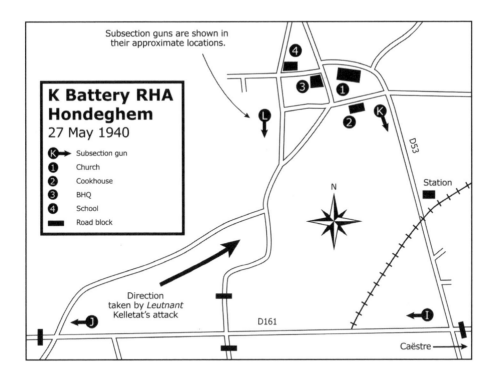

Although the village was in great danger of being enveloped, an element of impatience was creeping into the German assault which had now been held up for at least seven hours by a relatively small British force. *Leutnant* Kelletat on hearing he was the only officer remaining alive in his *kompanie* reported back to regimental headquarters where he was told brusquely to take command and 'mop up the village'. Returning to his men he ordered the observation post in the church tower destroyed and prepared for the final attack.

It would have been around this time that Rawdon Hoare decided the moment to withdraw had arrived, particularly as ammunition was low and there appeared to be little hope of reinforcements. Douglas Williams, in his 1940 account, says the withdrawal took place at 4.15pm when two columns left the village during a lull in enemy activity. The first, containing all the wounded and the two guns, was sent off ahead to rendezvous at St-Sylvestre-Cappel 2 miles to the northeast, with the second, which left a short time afterwards, taking a different route.

At St-Sylvestre-Cappel the column ran into units of the 6th Panzer Division which had already occupied the village. Douglas Williams again:

'A volley of hand grenades suddenly started from behind the tombstones in the graveyard. Germans appeared on all sides and the troop commander [Captain Brian Teacher] *decided they could only be dislodged by the desperate measure of a*

direct charge. Two parties armed with rifles and bayonets advanced round each side of the churchyard wall, each man shouting as he had been ordered to do, at the top of his voice. A terrible roar went up and the psychological effect was immediately apparent. Three or four Germans were shot and the rest throwing away their rifles broke into a panic stricken rout.'[6]

Despite both guns coming into action again the writing was on the wall for F Troop as German tanks moved in and destroyed the K Gun, leaving the crew of L Gun to put their own weapon out of action before clambering into the remaining lorries and departing in haste. But the drama was not quite over. One vehicle ended up in a ditch while another missed a turning and hurtled through a hedge into a field, regaining the road only after smashing through a set of railings. Incredibly, with machine-gun and rifle rounds whistling all around them, most of them got away. However, the final word must go to the startled expressions on the faces of the men of C Squadron ERY when they learned F Troop had driven over the very road they had mined with the loss of only one vehicle.

Predictably the casualty figures for the fight at Hondeghem and St-Sylvestre-Cappel were high. F Troop alone lost forty-five men out of the sixty-three that marched into Hondeghem but the majority would have been wounded as apart from the two casualties buried at Cassel Communal Cemetery there are only fifteen men of 5/RHA recorded on the CWGC database who were probably killed with F Troop. To those that survived, the award of the DSO to Major Rawdon Hoare and the MC to Brian Teacher served as an official recognition of the K Battery stand, while the award of the DCM to BSM Reginald Millard and the MM to Gunner Kavanagh, together with the three others mentioned in despatches, was further testimony of the bravery of those who manned the guns and ammunition limbers. Casualties from 5/Battery of 2/Searchlight Regiment are more difficult to find and the CWGC database record only two being killed on 27 May. There is no way of knowing the complete list of German casualties but at least seven men were killed in *Leutnant* Kelletat's *kompanie*.[7]

~

It was probably elements of von Ravenstein's combat group that came up against 133 Brigade after they resumed their advance from Hondeghem along the D161. The 4/Royal Sussex was under the command of another First World War veteran, 42-year-old Lieutenant Colonel Lashmer 'Bolo' Whistler, an outspoken individual but one renowned for his outstanding leadership. His battalion had been on the road from Lille since 24 May and was now ordered to defend Caëstre, but quite from whom – or even from what – remained a mystery to Second Lieutenant Peter Hadley in B Company:

'Why we were in Cäestre at all I did not know. Were we surrounded? It seemed quite likely. I did not even know whether we were operating as part of a higher formation or whether we were a "lost battalion" and I was too tired to care. We were evidently pawns in a game of some sort, and we were not in a position to see the chess board.'[8]

One thing was certain they were not operating as a 'lost battalion'. Although the 2/Royal Sussex – which we met briefly south of Hazebrouck in Chapter 10 – had been transferred to 132 Brigade, Brigadier Noel Whitty still had two infantry battalions at his disposal and it was these that were deployed to defend a line running from Eecke in the north to Strazeele in the south, a distance of nearly 4 miles.

At Cäestre Lieutenant Cecil Gould, commanding B Company of the 4/Royal Sussex, held the southern approaches while D Company stretched north towards Eecke. This left C Company to maintain contact with the 5th (Cinque Ports) Battalion, whose line ran down towards Strazeele where Whitty established brigade headquarters. Enemy shelling began on 26 May and continued intermittently throughout the day and night and realising that a German attack was only a matter of time, Whistler sent Private Bert Bleach from D Company 200 yards ahead of the company positions with orders to set up a reconnaissance post:

'We were given binoculars, a bike, paper and pencil, shovel and pick. We dug a hole or trench in the grass verge where we had good vision for about a mile across flat country, refugees were pouring past all the time carrying a few belongings such as blankets and chairs. We had to take turns at reporting back to battalion HQ on what we had seen. At first it was fairly quiet, but later in the afternoon we saw German tanks and heavy guns parked up and firing in our direction.'[9]

Bleach and his colleague had seen the advance units of what turned out to be some twenty enemy tanks approaching the south-east corner of the village under cover of an artillery bombardment that Hadley felt had not really stopped since the battalion first arrived. Private Bill Holmes would have agreed with him. 'We were in dugouts – two per trench. The time came to get our food. My mate asked me should he go or would I? You had to run, crawl and jump to reach the food. When I got back to the trench he was dead.'[10]

The shelling was not the first occasion this territorial battalion had been under fire but Whistler's apparent total disregard for the dangers of high explosive material did much for the morale of those present:

'[We] made no secret of our distaste for this sort of thing and crouched down unashamedly by the side of the road at the whistle of every approaching missile; but the CO merely stood there with his hands in his pockets laughing at us, for all

the world as if he were in the Royal enclosure at Ascot. Brave? Most certainly yes – if to be ignorant of fear can be termed bravery. Our brigade commander was exactly the same.[11]

As the tanks approached the village the guns of 226/Battery, 57/Anti-Tank Regiment opened up on the leading formation bringing six vehicles to a juddering halt. The remaining tanks withdrew and for the remainder of the day harassed the Sussex with machine-gun fire. Sometime that afternoon Peter Hadley and a fighting patrol from 11 Platoon was sent out by Whistler to deal with an enemy presence believed to be lodged in a farm three quarters of a mile to the west:

'We were just crossing road when – for the second time that day – I heard a shout of "Tanks!" This time there was not much doubt about it; for simultaneously with the warning came an ominous and unmistakeable rumble close at hand on our right. Never did ten men (and one officer) surmount a seemingly impenetrable hedge with greater speed: for we had no anti-tank rifles and it was without question a time for discretion rather than valour. In a matter of seconds eleven distinctly bewildered human beings were lying scratched and breathless behind the hedge listening to the sound of German tanks blazing away, barely 100 yards from us.'[12]

Hadley had found his Germans but very sensibly wanted to get a better idea of exactly what he was up against before making any decision as to what action to take. It was while he was keeping the tanks under observation that he and his men stumbled on another group of enemy tanks:

'One of the German tanks was just the other side of the hedge only a stone's throw away. There was no sound or movement and I presumed that the crew must be lying up inside in preparation for another move forward. Summoning what little courage I possessed, I crept forward stealthily on my own until I was actually behind the hedge with the tank barely ten yards from me on the other side. My forefinger was crooked somewhat nervously through the ring of a hand grenade and my heart was thumping away like a sledgehammer as I waited for some sign of human movement which would give me my chance. But nothing happened.'[13]

His anxiety soon turned to relief when he realised he had found six knocked out tanks from the earlier engagement and the 'terrifying monster which might at any moment turn and spit fire at me was as dead as mutton'. He admits to being somewhat embarrassed as a dozen Germans then advanced towards him with their hands above their heads in surrender. Having handed his prisoners over to an approaching unit of 226/Battery who had been responsible for the 'dead tanks', he returned to report to his company commander.

South of Cäestre the 5/Royal Sussex under the command of 47-year-old Lieutenant Colonel Farrah Morgan – known amongst the men as 'Monocle Joe' – were dug in around the D947. His battalion was fighting desperately to hold back the German advance which looked to have refocused its assault by attempting to outflank Cäestre to the south and attack the 5th Battalion's positions along the road to Strazeele. It was a tactic which had not gone unnoticed at Cäestre and Hadley for one 'had an uncomfortable feeling that the enemy was bypassing the little pocket of resistance that our efforts had provided'. His uncomfortable feeling was exactly right and it was the 5th Battalion that was about to feel the full force of the German attack. Captain Maurice Few, commanding D Company, wrote an account of the battle which, although completed in August after he had been taken prisoner, provides a flavour of the nature of the fighting south of Cäestre.

When D Company arrived at Strazeele at midday on 27 May, Lieutenant Colonel Morgan had been in command for just eighteen days but, despite this, was about to demonstrate his flair for battlefield leadership, skills he had honed since he first saw action with the Border Regiment in 1915. Thinking the road north was clear of enemy, Morgan's initial orders sent A and D Companies towards Cäestre to reinforce the 4th Battalion, a move that was delayed by a skirmish with enemy tanks which had concealed themselves behind hedges. Caught unawares the Sussex deployed for action and after a short and violent battle lasting some twenty minutes the tanks withdrew leaving behind seven Sussex casualties of whom four were killed.[14]

It was a taste of things to come but in the meantime the two companies, consisting of less than 100 men, continued north to Cäestre where D Company took up a position on the southern edge of the village with A Company in reserve. According to Few's account, C Company – which had arrived from the Bois d'Aval – then moved through Strazeele and took up temporary positions at the north end of the village before marching the one and a half miles to the crossroads east of la Croix Rouge where they found B Company heavily engaged and pinned down by enemy machine-gun fire. However, by directing artillery fire from 257 and 258/Field Batteries onto the main road, Lieutenant Ivan Austin, commanding the carrier platoon, enabled B Company to move along the road and dig in.

It had been touch and go but by nightfall on 27 May the battalion was in position on and around the D947 with C Company at la Croix Rouge and the remaining companies strung out along the road towards Cäestre. The next day the battalion came under a sustained attack which began with heavy shelling:

An enemy concentration of about 400 infantry was observed on the battalion front. The enemy attacked C Company who, together with 1/8 Middlesex Machine guns and 2 French tanks, assisted in the repulse of the enemy who retired soon after.

The whole Croix Rouge area was then heavily shelled, two machine guns being knocked out.'[15]

D Company came under fire at about the same time and enemy infantry were seen advancing towards them:

'They were engaged with some losses being inflicted. Eventually enemy mortar and machine-gun fire intensified making the buildings untenable. Fired SOS for artillery support at 5.15pm but without response. The company evacuated buildings and withdrew into the field in the rear, the Germans being about 150 yards away ... Lance Sergeant Pritchard and 2 men were sent back to investigate [the absence of 2/Lt John Hincks] but reported no one left alive in 2/Lt Hincks' buildings. Troops became restive and made a break for the rear. Captains Few and Hole were finally left with 18 other ranks of B and D Companies and 1 LMG [Bren gun] with a sandbag full of loaded magazines. The field of fire being limited to 50 yards it was decided to take up another position known to Captain Few on the right where some support could be expected from the 4th Battalion.'[16]

The distressing part of this account is the indiscipline which prompted the majority of men to 'break for the rear' leaving their officers to continue the fight with a handful of men and NCOs. Maurice Few and his men were now somewhere on the outskirts of Caëstre – still under spasmodic shellfire – but able to maintain the LMG fire along a fixed line down the road at intervals during the night. But by the time a runner arrived from the 4/Royal Sussex at 1.30am, there were only eight other ranks still capable of fighting. The runner brought word that the brigade was pulling out for Mont des Cats and it was likely they would find their battalion at Flêtre.

In the meantime, back at la Croix Rouge, the beleaguered 5th Battalion was still holding onto its positions but Morgan's only reserve was the Carrier Platoon under the command of Lieutenant Austin. Battalion headquarters was half a mile east of the village along the Voie Communale Botter Straete with C Company on the forward edge of the village. At 6.00pm on 28 May a runner arrived at battalion headquarters with a message from C Company stating that it had been overrun with heavy casualties and all that remained was Second Lieutenant Waters and a handful of men. Austin was ordered forward with a carrier which came under fire as he approached the crossroads:

'Lieutenant Austin went forward on foot carrying the Bren gun and a box of filled magazines. At about 200 yards from the village Austin came upon the flank of a German platoon, about 30–40 men were lying along a hedgerow with the commander slightly in the rear ... Lieutenant Austin proceeded to mount the gun on a stone heap and fire through the hedgerow, but before he could complete

this a German fired at point blank range by thrusting his rifle through the hedge. The bullet struck and splintered the butt of the Bren gun and passed through his respirator. He therefore came into action forthwith, standing up and firing from the hip. Magazines were expended until the entire German unit became casualties or withdrew. Having satisfied himself the village and immediate vicinity was clear of enemy, Lieutenant Austin reported to that effect to the CO.[17]

Austin's MC was announced in July 1940 and he later expressed amazement that the gun still worked after 'a bullet ricocheted off the return spring casing in the butt … After I returned to HQ to report I must have looked a bit shattered, as Major Grant gave me half a tumberful of whiskey with a raw egg in it.'[18] That night the battalion withdrew to Mont des Cats via Flêtre where they were reunited with Maurice Few and the remnants of D Company. All Peter Hadley remembered was that it was dark and still as they passed through Caëstre and at one point he caught sight of the brigade staff captain standing on a corner. 'Twelve hours later', he wrote, 'he was a prisoner.'

The CWGC database does not tell the whole story of the number of casualties sustained by the two battalions in the actions around Caëstre. The majority of the battalion was taken prisoner between Mont des Cats and Dunkirk with around 250 officers and men – including Hadley, Whistler and Cecil Gould – managing to get back to England. It was a similar story with the 5th Battalion: Maurice Few's diary records the strength of the battalion at Mont des Cats as 200 officers and men with at least another 10–15 being captured before they reached Dunkirk.[19] Both Whistler and Morgan were awarded the DSO in recognition of the 133 Brigade stand around Caëstre.

Chapter Twelve

Ledringhem, Wormhout and West Cappel

26 May–29 May 1940

'It is one thing to fight with proper equipment, but to fight and not run away without equipment is quite a different kettle of fish. The boys stood their ground – they were bombed, burnt out and sniped at and still they held. Who could ask for more?'
Corporal Eric Cole, HQ Company 1st Battalion Welsh Guards.

T he 48th Division's sector of the western face of the Dunkirk Corridor extended north from Cassel to the twin villages of Arnèke and Ledringhem and the larger town of Wormhout which lay a further two miles northeast on the D916. All three locations were held by Brigadier James 'Hammy' Hamilton's 144 Brigade. Hamilton was highly regarded by many of the officers in the brigade and was described by Captain Bill Haywood as 'fearless and imperturbable with a wonderful sense of timing and an uncanny anticipation of the enemy's movements'. Over the next 48 hours he was going to need all these qualities.

Lieutenant Colonel Guy Buxton and the 5/Gloucesters moved into Ledringhem on 26 May with the same orders given to the 2nd Battalion at Cassel – to hold on at all costs. Buxton, a former officer in 4/Hussars, had to spread his five companies across a front of nearly 4 ½ miles to cover the village of Arnèke which lay across the D52 to the southwest. Establishing his headquarters in the *Mairie* at Ledringham with HQ Company close-by, Buxton deployed B Company in Ledringhem, C Company astride the D52 Roman road and A and D Companies – supported by five anti-tank guns from 53/Anti-Tank Regiment – slightly forward in Arnèke.

Buxton's deployment of the Gloucesters was made in consultation with Hamilton's overall strategy in which he assumed – correctly as it turned out – that Arnèke, being the most westerly point in his line, would be attacked first, thus allowing the two companies of Gloucesters deployed in the village to fall back onto Ledringhem before they were overwhelmed. In this manner Hamilton hoped to divert some of the enemy units heading towards Wormhout where he had placed the 2/Royal Warwicks and the 8/Worcesters.

Early on 27 May both villages came under attack from artillery and mortar fire and Arnèke was assaulted by tanks and infantry of the German 20th Division with the intention of crossing the railway line running between Noordpeene and Esquelbecq. Initially the German attack was held with the Carrier Platoon doing some excellent work in ambushing the assaulting troops. By the end of the day, however, the village had been practically surrounded and during the night both companies were brought in across the Roman road to Ledringhem leaving five enemy tanks and a number of armoured cars disabled. That night Ledringhem was subjected to a heavy artillery bombardment which inflicted considerable damage on the already shell scarred village. By midday on 28 May assault troops from IR 90 and IR 76 were making their presence felt, forcing Buxton to pull in his companies and prepare an all-round defence.

As the intensity of German air and mortar attacks increased, information brought in from the Gloucesters' patrols added to battalion second-in-command Major F W Priestley's unease that the enemy were working round the flanks of the village and cutting off their escape route to the north. Priestley's suspicions were first raised when the telephone line to brigade HQ was severed and then by a later conversation with Private Albert Joines, who reported coming under fire from the north on four separate occasions while taking messages to and from brigade HQ at le Reit Veld on the D916. As Priestley said himself, 'It was pretty evident that the village was surrounded.'

Apparently frustrated by the lack of progress against the Gloucesters' dogged defence, IR 90 called upon the services of 3 *Kompanie*, 20/Pioneer Regiment which was equipped with *Flammenwerfer 35* flamethrowers, a weapon already familiar to British and Commonwealth troops in the First World War:

> '*During a second attack the enemy produced a flamethrower, the fuel of which did not ignite. He was disposed of, but not before much of this unpleasant oil had coated the defenders making it almost impossible to hold their weapons and giving rise to a temporary gas alarm, so pungent was the oil.*'[1]

Surrounded by the enemy on four sides, the battalion had resigned itself to fighting its last battle when Lance Corporals Ernest Barnfield and Reginald Mayo – who had been detached with their platoon to brigade HQ – arrived at the *Mairie* with orders to withdraw to Bambecque. The two men had volunteered to get a message through to the battalion and had taken nearly five hours to cover the three miles from le Reit Veld, an exploit for which both men were subsequently awarded the MM. Mayo was soon afterwards shot in the hip and eventually captured.

But withdrawing was no easy matter. By 10.00pm the enemy were well established by the church in the western end of the village. Buxton, well aware of the need to keep the village clear in order for the battalion to escape, ordered a counter-attack which pushed the enemy back at the point of the bayonet. 'The enemy,' wrote Major Priestley, 'had entered the churchyard and tried to get down the village street; this was stopped by heavy Bren gun fire, but he did establish himself in the end houses, they were evicted by a counter-attack with bayonets.'

Second Lieutenant Michael Shephard, who was later featured in the *Gloucester Citizen*, described how the Gloucesters charged past burning houses with the men shouting 'Up the Gloucesters'. In the light of the burning buildings he saw several German soldiers being bayoneted and all around him there were explosions from German stick bombs accompanied by the whine of machine-gun fire. 'Everywhere, our men were doing the same thing, bayoneting, shooting and bombing.' Three such charges were made, led by Captain Charlie Norris, Lieutenant Tony Dewsnap the Intelligence Officer and Lieutenant Donald Norris – brother of Charlie – respectively, all of whom were wounded.

Sometime after the counter-attacks 32-year-old Major Anthony Waller, who was the most senior officer killed at Ledringhem, was engaged by an enemy patrol at the back of the *Mairie* when he was badly wounded in the head along with Guy Buxton who was wounded in the leg. Sergeant Ivor Organ remembered the moment Waller was hit:

> *'We heard shouts and screams from behind a copse; two of our men were down. For one of them there was nothing we could do, but we took the other one to the cellar in the school, where the floor was already covered with wounded. Some were already dying in spite of being treated by the doctor who was working by candle light. The soldier we had brought in was none other than Major Waller* [commanding HQ Company] *who soon breathed his last, his head one bloody mass. Returning to the trench I saw that during my absence a grenade had wounded all the men there.'*[2]

The battalion was now closely surrounded by a large force of enemy; Buxton's problem was to disengage the battalion from the fighting long enough to assemble his men and issue orders for the withdrawal. Fortunately, during a lull in the fighting, a brief window of opportunity allowed him to do just that. Major Priestley described the moments after the battalion moved off:

> *'Two medical orderlies were left behind with the three wounded officers and the men in the school who were too severely injured to move. The remainder of the battalion moved off. Smoke from the burning buildings in the village helped cover movements. Complete silence was enjoyed and the battalion left the orchard at 1.15am. The battalion column was single file and fairly lengthy. Captain* [Leslie] *Hauting (Adjutant) kept the column on the right route.'*[3]

The odds against the chances of this column of men reaching British lines were high. Bambecque lay nearly 6 miles to the north-east, many of the 13 officers and 130 men were wounded, all were exhausted and it was dark. But five hours later, having found a gap in the German encirclement, they reached Bambecque via

Herzeele at 6.30am on 29 May, complete with prisoners whom they had taken en-route. It was a feat of arms that must rank alongside that of the 2/Dorsets. Their arrival was recorded by a delighted Captain Bill Haywood who had just been appointed adjutant of the 8/Worcesters and was convinced Buxton's battalion had been 'utterly annihilated':

> *'They were dirty and weary and haggard, but unbeaten. Their eyes were sunken and red from lack of sleep, and their feet as they marched seemed to me no more than an inch from the ground. At their head limped a few prisoners with Hauting the Adjutant, in close attendance … The column halted and two of the Germans flopped down exhausted, though a captured officer remained standing and tried to look defiant. I ran towards Colonel Buxton, who was staggering along, obviously wounded. He croaked a greeting, and I saw the lumps of sleep in his bloodshot eyes.'*[4]

There was one more journey for the battalion and that was to Dunkirk where they were evacuated. Altogether around forty men of the Gloucesters are identified on the CWGC database as having been killed between 26–29 May 1940. Twenty-four – including Major Anthony Waller – are buried at Ledringhem Churchyard Cemetery.

∽

The 2/Royal Warwicks arrived at Wormhout just before dawn on Sunday 26 May. At command level there had been a change of leadership and Major Phillip Hicks now commanded the battalion in place of Lieutenant Colonel Dunn who had been evacuated at Hollain with a burst gastric ulcer. It was raining when Captain Dick Tomes and the battalion's officers met Major Hicks in the town square to hear his orders, Tomes recalling that 'most of us fell asleep on the pavement where we halted.' The companies were allocated defensive positions on the western side of town while 8/Worcesters under Lieutenant Colonel James Johnstone were deployed on the eastern approaches. Even though the infantry were supported by Captain Sir John Nicholson and his two platoons of machine gunners from 4/Cheshires and a few guns from 53/Anti-Tank Regiment (Worcestershire Yeomanry), the two battalions still had a large perimeter to defend and life was not made any easier when C Company of the Warwicks under Captain Charles Nicholson, was ordered to move to Esquelbecq, a small hamlet about a mile and a half to the west.

Nicholson's move required some shuffling around on the Wormhout perimeter but even when this had been accomplished there were still holes in the defences. Haywood wrote afterwards that Colonel Johnstone thought 'it likely that the battalion was about to do its final job' and wished all his officers good luck in the coming battle. 'There was no hand-shaking, no solemnity, no fuss of any kind.'

As far as battalion headquarters were concerned there were plenty of locations to choose from the Warwicks took over a large house on the Esquelbecq road while the Worcesters' HQ based itself at a gardener's cottage in the grounds of a château on the D55 where Brigadier Hamilton had established his HQ. Just after midday on 27 May Wormhout was attacked by a wave of German aircraft that bombed the centre of the town and almost completely destroyed it. Fortunately this had little effect on the troops in terms of casualties but on surveying the wreckage Dick Tomes thought the place to be a shambles:

> *'Every house was either wrecked completely or partially and the square was a mass of debris, fallen trees, telegraph wires and smashed civilian vans. A few civilians were lying in the road either dead or badly wounded, and there must have been a lot killed in the houses. Most civilians were attended to by a French First Aid Post but our own RAP took in a few. We moved our HQ out of the house and to the far end of the park.'*[5]

That evening C Company reappeared from Esquelbecq having been ordered to move north to Bergues to guard divisional headquarters. Nicholson reported the presence of enemy reconnaissance parties west of the railway station, confirming a captured operational order already in Hamilton's possession indicating that Wormhout was the next target.

Soon after dawn on 28 May the inevitable shelling preceded the infantry attack which came in from the Esquelbecq direction forcing Captain Edward Jerram's B Company into contact with the enemy. The road block on the Esquelbecq road came under fire from German AFVs which appeared to be using a stream of refugees as cover. They were shot up by a 2–pounder anti-tank gun and machine-gun fire from Lieutenant Charles Dunwell's platoon but in the confusion a handful of German infantry managed to get away and establish themselves in a nearby house. There is no doubt that the initial German infantry attack was held up by the Warwicks and the machine guns of the Cheshires, so much so that *Obergruppenführer* Josef 'Sepp' Dietrich, commanding the 1st SS Division *Leibstandarte Adolf Hitler* (SS-LAH), made the decision to see the situation for himself. As he approached the outskirts of Wormhout his vehicle was halted by the B Company roadblock giving Gunner Rawlinson plenty of time to aim and hit Dietrich's vehicle, kill the driver and allow B Company to bring the remaining vehicles under a hail of rifle and machine-gun fire.

Dietrich and Max Wünsche, who was acting commander of 15 *Kompanie*, sought refuge in the nearby ditch which, fortunately for them, was deep enough to provide protection from the barrage of fire now being directed on them. All efforts to rescue the two officers ended in failure and at least three armoured vehicles from 6 *Kompanie* were knocked out by the Worcestershire gunners during the attempt.

The action now spread along the whole of the Warwicks' front as the attack was pressed home by three battalions of the SS-LAH, from the 20th Motorised Division and the 2nd Panzer Division. Although by noon the Warwicks' positions were still relatively intact it was not long before German armoured vehicles began pushing through the gaps in the line and in the process destroying the Worcestershire Yeomanry's anti-tank guns. But it was on B Company that the enemy focused the bulk of its effort using the Esquelbecq road to gain access to the town centre and in the process rescuing the hard-pressed Dietrich and Wünsche from their roadside ditch. Corporal Bill Cordrey described the advance of German armoured units:

> *'Everyone was firing now and I had my sights on the centre tank. I couldn't miss. I was giving it the whole round, and although I knew it was a bull's-eye the tank kept coming as if nothing had happened. Our ammunition, in spite of what the top brass had told us in England, was useless against armour. The situation was becoming critical and we were pinned to the spot by enemy fire. What should we do? Go while there was still time or wait to be massacred?'*[6]

Cordrey and his section took the only course of action open to them and got out, but not before they watched the tanks drive straight over a neighbouring position killing and wounding the men, some of whom were crushed beneath the tanks. At battalion headquarters Dick Tomes was philosophical about the outcome of the battle:

> *'The shelling increased. A smoke screen was laid and all the companies reported tanks, either attacking or preparing to do so, with infantry behind them. We had no tank obstacles and most of the 25mm and 2-pounder Anti-Tank guns had been destroyed and their crews killed after their fire had been cleverly drawn. It became obvious that we could not stop a tank attack and would be merely overrun. After all we were but a few scattered infantry posts, without our mortars, no carriers, very inadequate artillery support and no air or armoured support whatsoever. But the battalion had at any rate delayed the advance.'*[7]

Many were killed in the last desperate struggle; 47-year-old Major Cyril Chichester-Constable commanding A Company was last seen firing his revolver at the advancing enemy; Captain David Padfield lost his life while making his way back to A Company lines from battalion HQ and Charles Dunwell was killed with his platoon on the Esquelbecq road. At 4.00pm Major Hicks sent a last message to brigade headquarters and with no word from any of his three companies, prepared for the last stand. Dick Tomes was with him:

'Then two armoured cars appeared on the left and a real hurricane of fire descended upon us as they located our position. Luckily most of this seemed to go over our heads. Most appeared to be tracer …I saw a man with an anti-tank rifle – I didn't know where he had come from – I told him to follow me and started off up the road towards the armoured cars which were firing from behind a hedge some 200 yards away. He couldn't see where they were so I lay down in the middle of the road covered by a derelict truck. I fired two of the remaining three rounds … I was feeling curiously exhilarated now and still had a rifle and 50 rounds of [ammunition] *which I had taken off a carrier. After placing the man* [Private Fahey] *with the anti-tank rifle in position I got behind a hedge and fired off practically the whole bandolier at the crews in the turrets of the armoured cars – one became ditched – and at various vehicles and motor cycles coming up the road.'*[8]

It is quite possible that this last act by Tomes may have wounded the commanding officer of the 2nd Battalion, SS-LAH, *Sturmbannführer* Schützek, whose head wound sustained near the square at Wormhout left the battalion leaderless and in some confusion. Looking to his left Tomes saw two tanks heading towards him across the field and having directed his fire onto them ran towards Hicks who was shouting for him to come back. With German armoured vehicles all around them Hicks gave the order to those who were able, to make a dash for it. Joining them, Tomes was climbing a fence when a blow on the head knocked him unconscious.

The Worcesters were more fortunate. Seeing little point in sacrificing another battalion in what Haywood described as 'futile attempts' to rescue the Warwicks, they were withdrawn to Bambecque but not before they were able to leave a memento in the form of two of Captain Ted Berry's carriers:

'Our lugubrious Ted accepted this dangerous task with his characteristic lack of eagerness, and his equally characteristic lack of hesitation. Off went the carriers in the pouring rain and in a moment or two we heard their Bren guns firing. Ted found the Bosche in Wormhout still unorganized, and he drove round the square, gunning them as they ran into houses and shops. Not long afterwards Ted was back, cadging a cigarette from me.'[9]

Tombes was captured along with Captain Tony Crook, the battalion medical officer, after he had been taken to the RAP in the park. Others, such as Hicks and Jerram, managed to evade capture but of the three companies that had fought at Wormhout only 7 officers and 130 men were finally evacuated from Dunkirk.[10]

⁓

Halfway along the D17 between Esquelbecq and Wormhout is a memorial that stands as a permanent reminder of the appalling conclusion to the battle at Wormhout. Many historians feel that the nature of the battle changed after

Deitrich was forced to take cover on the Esquelbecq road and heavy German armour was required to subdue the Warwicks' defence. That may well be the case, but whether the subsequent massacres were a direct result of the indignity suffered by Deitrich and the wounding of Schützek is a matter of conjecture. However, there is little doubt that the SS troops who took Wormhout were in a murderous and vengeful frame of mind which manifested itself in the form of the brutal behaviour which came to be associated with the Waffen-SS.

Several contemporary accounts highlight the incidents which were witnessed by Private Arthur Baxter of the Worcestershire Yeomanry when an officer and the driver of a British 15cwt truck were murdered after they had surrendered and another soldier was shot after refusing to hand over his watch. In another incident Lance Corporal Thomas Oxley of 4/Cheshires was amongst a group being driven into the main square from the Wormhout-Cassel road when they were fired upon by a group of German soldiers at 1.50pm. Most of the men on the trucks were killed or wounded but Oxley and three others were thrown off as his vehicle lurched round a corner in its attempt to get clear. Finding themselves surrounded, they raised their hands in surrender:

'After a matter of minutes, they fired upon us. Whether they all fired, I cannot say, but definitely one of them, who I had been watching, let go a burst on his Tommy-gun at the four of us. I was hit twice on the arm and leg, and was knocked out immediately ... After coming to, I saw some Germans sitting around the shop fronts ... Three Germans brought an English sergeant who was not known to me, out of a house. He appeared to be badly wounded, and a German officer immediately shot him down with a revolver. He emptied the revolver into the sergeant while he lay on the ground.'[11]

If his account is correct and this did take place at 1.50pm, then the German attack must have already broken through and entered from the south, however it appears they left the square at about 4.50pm after gunfire was heard nearby, giving Oxley and another man the opportunity to escape.

Hugh Sebag-Montefiore points out that if these incidents had been the only acts of violence perpetrated that afternoon then they could have been viewed to some extent as the result of soldiers reacting with brutality in the immediate aftermath of a fierce battle. After all, it is those few moments following the act of surrender which are the most dangerous for the defeated soldier. Tragically this was not to be the case with some fifty men from D Company whose surrender had already been accepted near the Wormhout-Cassel road. As this group were being marched into the town they witnessed fifteen to twenty men being lined up against a wall and shot, which not only left them numb with horror, but wondering if they too were to be dealt with in the same manner.

The D Company men were soon joined by Gunner Richard Parry from D Troop, 69/Medium Regiment (Caernarvonshire and Denbighshire Yeomanry) which had been ambushed at Wormhout on the way to Dunkirk. Under the command of 31-year-old Captain Heneage Finch, the 9th Earl of Aylesford, who was killed in the lead vehicle, the surviving gunners were ordered to scatter and make their escape. Parry headed towards the Penne Becque, swimming downstream in an attempt to get away but in vain; wet and exhausted he was taken prisoner. Private Edward Daly, who surrendered with A Company after their ammunition had given out, remembered being shot in the shoulder by a German soldier armed with a revolver and then marched to where the remnants of D Company were being held:

> *'From this point, with some other ranks of the Cheshire Regiment and the Royal Artillery, we were marched to a barn some distance away, rather more than a mile I judged. According to my estimate there were about ninety altogether who were herded into the barn, more or less filling it ... Captain Lynn-Allen who was commanding D Company* [Warwicks] *and who was the only officer amongst the prisoners, protested against what appeared to be the intention, namely to massacre the prisoners.'*[12]

Private Albert Evans recalled the forced march to the barn on la Plaine au Bois during which several men – despite the fact that many were badly injured – were bayoneted or clubbed with rifle butts by the accompanying soldiers from 8 *Kompanie*, 2nd Battalion SS-LAH.

The exact chronology of the cold-blooded slaughter of British soldiers which took place in and outside the barn on the afternoon of 28 May 1940 is difficult to piece together accurately, but the testimony of survivors paints a grim picture of the horrific circumstances that unfolded in the barn. It began with the surrounding SS infantrymen throwing grenades into the tightly-packed structure which, apart from killing and maiming those who were closest to the explosions, shattered the arm of Albert Evans. These first grenade explosions killed 36-year-old Rugby born CSM Augustus Jennings and Sergeant Stanley Moore who courageously shielded their comrades with their own bodies; their sacrifice undoubtedly saving a number of men from being killed. Gunner Parry counted five explosions, one of which blew him through a gap in the side of the barn where he witnessed a group of five men being herded out of the barn and shot. 'I could see them round the back of the barn, and their last act, was to turn round of their own accord, and face the firing squad.'

Albert Evans was standing next to 28-year-old Captain James Lynn-Allen when the officer grabbed him by the arm and dragged him out through the corner of the barn:

'Captain Lynn-Allen practically dragged or supported me the whole way to a clump of trees, which was about 200 yards away. When we got inside the trees, we found there was a small stagnant and deep pond in the centre. We got down into the pond with the water up to our chests … Suddenly without warning a German appeared on the bank of the pond just above us showing we must have been spotted before we gained the cover of the trees. The German who was armed with a revolver, immediately shot Captain Lynn-Allen twice … I was hit twice in the neck, and already bleeding profusely from my arm, I slumped in the water.'[13]

Lynn-Allen was dead but Evans survived by initially feigning death and later crawling to a nearby farm where he received medical attention from a German ambulance unit.

It is still unknown how many men were killed in the barn but the figure is thought to be between eighty and ninety. Altogether there were some fifteen survivors, some of whom came forward to give their testimony, and others who perhaps preferred to forget behind the wall of anonymity. The dead were buried in a mass grave on the Plaine au Bois but as their identity tags had been removed many remained unidentified when the grave was exhumed in 1941 and the bodies reburied locally. Realising a crime had been committed it is thought the Germans dispersed the bodies resulting in the exact location of all the dead being lost. It is possible that many may be amongst the forty unknown burials at Wormhout Communal and Esquelbecq Military Cemeteries and it is not beyond the realms of credibility to assume that some are still buried somewhere on the Plaine au Bois.[14]

The War Crimes Interrogation Unit began reconstructing the events at Wormhout in 1943 but regrettably failed to bring any of the 2nd Battalion SS-LAH to justice. Several had been killed on the Eastern Front by the end of the war and others, such as Josef Deitrich, managed to escape the noose protected by an oath of silence and the failure of the survivors to positively identify any of those who had actually committed the crime. *Hauptsturmführer* Wilhelm Mohnke who was in command of the 2nd Battalion SS-LAH at the time of the atrocity led a full and active life after his release from Soviet captivity and died, aged 90, in 2001 in a Hamburg retirement home.

∽

On the same day as the Wormhout massacres were being perpetrated Brigadier Norman and the 1/Fife and Forfar Yeomanry under Lieutenant Colonel Ronald Sharp, were ordered by Major General 'Bulgy' Thorne to travel north from Cassel to Socx where enemy tanks were reported to be menacing the flank of the Dunkirk Corridor:

'At about the same time the Welsh Guards received orders from III Corps to go to the same area to "clear up the situation". I contacted Colonel Copland-Griffiths who agreed to move under my command. As 5/RHA in the area could no longer be protected by the reduced Cassel garrison their CO also agreed to move under me. I agreed to leave the East Riding Yeomanry at Cassel because 145 Brigade could no longer hold their perimeter without their help.'[15]

The move of Norman's composite brigade was fraught with difficulties particularly as the enemy were by now across the main Cassel-Bergues road forcing the convoy to move along minor roads to the east which were jammed with refugee traffic and horsed French artillery units. Norman was well aware that if the 'Germans had attacked us on the move there would have been a complete disaster'. As it was, a journey of 15 miles took five hours to complete.

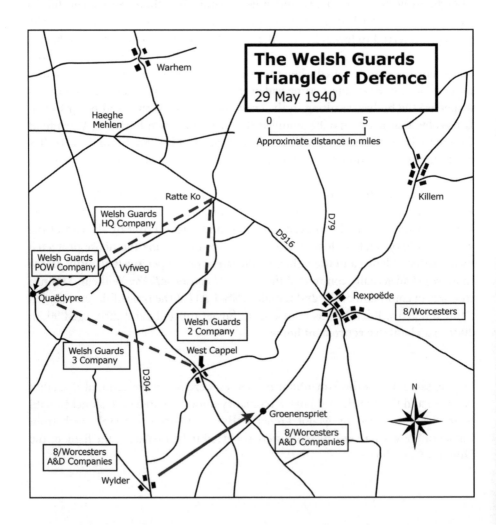

It was dark by the time Norman met his commanding officers at Vyfweg (les Cinq Chemins) where he explained the brigade was to defend a 5-mile sector between Bergues and West Cappel. Regardless of the addition of 6/Green Howards – who had arrived before Norman – it must have been apparent to the brigadier that he did not have enough men to hold the sector for more than a few hours. The 5/RHA guns he placed behind the Canal de Basse Colme, leaving two sections in forward positions ready to engage German AFVs.

Norman's initial meeting with Lieutenant Colonel Mathew Steel, commanding the Green Howards, was not one which filled him with confidence, especially after Steel explained his battalion had little combat experience and had been brought back to Vyfweg from the beaches where they had been told they were going home. 'They will stay just as long as they do not see a German,' said Steel. 'At the first sight of the enemy they will bolt to a man. I thought it only fair to let you know.'[16] Serving with the Green Howards at the time was Lance Corporal Stanley Hollis who was Steel's despatch rider. Promoted to sergeant when they got home, Hollis would go on to be awarded the VC with the same battalion during the Normandy landings in June 1944.

Giving Copland-Griffiths the freedom to deploy his battalion as he saw fit, Brigadier Norman established his headquarters at the Vyfweg crossroads, a hamlet that was contained within the wide triangle of ground around which Copland-Griffiths had deployed his Welsh Guards. With strong-points at Vyfweg, West Cappel and Ratte Ko (la Forge du Rattekoot) and using the Fife and Forfars' tanks and 3 Company to fill the gaps, a triangle of defence was created. It was, however, very fragile: many of the 3 Company platoon posts found themselves in isolated farms with orders to hold on as long as possible before retiring. Even with the main body of 8/Worcesters south of Rexpoëde there was still a one and a half mile gap between them and West Cappel which made the whole defence a rather tenuous arrangement, an opinion Lieutenant John Miller may well have agreed with at his isolated platoon post at the Hoymille crossroads south east of Bergues!

However, Copland-Griffiths' battlefield instinct proved to be correct in that West Cappel appeared to be the focal point of the main German attack, although, there had been earlier indications of this from the skirmish at Wylder, when the Worcesters' A Company – with three anti-tank guns from 211/Battery – was involved in a three-hour battle before they were withdrawn towards Groenenspriet by Captain John Farrar.

Sent to the small village of West Cappel Welsh Guards Captain Jocelyn Gurney and 2 Company, arrived in a small convoy of trucks early in the morning of 29 May. Keeping HQ Company and the RASC drivers with their vehicles in the grounds behind the seventeenth century château, he positioned PSM Hubert 'Bert' Maisey with 6 Platoon to cover the northern approaches and 19-year-old Second Lieutenant Rhidian Llewellyn with 5 Platoon to cover the south and south-eastern roads towards Wylder and Bambecque. This left Second Lieutenant Nick Daniel and 4 Platoon to dig in around the area of the church. The first sign of enemy activity came at 12.30pm when 5 Platoon reported a German patrol on their front but it was not until 3.00pm that Llewellyn reported that a strong force of enemy tanks and infantry were advancing from the direction of Wylder. Concerned that they would be overrun, Gurney sent a runner and ordered 5 Platoon to withdraw to the château.

From Llewellyn's account it appears that the withdrawal was going relatively smoothly until his last section was about to leave:

'The section was shot up as they went down the road ... I raced back to the last Bren gunner, Guardsman Warwick, who was firing in bursts to his front. Our time to leave had come but which way to go? I knew our retreat had now been cut off and as Warwick had been firing for some time I found it difficult to get him out of his slit trench, he was very stiff. I picked up his Bren for him ... I put the gun into the hip firing position and Warwick was close at hand with loaded magazines. We worked our way down the hedge towards the church and the 4 Platoon position. When Warwick and I came out of the [church] *gateway, the lane was full of Germans. I fired several bursts at them and sent them scampering down the lane. I fired after them and used up a full magazine. We ran into more Germans at the rear of the houses, some were firing at us and one or two with their hands up. We ran through them and I kept firing all the time.'*[17]

Llewellyn and Warwick made it back to the 4 Platoon position where there was a short conversation with Nick Daniel who by this time was coming under considerable pressure himself – presumably from the same body of German troops that Llewellyn had just dispersed with his Bren gun.

Llewellyn then made his way back to the rear of the château to report to Captain Gurney at HQ Company; telling him to wait for his return, Gurney left to assess the situation facing Nick Daniels and 4 Platoon for himself:

'I crawled away towards the moat and as I was in the ditch two tanks came into the garden and shot at me. I dived under the moat bridge and there I was, with a tank pounding at the bridge above me; luckily he didn't see the moat, went into it and stuck; but his gun was trained on the château door. Eventually my servant crawled to me and I decided that we must make for the château. As we got out of the moat Daniel and some of 4 Platoon came in. They had a man on a stretcher and I said we must make a dash for it and picked up the front end of the stretcher. Guardsman [Ivor] *Llewellyn had the other end. As we made for the door of the château the tank in the moat fired and caught Llewellyn and killed him.'*[18]

Daniels had been lucky to get away with a few survivors from his platoon and had no idea that PSM Maisey and 6 Platoon had already been overrun in the north of the village. But there was little time available for empathy as tanks now crashed through the château grounds scattering all before them. At the same time as Gurney and his party were making a break for the château door another tank moved in on HQ Company and 'shot them up' as they ran for cover. Llewellyn again:

'*Guardsman Andrews and I were the last to leave Company HQ and we worked our way back to the château but reached the bridge over the moat at the same time as the tank, fire from which wounded me in the right hand. Andrews and I dived under the bridge from where Captain Gurney and party had just made it to the château door some minutes before.*'[19]

And there they remained for the next two hours while the battle raged on above them, Llewellyn admitting they were most concerned their presence would be discovered at any time by the tank crew.

Meanwhile at Groenenspriet, less than a mile to the south west, 30-year-old Captain John Farrar and two companies of Worcesters were putting up a spirited defence against tanks and infantry which had encircled them. Fighting back with Boys rifles, at least one tank was put out of action and its crew shot up by Private Turton before fresh enemy infantry was seen to arrive in lorries:

'*At 5.15pm Captain Farrar wrote a message saying that three large and five small tanks had passed his HQ and were heading due east. A few minutes later other tanks closed in on D Company HQ and set it on fire. All platoons of that company were overwhelmed, but men in twos and threes continued to resist. Captain Farrar, we gather, refused to leave and was last seen firing an anti-tank rifle at enemy tanks. At 5.30pm enemy infantry made a strong attack on Groenenspriet. Many of these, wearing British uniform, were shouting 'British' and pretending to surrender. They were allowed to approach more closely, but their colleagues in the rear spoilt the ruse by opening fire. [The] A Company Platoons returned the fire and a heavy engagement ensued until about 6.00pm. By this time both A and D Companies were so badly cut up that further organized resistance was impossible, and the survivors from the scattered platoons of both companies – 3 Officers and about 60 men – arrived by fours and fives at battalion HQ to re-organize.*'[20]

At West Cappel a lull in the fighting at 7.30pm enabled Llewellyn and Andrews to creep out of the moat undetected and enter the château by a side entrance:

'*Inside the chateau we now had about 35 of our people, these included Captain Gurney, Nick Daniels and a few of 4 Platoon, Guardsman Savage, a stretcher bearer who did magnificent work throughout the battle, PSM Christian and most of my platoon ... The company had already lost about 100 men ... By 9.00pm Captain Gurney thought the Germans were about to renew the attack on the château, so while he and PSM Christian covered our withdrawal we crawled down the steps ... Private [Austin] Snead reported the Germans were creeping closer and they opened fire. We fled crossing the road under fire and met up near the 6 Platoon position from where German voices were heard.'[21]*

It would appear that the first contact with the enemy at the Vyfweg crossroads came much earlier than at West Cappel. Brigadier Norman noted that the first indication of an enemy attack came at about 7.00am when a crowd of Green Howards came running past his position:

'One of their CSMs and I did our best to rally them and get them into neighbouring ditches – then came the German tanks that had driven them in. I and Major Murray Prain, 1st F & F Yeomanry, who was with me, got into a friendly deep ditch which had water in the bottom. As the tanks approached firing their machine guns we watched them under our tin hats over the edge of our ditch firing at them with a Boys rifle. The bullets bounced off their front plates like peas. When they got to within thirty or forty yards they could not depress their guns enough to hit us. We went to the bottom of it and lay flat on our fronts in the water, I wondering what it would feel like to have bullets going into my behind and coming out of my mouth.'[22]

Fortunately for Norman it was a feeling he never had to experience as at that moment the forward guns of 5/RHA opened up on the tanks forcing them to withdraw and both men – very wet by this time – emerged intact.

According to the 1/Armoured Reconnaissance Brigade war diary, later that morning Norman moved his HQ from Vyfweg 'towards Ratte Ko' which the diary says was forward of the Welsh Guards and the Fife and Forfar headquarters. There is also a suggestion in Ellis's account that the Welsh Guards Prince of Wales Company was withdrawn from Quaëdypre and moved further east, although this is not made clear in the war diary.[23] At 6.00pm Major General Thorne arrived for a roadside conference with Norman at which time it is likely that plans for the withdrawal of the brigade were discussed. Sometime later Captain Jimmy Haggas – whom we last met at Hondeghem – was asked by Copland-Griffiths to take his adjutant, Captain Archie Noel, to brigade HQ for further orders:

'On our way we were fired upon by machine guns and I think some heavier stuff. I found Brigadier Norman with Lieutenant Colonel Sharp under heavy machine-gun fire. They were standing in a shallow pit. The brigadier gave us orders to take back to Copland-Griffiths instructing him to withdraw the Welsh Guards.'[24]

Minutes after Haggas left the crossroads Lieutenant Colonel Sharp and Captain Foster Jennings, the Fife and Forfar medical officer, were killed by a shell which obliterated regimental headquarters and wounded several others in the vicinity.[25]

Captain Otho Bullivant, the Fife and Forfar adjutant, thinks that the orders for a withdrawal were passed on to Norman's units at around 7.00pm that evening when they moved north towards Bergues. Most managed to get away but German infantry rushed the Guards HQ Company building before the last group were able to leave, taking – amongst others – Archie Noel and RSM Richards prisoner.

But for the Welsh Guards at West Cappel it was a little more complex as they were by now surrounded and cut off from their escape route. Rhidian Llewellyn writes that they began their night march across country at 10.00pm, and during the journey they were forced to fight on at least two occasions as they passed through German lines. Inevitably the little party became fragmented in the darkness and, reduced to twenty-three officers and men, they arrived at the Canal de Basse Colme at 3.00am on 30 May. Llewellyn's last words on the West Cappel episode simply stated that they reported to Copland-Griffiths on the beach at La Panne and the battalion sailed for England at 10.00pm that night. His award of the MC was announced with that of Jocelyn Gurney in October 1940.[26]

Near Rexpoëde, Captain Arthur Steele, a Liaison Officer with 144 Brigade, arrived outside the Worcesters' HQ as it was getting dark. Haywood watched his arrival:

'He pulled up quietly in the road outside, stepped out, ignored the enemy's fire, calmly shut the door of the car and ordered it to be pulled off the road, then walked slowly into battalion HQ. He brought a message informing us that we were to withdraw at 8.00pm and gave us our route to Bray-Dunes on the coast … From B and C Companies few escaped. B Company, which was widely deployed, fought on until its ammunition was exhausted, and then had no alternative but surrender, since the net was closed so tightly around it.'[27]

Private Bailey serving in the Signals Platoon was one of the lucky ones who got home to England and recalled the battalion's last march to Bray-Dunes:

'On May 30th the beach at Bray-Dunes was reached after a march of seven hours. There were about 100 men out of a battalion of 750 but eventually the number reached 150. There was no-one from B Coy but later seven men from C Coy arrived, some having had to stand up to their necks in water under a river bank to avoid being taken prisoner.'[28]

Chapter Thirteen

The Ypres – Comines Canal

25–28 May 1940

'During the course of the afternoon we were subjected to an intense artillery bombardment. Although the holes we had dug were often blocked with earth from the explosions we only mourned the loss of one soldier. But a hundred paces to our right, seven men from the first platoon of 13 Kompanie were hit on a terrace where five were wounded and one killed.'

Feldwebel Muller-Nedebock IR 162 on being shelled
by British artillery on 27 May

In Chapter 6 the situation on the Lys and the breaching of the Belgian line at Courtrai – which left a dangerous gap of some eight miles on the BEF's right flank allowing German units to cross the Lys east of the town – was touched upon briefly. Gort's historic decision to send the four brigades of the 5th and 50th Divisions to the line of the Ypres-Comines Canal was almost certainly precipitated by the intelligence he was receiving regarding the Belgian collapse (the capture of documents by 1/7 Middlesex serving only to substantiate what was already suspected). Confirmation of the Belgian lack of resolve – if indeed it was needed at this stage – was also being fed back from the 12/Lancers, their two messages of 25 May making plain that von Bock's Sixth Army units were exploiting the gap. The first message timed at 5.00pm stated that the Germans were pushing into the outskirts of Menin and advancing north through Moorslede with little or no resistance from the Belgians. If that were not bad enough, the second message received at 5.25pm advised that the Lancers were now becoming involved in an infantry battle between Menin and Roulers (Roeselare) 'in which the Belgians are taking no part'.[1]

It was now clear that the Belgians were retreating north-east, away from the BEF and if Gort did not defend the line of the canal running north from Comines to Ypres then the BEF would be denied access to Dunkirk by von Bock and a military disaster of gargantuan proportions would ensue. The decision by Gort to send the 5th Division to the Ypres-Comines Canal was as significant to the outcome of the Dunkirk evacuation as Hitler's Halt Order of 24 May would prove to be.

The canal had never been used since its completion in 1913 and much to the surprise of both German and British units was largely dry with a railway line running south from Ypres on its raised eastern bank. Yet in spite of being described as 'a poisonous position to hold' by Lieutenant Colonel George 'Pop' Gilmore commanding the 2/Cameronians, the canal did form a barrier of sorts and, amid the surrounding flat landscape, was the only line of defence available.

Major General Howard Franklyn was summoned by Gort late on 24 May and informed that the 5th Division was to hold the line of the canal and 143 Brigade was to come under his command. 'It was now a matter of time', he wrote, 'as to whether the 5th and 50th Divisions could be brought into position before the arrival of the Germans. A subsequent discussion with Alan Brooke took place at Ploegsteert Château 'on the grass with a map between us' during which the commander of II Corps explained that 'there were three German divisions advancing through Belgium with nothing to stop them except one British brigade, the 143rd, strung-out along the Ypres-Comines Canal on a front of ten thousand yards'.[2]

Brigadier James Muirhead, commanding 143 Brigade, was already acutely aware that his three battalions were 'strung-out' while they awaited the remainder of the 5th Division to arrive and no doubt sharing Franklyn's hope that the Germans would not arrive first. In the event the British were only just in time and Muirhead may well have breathed a sigh of relief as his frontage was reduced to 3 miles of canal bank from Comines to Houthem.

But even when reinforced by the 4/Gordons machine gunners, 97/(Kent Yeomanry) Field Regiment and 53/Anti-Tank Regiment, 143 Brigade historian Peter Caddick-Adams is of the opinion that its defences were 'little more than a string of fortified farms'. Brigadier Miles Dempsey's 13 Brigade covered the 2-mile stretch between Houthem to Hollebeke while Monty Stopford's 17 Brigade dug in on their left and continued along the railway line to Zillebeke, 3 miles south-east of Ypres. The 50th Division did not begin arriving until 27 May when they took up their positions on the left of 13 Brigade in and around Ypres.

Against this thinly held line were the three divisions of Viktor von Schwedler's IV *Korps*, the 61st Division – nicknamed the 'Lion' Division – and the 31st and 18th Divisions, all of which had fought in Poland. A fascinating account – referred to by Charles More in *The Road to Dunkirk* – relates to the initial direction of the attack by IV *Korps* on the canal. Apparently von Bock countermanded the orders which placed Ypres as the midpoint in the attack and ordered IV *Korps* to 'continue straight ahead' with the axis of the attack falling between Houthem and Hollebeke. It was fortunate for the British that he did as Ypres itself was largely undefended and the ground to the north practically unoccupied. More's point that 'Bock's single-mindedness' may have deprived the Germans of a significant prize serves to illustrate the 'touch-and-go' nature of a battle that could so easily have had a different outcome.

The attack on the 5th Division began early on 27 May and was marked by the absence of tanks. In the south, opposite 143 Brigade, the intensive fire from four battalions of IR 67 and IR 162 drove the forward defences back some 500 yards from the canal and overwhelmed the forward companies. Captain Purchas, commanding A Company of 1/7 Warwicks, was soon overrun defending the approaches to Houthem station as was B Company, positioned in Houthem itself. Captain Neil Holdich was commanding C Company on Purchas's right flank around Soenen Farm:

> *'The attack came in tremendous strength across the whole front. Heavy, almost continuous firing from rifles, automatic weapons and very quickly we were in serious trouble. 15 Platoon was badly hit ... 13 nearly as bad, but strongly supported by Sgt Flook, for whom I later got a 'mention'. Suddenly two trucks came whizzing across from the right, into our area, containing a Lt Colvin and two heavy machine-gun sections from the 4th Gordon Highlanders. I thought they had arrived in answer to my earlier request for reinforcements from battalion HQ but no! He said none had given him orders for this but we seemed to be the only people in the area still fighting. Within minutes he had one gun up in the attic, and the other on the left of our building, slamming fire at anything that moved.'*[3]

While the 1/7 Warwicks were battling to hold on to some sort of defensive line the 2/Cameronians on their left were having similar problems with their forward positions giving way. According to the Warwicks, the Cameronians had begun to withdraw in some disorder and Lieutenant Colonel Gerard Mole sent his intelligence officer, Lieutenant Blyth, who 'intercepted the Colonel [George Gilmore] about 1 mile away and turned him round'. A damning indictment if taken on face value! In reality it is unlikely that Gilmore was retiring, indeed in his own account he writes that after his front-line posts were forced to withdraw the battalion was ordered by Brigadier Dempsy to form a new line on the Kaleute Ridge about 1 mile west of the canal which, in the heat of battle, was confused with the Warneton-Ypres road – where presumably Blythe found Gilmore preparing to counter-attack. Regaining the ridge was costly but together with the 2/Wiltshires and to some extent the Inniskillings, the 13 Brigade line was still intact at nightfall.

On the 8/Warwicks front it was a similar story: Major Kendall – who assumed command at Calonne from Lieutenant Colonel Baker – only remained in touch with his rifle companies for a short while before all communication ceased. Already seriously depleted before they arrived on the canal, the battalion could hardly muster 200 rifles. The last message from B Company at Woestyn was cut off mid-sentence as Captain Burge's company fought hard to remain intact. For a time Corporal Bennett managed to keep the enemy infantry at bay with his Bren gun before capture became inevitable. Captain Cyril Lewthwaite's C Company held out at company HQ most of the morning against units of IR 82 and IR 162 until they were overwhelmed at about 11.00am. Private William Watts was taken prisoner with Lewthwaite:

> *'We were grouped together in the small kitchen looking to Captain Lewthwaite for guidance. He said, "I think we are now completely surrounded". As he said this, the window was broken and a grenade or stick bomb was thrown in. There was a very loud explosion but as I was half lying against the staircase I felt no shrapnel. We were all very dazed and the front door was thrown open. There were lots of shouts of 'Raus, Raus!' We stumbled through the door, Capt Lewthwaite going first.'*[4]

As far as Lieutenant Colonel Whitfeld's 43rd Light Infantry were concerned the 27 May could not have had a worse start. Whilst visiting the forward companies Whitfeld was hit in the arm by one of the B Company sentries and had to be evacuated, command falling to 42-year-old Major David Colvill who perhaps had one of the most difficult sectors to defend. Much of Comines was on the eastern bank of the canal and German units were able to infiltrate through the town to its very edge. *Feldwebel* Muller-Nedebock's account of his service with IR 162 indicates his *Kompanie* were on the lip of the eastern bank on the night of 26 May and next morning led the assault on 'some farms beyond the canal which were not very closely defended'. He may well have been describing the attack on A and B Companies. But their advance was not without cost: he also writes of the large number of casualties his battalion sustained from the British artillery bombardment – which could have been the work of the guns of 97/Field Regiment or those positioned further west on the Messines Ridge.

Captain 'Plum' Warner, the adjutant of the 43rd was at battalion HQ at the farm owned by Jules Dugardin at Mai Cornet and writes that the situation was giving cause for anxiety as early as 5.30am:

> *'Regimental headquarters was being sniped. Communications had broken down. No one knew where C Company* [Major Richards] *was. Regimental headquarters took up alarm posts at about 7.00am and soon afterwards the enemy was seen working up a stream in a north-westerly direction on the left flank. These were engaged with Brens and 3-inch mortars and must have suffered many casualties … The posts held by regimental headquarters were shelled and there was a small amount of small arms fire. There were 12 casualties including Captain* [Tony] *Jephson, who was hit in the hand, and all were successfully evacuated … information was very scarce. The situation was obscure and brigade sent no orders. At about 2.45pm the enemy were only fifty yards away* [from the most forward post] *… Major Colvill decided, therefore, to withdraw to Warneton, where more effective resistance could be organised.'*[5]

Colvill had little choice: both A and B Companies had been overrun and the company commanders killed and no word had been received from C Company, leaving him to assume the worst. In fact the worst had not happened and Richards – apparently surrounded and curiously unable to communicate with Colvill – broke out with the surviving men of his company and they fought their way back to Warneton. Lieutenant Giles Clutterbuck remained behind and was last seen

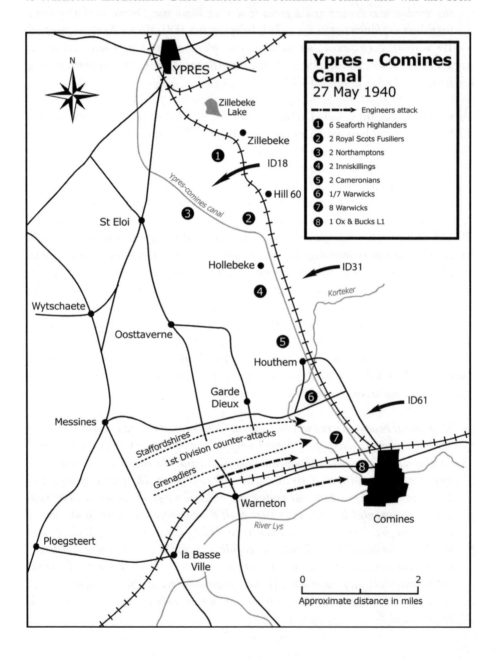

firing his revolver at the enemy. Colvill, by now wounded and evacuated, left the battalion in the hands of Major Richards.

By the afternoon of 27 May the British line on the 143 Brigade sector had been pushed back almost a mile from the canal. Houthem itself was surrounded and IR 162 had occupied Bas-Warneton. At Ploegsteert Château Franklyn recalled coming to the conclusion that the situation on the right flank at Comines had become too precarious to leave to the defending troops on the ground and ordered the first of two counter-attacks. The first consisted of Royal Engineers from the 4th Division, the 13/18 Hussars with their light tanks and part of A Company from 6/Black Watch. Launched at about 7.00pm towards Bas-Warneton and Comines, Corporal Thomas Riordan from 7/Field Company (FC) remembered that 'farms were burning and tracers were streaming in all directions':

'Our own and the enemy's positions were intermingled so much that the Germans could not use their artillery to full effect and as dusk fell the enemy advantage of perfect observation was lost. 59 [FC] came up on the left of 7 [FC] and the Black Watch to take up their position walking through the smoke of the burning farm buildings with fixed bayonets. Major MacDonald 59 [FC] OC was mortally wounded. Major Gillespie [OC 7/FC] although wounded remained in action until 7/FC were relieved. 225 [FC] took up their position on the left of 59/FC but were not fired upon. It was now a matter of holding on and consolidating the position.'[6]

~

Franklyn's rather sour comment that the first counter-attack 'met with some success but was not strong enough to have any real effect' is puzzling. Clearly he did not fully appreciate the strength and size of the attack although he grudgingly admits their attack 'facilitated the much bigger counter-attack' which he had planned for later that evening.

The second counter-attack involved the Grenadier Guards and the North Staffordshires from the 1st Division who had arrived at Le Touquet after a punishing march from Roubaix. Major Adair, commanding the 3/Grenadier Guards, received orders from Brigadier Beckwith-Smith to march immediately to Dunkirk and embark for England. It was while Adair was discussing the details with his adjutant that a second order arrived countermanding the first and placing his battalion under the orders of General Franklyn. Similar orders had been sent to Lieutenant Colonel Donald Butterworth, commanding the 2/North Staffordshires, both men and their battalions arriving at Ploegsteert by 7.30pm where they were briefed by Franklyn.

Forbes and Nicholson, in their history of the Grenadier Guards, underline the extent of the task now facing Adair and his battalion, circumstances that applied in equal measure to the Staffordshires:

> *'Divorced from their own familiar division and brigade – whom they were not to see again until they reassembled in England – without even the time to snatch some food, the battalion now had a further 9 miles to march before they reached their start line, and from there it was a further 3 mile advance over unknown country to attack an enemy whose strength and exact positions were likewise unknown.'*[7]

All that Adair and Butterworth knew was that the Germans had broken through and their battalions were to attack from La Basse Ville – Messines road with the Staffordshires on the left and re-take the ground up to the canal.

Advancing with 1 Company (Lieutenant Richard Crompton-Roberts) and 2 Company (Captain Roderick Brinkman) in the lead, the battalion crossed the start line at 8.30pm with Brinkman using the railway line on his right as guidance. The first 2 miles was only interrupted by the addition of some of the Warwicks and the odd badly-aimed shot but as they drew closer to the canal the Grenadiers' casualties began to mount and Brinkman was hit by a mortar fragment in his right eye and soon afterwards by machine-gun fire. It was probably the same fire that hit and killed Crompton-Roberts and wounded Lieutenant Aubrey Fletcher. Roderick Brinkman found he had very few men left when he reached the canal:

> *'There was a cottage on the canal which seemed to be the centre of activity of some Germans. I had five hand grenades in my haversack and four of these I threw into the windows of the cottage. Those Germans who were not killed or wounded fled back across a small bridge on to the other side of the canal … I sent a guardsman back to Major Adair, Sgt Ryder and myself then proceeded to crawl back to where I had left my reserve platoon. On the way back I was hit again through the back of the right knee and became unable to crawl or walk.'*[8]

Butterworth's Staffordshires must have crossed the start line a little earlier, the darkness cloaking any contact they might have made with Grenadiers. The battalion ran into heavy German artillery and mortar fire in the vicinity of Garde-Dieux but pushed on across the Kortekeer stream at Pont Mallet having picked up a number of Warwicks on the way. According to Henri Bourgeois some of the Staffordshires reached the canal but heavy casualties appeared to have pushed them back to where Butterworth stabilised the line east of Garde-Dieux. Likewise the Grenadiers consolidated their line on the low ridge overlooking the canal after some desperate fighting to clear the west bank of enemy.

As courageous as the second counter-attack was, it is likely that its success was, in part, due to the first attack. The Grenadiers' advance on the right appeared to be more successful than that of the Staffordshires and this is probably due to the actions of 7 and 59/Field Companies, which reached the Kortekeer stream and in a few cases advanced beyond it. The first attack was much stronger than Franklyn originally thought, but had the Grenadiers and Staffordshires not counter-attacked and knocked the German 61st Division off balance, the British would have been in a much weaker position the next morning.

Further north, along Monty Stopford's 17 Brigade sector, the canal bent back to the north-west, widening the gap between it and the railway line along which the 6/Seaforth Highlanders and 2/Royal Scots Fusiliers (RSF) were deployed, Stopford realising early on that the brigade had far too few men to hold the sector between them and the 50th Division at Ypres for very long. Assaulted by the German 18th Division, an early casualty was the battalion of Seaforth Highlanders whose rearward drift may also have been influenced by the retirement of the 13 Brigade units on its right. Poor communication was certainly responsible for some battalions confusing the movement of others for unneccesary retirement and withdrawal, which may have ultimately contributed to Stopford's orders to retire to the line of the canal where the 2/Northamptons were in position. This was easier said than done for the RSF whose left flank company was on the infamous Hill 60 – one of the iconic landmarks in the defence of Ypres during the previous war:

> 'By this time the forward companies were heavily engaged ... and before the operation could be carried out it was necessary to mount and deliver a local a counter-attack in order to give breathing space for the withdrawal. The commanding officer considered it inadvisable to use the reserve company for this purpose ... Therefore he decided to use the fighting patrol to deliver the counter-attack. This attack, gallantly led by Lieutenants [Richard] Cholmondeley and [Hamilton] Maitland-Makgill-Crichton, both of whom were killed, achieved the purpose at considerable cost, and the forward companies disengaged.'[9]

In his history of the RSF Kemp tells us that Lieutenant Colonel Bill Tod established his new positions on the west bank of the canal in the early afternoon where IR 54 engaged his forward companies. 'In spite of the inadequacy of our position he [the Germans] was again successfully held, but before darkness fell contact had been lost with the brigade on our right [13 Brigade]. Forward elements of the enemy had crossed the canal and were pressing round both our flanks.'[10]

On the morning of 28 May few, if any, of the British troops would have heard the news that King Leopold of the Belgians had capitulated and arranged a ceasefire from midnight on 27 May. Not that the information would have affected Lieutenant Colonel Tod and the RSF who were preparing to make their last stand in what the 17 Brigade war diary described as 'a small isolated farmhouse'. It was not until 1945 after Tod was released from captivity that he was able to relate what actually took place that morning:

> 'At first light I extended what was left of the battalion and advanced from the farmstead, sending Ian Thompson and his carriers to try and contact the unit

on our left. No sooner had we taken up a position on the edge of a wood than the German attack began. Very soon they had broken through our thinly-held position and at the same time had come round both flanks and were behind us ... I then decided that our only hope was to fall back on the farmstead again. There at least we could put up some sort of all-round defence. This was done and on the way back I was hit and knocked into a stream ... The situation soon became quite hopeless. The Germans were still around, the barn was full of wounded and our ammunition was all but expended. Rightly or wrongly, I surrendered. The time was about 11.00am.'[11]

Lieutenant Colonel Tod and the forty-five officers and men of the RSF who surrendered that morning would surely have applauded the action at Houthem involving 35-year-old Private Anthony Wynne of the 1/7 Warwicks. Much like Private John Lungley of the 5/Buffs at l'Arbret, Wynne was holding the first building behind the bridge and resolutely prevented any German attempts to cross the canal with his accurate Bren gun fire. He held out until midday on 28 May when he was killed by a shell. His body was buried in the canal bed and later reinterred at Esquelmes War Cemetery.

The lack of an effective German attack on 28 May provided the British with the opportunity to withdraw, the rain which had extended across the whole sector by lunchtime perhaps masking the movement of British units and reducing German enthusiasm for offensive action. Caddick-Adams writes that the Germans were unaware of the British departure which was certainly the case with Major Neil Holdich and C Company of the 1/7 Warwicks who received their orders to withdraw under the cover of darkness:

'Over the next two hours I gathered everybody together and at 9.00pm we moved out. We got to battalion HQ in good order and all that were left of us crossed the Messines Ridge, on foot, in total darkness, by 10.30pm. As we reached our transport at the crossroads, two artillery shells crumped down, causing more casualties, but fortunately they were the last of the battle.'[12]

Although the casualty figures are vaguely reminiscent of those of the First World War, it should be remembered that three German divisions were held along the canal between 26–28 May by three depleted British infantry brigades. German casualty figures are estimated at 600 killed with the greater proportion from ID 31 and 61, IR 151 for example reporting 127 killed and wounded for virtually no ground gained at all. The British appeared to have had a similar number killed but over 600 were taken prisoner. Interestingly the battalion returns for June 1940 show that the 5th Division battalions involved in the fighting on the canal each mustered some 400 officers and men on arrival in England but whether this applied to the Warwicks is not clear as Cuncliffe reports that the 1/7 had lost almost half its fighting men and only fifty-eight officers and men of the 8th returned home with Major Kendall.

Ypres has been omitted from the story so far as German intentions appeared to be concentrated on the canal line to the south. The town was in the German 18th Divisional sector and apart from occasional shelling – the Menin Gate was hit twice for example – it was never seriously attacked. But from the British point of view the discovery by the 12/Lancers that the town was undefended apart from a handful of Belgian sappers accounts for the hasty movement of the 1/6 South Staffordshires to defend the town. The South Staffordshires were a territorial battalion embodied at Wolverhampton in September 1939 as infantry pioneers and their presence at Ypres has been almost completely overshadowed by 150 Brigade and the 12/Lancers and it may well have been their status as a pioneer battalion that saw them discounted from Ellis' *Official History*.

The South Staffs spent the night of 26 May erecting tank-blocks from the stones intended for the reconstruction of the famous Cloth Hall in the Grote Markt and digging trenches on the old ramparts. According to the 12/Lancers war diary for 26 May, 'B Squadron remained to hold Ypres at all costs'. They make no mention of the South Staffords who, like the Lancers were placed under Brigadier Cecil Haydon's command when 150 Brigade arrived the next morning. The South Staffs continued to hold the ramparts from the Menin Gate round to the Lille Gate on the southern edge of the city and, although Ypres was heavily shelled during the day, no enemy advance was seen until that evening when troops began probing the British defences. German sources indicate the cyclists of 18 *Aufklärungs-Bataillon* came under fire from the Menin Gate – presumably from 150/Brigade Anti-Tank Company and the South Staffords – whilst heading north over the crossroads on the Menin Road at approximately 2.30pm. Fire was returned by two German AFVs and supported by the guns of 54/Artillery Regiment, who were just north of Zillebeke lake.

It was undoubtedly this action that gave rise to Lieutenant Smith and his sappers from 101/Field Company blowing the bridge at the Menin Gate which takes the N8 over the old moat. Positioned on the ramparts, Second Lieutenant James and 13 Platoon of the South Staffords would have had a grandstand view:

'*By afternoon advance units of the enemy were definitely within striking distance of the canal and there seemed to be no reason for further delaying the orders to fire the charges. The anti-tank guns were brought up and put into position at the Gate and at 4.00pm orders were given that the bridge at the Menin Gate should be fired. This was done with complete success and without causing any structural damage to the Gate but causing irrepairable damage to the car of the Colonel* [of the] *East Yorks, the machine being completely werecked by falling masonry.*'[13]

On 28 May the 1/6 were still at Ypres but enemy pressure was increasing along the canal. At around lunchtime the Green Howards, on the south-eastern sector of the town near Zillebeke Lake, were attacked by units of IR 54 – the same regiment that had overrun the RSF that morning – and before long the South Staffs at the Lille Gate also came under fire. Due largely to the courage of Corporal Rushdon, however, who continued to bring fire from his Bren gun down on the enemy despite his wounds, the attack fizzled out.

The 50th Division battalions withdrew from Ypres in the early hours of 29 May, the 1/6 marching to Poperinghe where it was reunited with the B Echelon transport and Captain Derek McCardie, who would later achieve fame at Arnhem in command of the 2/South Staffords. Later that morning IR 30 entered Ypres through the Lille Gate and raised the Swastika over the Cloth Hall at 11.25am, finally achieving in a matter of days the occupation of a town that had been denied them for four years a generation previously.

Chapter Fourteen

The Final Line

27 May–3 June 1940

'One of my section commanders asked what he should do with all the unopened tins and I was engulfed with a wave of hatred for the Germans. Why should these bloody bastards invade other people's countries, destroy their homes, villages and towns and machine gun and bomb them on the roads, and take what did not belong to them?'

Lieutenant Jimmy Langley, 2/Coldstream Guards,
on the Canal de Basse Colme.

While Cassel was being prepared for battle by 145 Brigade on 27 May, the Hotel du Sauvage in the town square was the venue for a meeting between General Robert Fagalde and Lieutenant General Sir Ronald Adam where plans were agreed for the defence of Dunkirk. The perimeter line was to run between Nieuport Bains in the east and Gravelines on the western edge of the Dunkirk Corridor. Thirty miles wide and some 7 miles deep, the western sector between Gravelines and Bergues would be the preserve of the French while the British would defend the line from Bergues to Nieuport.

Lieutenant Colonel the Viscount Robert Bridgeman had already drawn up plans for Dunkirk's defence which divided the bridgehead into three corps sectors. II Corps would defend the eastern sector and be evacuated from the La Panne beaches; I Corps in the centre would use Bray-Dunes as their evacuation point and II Corps, after holding the western end of the line, would evacuate from Malo-les-Baines. Adam established his HQ in the town hall at La Panne while Brigadier Frederick Lawson, who had been attached to Adam's staff from the 48th Division, began the more difficult task of organising the defence line with those troops 'filtering into the perimeter'.[1]

By 28 May Lawson had improvised a defence along the perimeter using gunners and infantry stragglers – dubbed 'Adam Force' – expecting that his scratch command would be reinforced with infantry units as they became available. His efforts were given an additional air of urgency by the Belgian capitulation which effectively opened the Nieuport flank to the German advance; fortunately Second Lieutenant Edward Miller-Mundy's troop of the 12/Lancers arrived in Nieuport at 9.30am just before the first German units arrived. Yet it was a touch-and-go for a while. Smith and his sappers arrived at the Dixmuide-Furnes road bridge in time to assist Second Lieutenant Edward Mann whose drawn revolver was enough to persuade the Belgian sapper officer the bridge needed to be destroyed:

> '*He finally pressed the switch but there was no result; 2/Lt Mann then inspected the charges on the bridge, which had obviously been tampered with, and on his return found a French major, who told him he would now take command, that his troops were fast approaching and 2/Lt Mann need bother no more about blowing the bridge.*'[2]

Smith's account states that the 'bridge was completely destroyed in spite of the two [sic] Belgian officers who said that the bridge was to be blown on their instruction'. He makes no mention of the French officer who Mann says attempted to take command but goes on to say, 'The destruction had only just been completed when German motorcyclists arrived at high speed closely followed by infantry in lorries and it seems certain they hardly expected the kind of reception they received.'[3]

It appears that the German infantry anticipated the bridge to be intact and the barrage of fire they received on arrival was not in the 'French' major's plan as he had by now melted away leaving the Lancers to deal with the enemy infantry. Smith writes these were soon seen off and he then left for Schoorbakke to destroy another bridge before moving to Nieuport to give assistance to Second Lieutenant Henderson's troop who were struggling with the canal bridges. At 11.00am the first patrol of German motor cyclists from the 256th Division

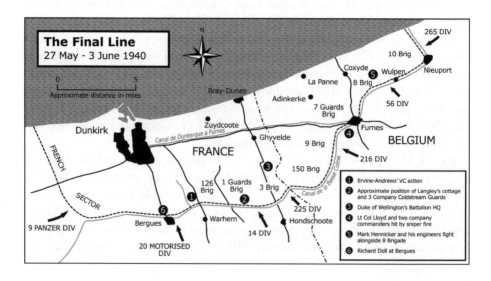

approached Nieuport along the coast road – sandwiched between refugees – and were swiftly dealt with by the Lancers in a 'short and intense fire fight'. The Lancers' war diary records that soon afterwards reinforcements in the form of 100 gunners and engineers of Adam Force, took over the line. For the time being the eastern end of the perimeter was intact.

The precarious nature of the line is illustrated by the defence that was assembled between Wulpen and Nieuport, a sector under the command of Lieutenant Colonel Edward Brazier. It was hardly an ideal position but despite the ground resembling a 'chequer-board of dykes and ditches, crossed only by occasional bridges', the difficulties faced by the defenders were also faced by the attacking infantry. Brazier was not alone in giving thanks that the ground did not favour tanks. Close to the bridge at Wulpen Lieutenant Beasley, a gunner officer from 210 Battery, 53/Medium Regiment, found himself turned into a front-line infantryman:

'*The Germans arrived the following morning and shelled and mortared us heavily. This was our first taste of real war and the casualties in our mixed force were pretty heavy. The regiment was pretty lucky on the whole but lost a lot of young boys and we were all stunned to hear that* [Lieutenant] *Bruce Thornton had been killed trying to rescue a Bren from an impossibly exposed position ... The Boche threw out strong patrols over the bridge and it was decided to send out a party to blow the bridge (the gunners had already tried with their 25-pounders but had not been successful). A young sapper officer volunteered to take a small party but he was unlucky enough to meet a German patrol on the bridge. He managed to get away after a scuffle but the party suffered some casualties and the bridge remained ... On the second day this cosmopolitan force was relieved by the 2 Battalion Royal Fusiliers* [12 Brigade]. *We felt pretty embarrassed at handing over a folorn task to infantry who had been marching and fighting for five days without any sleep, well knowing that they had come so that we, amongst others, could get away – a rotten mission to give anyone.*'[4]

Edward Brazier and the men of 'Brazier Force' were taken off the beaches at La Panne on 30 May.

Although not part of Brazier Force, Mark Henniker, who by this time had been promoted to command 253/Field Company, was amongst several RE units sent up to Furnes to bolster the line. Arriving in the town square he was surprised to find himself in command of nearly 1,000 officers and men and, as he later observed, they were hardly organised or trained for an infantry battle:

'*There were men and vehicles from the other two Field Companies of 3 Division, and the more cumbersome vehicles of the Field Park Company. The OC 17 Field Company was a regular officer and senior to me, but it was reported he had been killed that afternoon. The OC of 246 Field Company was also a regular and senior to me but out on a reconnasiance somewhere and the OC 15 Field Park Company was only a captain, so I was evidently the Head Boy of all those present.'*[5]

Captain Dick Walker, the 3rd Division RE adjutant, lost little time in sending the engineer detachments up to Coxyde (Koksijde) at great speed where they were deployed along the canal and ordered to hold until the arrival of Brigadier Christopher Woolner's 8 Brigade. Here they were tucked in alongside the 1/Suffolks who were, by this time, without Lieutenant Hugh Taylor who had been a casualty of the 8 Brigade attack of 23 May at Watrelos on the Gort Line. Henniker's concern that his engineers would not live up to expectation was soon dispelled by the Suffolks' adjutant who praised their soldierly behaviour under fire, leaving Lieutenant Colonel Desmond Harrison to proclaim that 'Morale was beginning to drop a bit, but Henniker and 253 sat like a rock in the brigade reserve line and did a lot of saving the day.'

Also approaching Furnes at the end of a 15-mile march were two battalions of 7 Guards Brigade. The clatter of small arms fire and the presence of harassed staff officers was the first indication that part of the town was already in enemy hands, an observation Guardsman George Jones of 1/Grenadiers had already made for himself. 'About a mile away and out of range as far as we were concerned, a party of Germans could be seen marching and wheeling bicycles at about the same speed as us. Friend and foe arrived in Furnes at about the same time.' Despite the enemy presence and 'rather annoying sniper fire' the Grenadiers moved up to reconnoitre their allocated positions. But it was here that tragedy struck the 2nd Battalion when Lieutenant Colonel John Lloyd and two of his company commanders, Captain Christopher Jeffreys and Major Hercules Pakenham, fell victim to German sniper fire. The three officers were lying in a very exposed position on the canal bank, the colonel was obviously dead but Pakenham and Jeffreys were still alive and it was probably their plight that drove Lieutenant Jack Jones to drag their bodies to safety.[6] Command of the battalion fell on the broad shoulders of Major Rupert Colvin who eventually led the battalion home via the beaches at La Panne.

Thus on 28 May Montgomery's 3rd Division was moving into the Furnes salient with 8 Brigade to the north and 9 Brigade to the south and – sandwiched in between – were the two Grenadier battalions of 7 Guards Brigade holding the centre and southern outskirts of Furnes. The 1/Coldstream arrived during the night of 29 May and was placed in reserve on the Coxyde road. What followed was a messy and sustained battle characterized by almost continuous shell fire that systematically destroyed the buildings of Furnes and causing George Jones to remark that 'We saw the town of Furnes tumble about us. The Germans expended untold quantities of ammunition upon the area, and us!'

But shellfire and sniping were not the only dangers. On the night of 30 May enemy infantry attempted to cross the canal using inflatable rafts and pontoon bridges resulting in a fire fight that drew in the 1/Coldstream Guards. Here an enemy foothold on the northern bank was counter-attacked by 35-year-old Major John Campbell, commanding 1 Company. 'He and his runner went forward with grenades under cover of fire from one of his platoons, to dislodge the enemy. He silenced one machine-gun and damaged one pontoon, but as he was attempting to rush another enemy post he was fatally shot and his runner was wounded.'[7] The news of this may well have contributed to the death of Campbell's father, Brigadier General John Campbell had been awarded the VC at Ginchy in October 1916 whilst commanding 3/Coldstream.

Support from 3 Company managed to staunch any further incursions but the determination of the enemy to force a crossing cut down almost all the company officers leaving 21-yearold Second Lieutenant Peter Allix and Captain Cecil Preston dead on the canal bank. The Coldstream counter-attack had taken place in the nick of time: dawn revealed the enemy outpost had withdrawn which enabled British mortars and artillery to target the enemy pontoons, persuading the Germans to cease in their efforts to cross the canal.

The focus of the enemy assault next day fell on 8 Brigade which was already running short of ammunition and for a while it looked as if the enemy would manage to encircle the salient. Rallied by Lieutenant Jack Jones and his carrier platoon, resistance was stiffened and the line restored. Jones was awarded the MC for his 'prompt and determined actions that undoubtedly saved a situation that would otherwise have had disasterous results'. But it was only a matter of time before the enemy broke through what had become a very thin line of defence. Fortunately the orders to retire to La Panne came at exactly the right moment and in the early hours of 1 June the brigade slipped away without further mishap, reaching La Panne around 3.00am. George Jones remembered it well:

'For us the miracle of Dunkirk then began. This curtain of ragged steel began to lift just before 10.00pm and, in the bright red glow of a hundred fires, we walked from Furnes without a bomb, shell or bullet arriving within half a mile of our scrambling single files. Twice we took wrong turnings almost walking down the throat of the enemy ... but at last we were clear.'[8]

On 27 May the 1/Duke of Wellington's Regiment from 3 Brigade was on its way to Dunkirk when they were diverted to Les Moëres, just south of Bray-Dunes, and ordered to hold a 5,000 yard sector of the Canal de Basse Colme between the bridge at la Cartonnerie and the bridge carrying the D79 at Pont Pauwkens Werf. With battalion HQ at a farmhouse in les Moëres, C Company, under Captain William Waller positioned itself astride the bridge at la Cartonnerie, leaving A and B Companies to hold the remaining canal bank. As the regimental historian points out, the front may have been protected by the canal but the field of fire was in places less than 30 yards, as the D3 running along the southern bank was packed with abandoned vehicles and, in the case of C Company, a number of residential buildings.

Abandoned vehicles were also causing problems for the men of 2/Coldstream who had taken up positions on the Dukes' right flank. The difficulty posed by the tangle of immobilized trucks and lorries was that they afforded cover to the approaching Germans and made it possible for their infantry to get close to the canal bank almost completely unobserved. Nevertheless, Bootle-Wilbraham deployed his Coldstreams along the northern bank to await the arrival of the enemy:

> 'We had a front of 2,200 yards to cover, with two important bridges over the canal. No. 1 Company was on the right, No. 3 Company right centre, No. 2 Company left centre and No. 4 Company on the left. Headquarters was badly placed in a little farmhouse to the south of the windmill at Krommelhoeck. The mill was used as an OP and was an obvious landmark in this flat, open country. The canal was a reasonable anti-tank obstacle; a second canal, called Digue des Glaises, ran parallel to the front, about 400 yards behind it, and there was yet another canal behind battalion headquarters by the windmill.'[9]

Dawn on Thursday 30 May saw water in the canals gradually rising as the open sluices slowly flooded the surrounding countryside. Concerned that the floodwaters would channel the Germans towards the bridges, Bootle-Wilbraham ordered the bridges on his front to be blown, the Dukes following suit at 11.00am at Pont aux Cerfs. Apart from some heavy shelling and 'a great deal of small arms fire' there was no serious assault during the day, the Dukes reporting that 'the Germans who reached the banks of the canal did not return to tell the tale'.

Commanding 3 Company of the Coldstream was 35-year-old Major Angus McCorquodale, a larger than life figure whose brother Hugh had married the novelist Barbara Cartland in 1936. The only other officer in the company was Lieutenant Jimmy Langley whose reponse to Brigadier Merton Beckwith-Smith's 'absolutely splendid' news that the battalion had been given the 'supreme honour' of being the rearguard was muted to say the least. Suggesting the brigadier should inform the men of the 'splendid news' himself, he listened quietly as 'Becky' told them that not only were they about to fight one last battle, but also how they should deal with Stuka dive bombers with a Bren gun, 'taking them like a high pheasant and giving them plenty of lead'.

McCorquodale based his company HQ in a small cottage on the banks of the canal east of le Mille Brugge and while the company dug their weapons pits a continuous stream of British and French troops crossed the canal watched by Jimmy Langley:

'They varied from two platoons of Welsh Guards, who had been fighting near Arras – though they looked as though they had performed nothing more arduous than a day's peace time manoevering – to a bedraggled, leaderless rabble. I also came across some outstanding individuals. One corporal in the East Kents, particularly excited my imagination. Barely five feet tall, wearing socks, boots and trousers held up by string, he had a Bren gun slung on each shoulder with a rifle slung across their barrels. The slings of the Bren guns had cut deep into his shoulders, his back and chest were caked in blood and I could see part of both his collar bones. I offered him a mug of tea and ordered him to drop the Bren guns as I would be needing them.'[10]

Resolutely holding onto his guns the corporal explained that his major, who was 'dead somewhere back there' had told him to get both weapons back to England as they will be needed soon. Looking Langley straight in the eye he made it quite clear that that was exactly what he intended to do. Langley's reply was to put a generous tot of whiskey in the man's tea, patch him up and send him on his way.

The 1 June – 'a glorious day' wrote Bootle-Wilbraham – began with a ground mist which lifted as the sun rose. To Langley's astonishment it revealed a hundred or so Germans 'standing in groups about 600 yards away in a field of corn'. Opening fire on the mass of enemy soldiers in front of them resulted in, what Langley called, a massacre leaving him feeling slightly sick; a sensation which was quickly forgotten with the enemy attack on the area of the blown bridge at le Mille Brugge. Langley was observing from the attic in the cottage:

'This was partially held by No.1 Company, under Evan Gibbs, on our right, and partially by a company of a regiment from the North of England, the road leading back from the bridgehead to Dunkirk being the boundary line … We had seen the Germans rush up what looked like an anti-tank gun on wheels and watched with interest as it pointed our way and fired. Nothing happened and we turned a Bren gun onto it. Then there was the most awful crash and a brightly lit object whizzed round the attic, finally coming to rest at the foot of the chimney stack. One glance was enough – it was an incendiary tank shell … The Germans put four more shells into the attic and then desisted.'[11]

The enemy assault was enough to encourage the 5/Border Regiment on the right of Captain Evan Gibbs' company to contemplate withdrawing, a notion that was greeted by McCorquodale's threat to shoot them! The Borders' war diary simply states that on 31 May all ranks that were considered non-essential were ordered to withdraw to the beaches and A and C Companies came under heavy shellfire. Sadly war diaries are notorious for reporting the facts as seen by a particular battalion and there is no mention of why they withdrew or who gave the orders. One can only assume that their move – which opened a gap in the line on the Coldstreams' right flank – was sanctioned by the CO, Lieutenant Colonel Law.

By now it was clear the enemy were massing for an attack which the defending troops would have little chance of holding – rather, it was merely a question of how long they could contain it before being overwhelmed. Evan Gibbs was killed attempting to retrieve a Bren gun leaving an inexperienced Lieutenant Ronnie Speed in command. McCorquodale sent Langley with a flask of alcohol with orders to make Speed drink it and shoot him if he retired the company. 'Ronnie was looking miserable, standing in a ditch up to his waist in water and shivering. I offered him Angus's flask and advised him to drink it, which he did.' Half an hour later Speed was killed and the remaining men of 1 Company fell back on Langley's cottage.

The end came shortly afterwards. McCorquodale – determined not to die in the new British battledress which he abhorred – had changed into his First World War service dress – while Langley was dealing with a German machine gun firing from a cottage on the opposite side of the canal:

'I started my favourite sport of sniping with a rifle at anything that moved. I had just fired five most satisfactory shots and, convinced I had chalked up another 'kill', was kneeling, pushing another clip into the rifle, when there was the most frightful crash and a great wave of heat, dust and debris knocked me over. A shell had burst on the roof. There was a long silence and I heard a small voice saying, 'I've been hit,' which I suddenly realized was mine.'[12]

Langley had been hit in the head and left arm and was soon after evacuated to Dunkirk but being a stretcher case was refused access to a boat on the grounds that he was unable to sit or stand up. Returned to the care of 28-year-old Captain Phillip Newman at 12/Casualty Clearing Centre, he was taken to Château Cocquelle in Rosendael to await the arrival of German troops.

News of the German assault on the canal was received by Bootle-Wilbraham with some sadness; there is little doubt he apportions the demise of two of his companies on the withdrawal of the 5/Border Regiment:

'The Germans had outflanked No.1 Company, having got across the canal where our neighbours had abandoned their positions. The three officers of the company had been killed – Evan, Charles Blackwell and Ronnie Speed. The warrant officers and senior NCOs had been killed, including PSM Dance and Sgt Hardwick who had done so well at Pecq; and then the leaderless company had been forced back on to No. 3 Company. Angus had been killed when his bit of trench was enfiladed. Jimmy Langley put up a magnificent fight in a cottage on the canal bank and continued to fire his Bren until he was put out of action. It was Nos. 1 and 3 Companies that bore the brunt of the attack. Nos. 2 and 4 Companies had a comparatively easy time and few casualties. Jack Bowman brought out the remainder of the much reduced right half of the battalion ... The battalion was allowed to slip away in the darkness, and they were not followed up. There was no moon.'[13]

Both the Dukes and the 2/Coldstream were evacuated from the Dunkirk Mole late on 2 June joining the 6,695 British troops who finally left France that day. Over the course of the short campaign the 2/Coldstream had sustained 195 casualties of whom 70 officers and men had been killed.

~

A little to the east of the small tributary which joins the Canal de la Basse Colme near the bridge at le Benkies Mille was the ground defended by 1/East Lancashires. On 31 May Second Lieutenant John Arrigo and his platoon from D Company were in position around the destroyed bridge and reported being under fire from snipers, two of his men being shot and killed near the bridge during the morning. The battalion had initially been allocated a 3,000 yard frontage to defend which Lieutenant Colonel Pendlebury realized immediately was an almost impossible task given the depleted strength of his men and their lack of fire power. We shall never know whether Pendlebury's decision to replace D Company with the Stonyhurst-educated Captain Marcus Ervine-Andrews and B Company was a purely tactical judgment, or was motivated by the fighting spirit already displayed by Ervine-Andrews. But whatever the reason the move set the scene for the award of the final Victoria Cross of the campaign.

Ervine-Andrews had C Company of the 2/Warwicks under Captain Charles Nicholson on his right, whom the reader will recall had avoided the Wormhout fighting being ordered to Bergues on 27 May. On his left were the 5/Border who at least reduced the East Lancashire's frontage to a more reasonable defensive line. Dawn on 1 June began with a crash of explosions and Ervine-Andrews recalled that:

> *'There was a tremendous barrage of artillery and mortaring throughout the first attack. It must have gone on for two to three hours ... During the course of the morning most of my four positions were pretty all right – the odd casualty here and there, but one position was in desperate straits. They were running very short of ammunition and were forced to search the dead bodies to find some more ... They now asked for urgent help. I had no reserves whatever. I picked up my rifle and some ammunition and, looking at the few soldiers with me in company headquarters, said "I'm going up. Who's coming with me?" Every single man came forward.'* [14]

The section in trouble was fighting from a barn close to the junction of canals. When Ervine-Andrews and his men arrived the roof was ablaze and the enemy were attempting to cross the canal using inflatables:

> *'My men didn't fire much because we were too short of ammunition. They realized it was better that I should do the firing rather than waste the few bullets we had. If you fire accurately and hit men, then the others get discouraged. It's when you*

fire a lot of ammunition and don't do any damage that the other chaps start being
very brave and push on. When they're suffering severe casualties they are inclined
to stop or, in this case, move round to the flanks.'[15]

Holding off the attack Ervine-Andrews personally accounted for seventeen
Germans with his rifle and several more with Bren gun fire. At 3.00pm he
sent his second-in-command, Lieutenant Joe Cêtre, to battalion HQ to report
on the situation and Cêtre returned with a fresh supply of ammunition and a
handful of reinforcements along with instructions from Pendlebury to hold the
position until the last round. Incredibly they did and it was early evening when
the survivors withdrew. But the story does not end there; left with two badly
wounded men Ervine-Andrews assigned the one remaining carrier to transport
them to safety leaving himself and eight men to reach the beaches on foot. They
arrived at their evacuation point on 3 June and were taken off by HMS *Shikhari*
on one of the ship's last evacuation runs.

The announcement of Ervine-Andrew's award of the VC – the seventh to
be awarded to former Stonyhurst pupils – came as a surprise to the 28-year-
old captain who considered the fight to have been a company action and always
maintained that 'Anything that I was able to achieve was made possible by the
support and bravery of my men.'

Another kind of bravery was exhibited by Lieutenant Richard Doll who had
left Aldershot with the 1/Loyal Regiment on 22 December 1939. Appointed as
the medical officer to the battalion, Doll's war in 1940 was very much governed
by the movements of 2 Brigade which, on 29 May, was ordered to take up a
position east of Bray-Dunes in preparation for evacuation. Lieutenant Colonel
John Sandie was probably more aware of the overall situation along the Dunkirk
perimeter line than his battalion was, but even so, the order to turn round and
march back towards the enemy was not greeted with enthusiasm. Richard Doll
recalled the moment:

'*During the previous night fifty of the battalion had been allowed to go down to the*
beach and embark, so we were expecting to get off at any minute. However, we were
to be disappointed, for we were suddenly ordered forward to Bergues where we were
told the Germans had broken through. The adjutant borrowed four lorries from an
artillery regiment and sent off D Company to hold the canal in front of Dunkirk
while the rest set off the seven miles on foot.'[16]

Doll was convinced that the battalion had been tricked into relieving the
Bergues garrison whom he says consisted of a mixed force of stragglers from
the Lincolnshires, Welsh Guards and Royal West Kents together with 'a reliable
French battalion with an able commander'. He records his anger at finding a
number of British officers 'feasting off roast chicken and champagne in a large

and beautifully furnished house' who were apparently delighted at seeing their relieving force arrive and left the town an hour or so later. Harsh words indeed from a junior officer but, in the circumstances, perhaps understandable.

Clearly the Germans had not broken through and although Doll's rather emotive view of the situation may have been shared by others, the 470 officers and men of the battalion who entered Bergues were welcomed by Major General Curtis to reinforce the 46th Division units deployed in and around the town. In 1940 Bergues was an old country town built on the side of a hill at the junction of three canals and was entirely surrounded by the 17th century ramparts which were pierced by four gates. It was around these gates that Sandie deployed the Loyals and together with the remaining troops who had been formed into companies by Captain Arthur Walch, they constituted a rather chaotic defence.

During the night of 30 May Bergues was shelled and the 2/5 Sherwood Foresters, who were to the east of Hoymille, came under severe artillery and mortar attack which ultimately forced them back behind the Canal des Moëres. Enemy shelling continued throughout the next day, Private Hector Morgan in D Company near the Ypres Gate recalled how:

'We were jumping from door to door. The German gunners were dropping shell after shell and as soon as they had dropped one, off we'd go into another doorway. It so happened that I was flattening myself in one of the doorways when he [the Germans] *dropped one about fifty yards from us. All of a sudden I felt this terrible bash on my back and I said to one of my mates, that's my lot. I've had it.'*[17]

Morgan lived to tell another tale as the projectile that had hit him was a large cobblestone thrown up by the explosion but there were many other casualties, Richard Doll reported a continual stream of wounded pouring into the cellar where he had established his RAP: by midday it was overflowing.

By daybreak on 1 June fires had taken hold near the church and town hall and whole rows of residential buildings were in flames. The heat was so intense that even the troops dug in around the ramparts were feeling its effects while terrified horses galloped up and down the streets into which debris from burning buildings was falling. Casualties were mounting steadily: one shell alone accounted for nine men killed and two officers and another fifteen men wounded. At midday Curtis ordered the Loyals to evacuate the burning town and take up positions along the canal outside the northern ramparts.

At 1.50pm news reached Sandie that the Germans had forced passage across the canal – this was the action involving the Coldstream and the 5/Border which also overwhelmed one platoon of the 2/Warwicks – and enemy units were reported to be advancing north. Two companies of the Loyals were ordered north to counter-attack leaving D Company to oversee the last British units leaving the town. For Richard Doll the evacuation from Bergues was far from straightforward. Finding the town almost deserted he was determined not to leave the wounded behind:

> '*I sent Stansfield (my driver) to get the 30cwt lorry and filled it with all the able bodied men and those of the wounded who could fire. I removed the hospital tags from them as, if they were to fight, they could not claim to be wounded. Each was armed with a rifle ... A difficulty soon arose, for the town was so shattered that we were unable to recognize our way about. We made one false attempt to get out, being halted by a blown-up bridge, when to our delight we found a soldier who was apparently still on duty; he turned out to be a Royal Engineer who was dealing with the last bridge, and he redirected us to it. Once again we lost our way, and following a dispatch rider, we came out near the crest of the hill well in sight of the enemy. We turned round at full speed and tore back over heaps of bricks and rubble into the town; two shells must have landed very near us, for twice the car was shaken as loud explosions seemed to crash above us. This time I was luckier, for I took the right turning and saw Captain Leschalles, D Company commander, and I breathed a sigh of relief.*'[18]

Doll's journey to Dunkirk was accompanied by a cacophony of enemy shellfire which periodically sent him and whoever was with him at the time scuttling into drainage ditches to seek shelter. Eventually he and half the battalion were taken off the beaches at Malo les Bains aboard the SS *Maid of Kent*. The other half of the battalion was not so lucky; they marched out along the mole but missed the last boat and had to spend all Sunday on the beach before getting away on 3 June.

Frustrated by the inactivity that presented itself at Bray-Dunes, Major Mark Henniker found two beached rowing boats with *Teddington* painted on the transom. Stocking them with food and water he and his group of two officers and thirty men hauled the two boats into the water and began to row towards England. Having swapped boats *en-route* and collected three more men who were drifting aimlessly without oars, they waited for the tide to turn in their favour, which it did early the next morning:

> '*After we had been rowing for about two hours we were out of sight of land. We then saw what I took to be a Royal Naval pinnace pointing towards us. The sea was like glass and, as we got closer, it seemed to be stationary or moving very slowly, for she had no bow wave ... We rowed towards her and found she was deserted, so we tied up astern and boarded her, there was a half eaten meal on a table and food and water in plenty aboard. A lieutenant commander's jacket was hanging on the back of the stateroom door with his name on the tailor's tab in the back.*'[19]

They had come across their own *Marie Celeste* and while there was plenty of evidence on the boat from what looked like an air attack, the crew had completely vanished. Henniker writes that they soon got the boat moving and were eventually taken aboard HMS *Locust* just before reaching Dover.

But for thousands of men like Private Bill Holmes of 4/Royal Sussex who had marched out of Caëstre to Mont de Cats in the early hours of 28 May, their arrival at Dunkirk was too late. Joining the hopeless groups of tired and hungry men now stranded on the beach Holmes and his mates stared across the water towards England as if willing a ship to appear:

> '*Then before we knew what was happening, several of these German motorcycle combinations arrived. They fired traced bullets at us, so we had no choice. You either gave up or died. I never thought I'd ever be a prisoner. I thought I might be killed. But one thing I thought was if I'm going to die I'd like to die at home. I didn't mind being shot but I didn't want to die out there. I was a long way from home.*'[20]

Holmes and those like him who had been left behind were destined to face an uncertain future behind the wire of captivity which for many would last for five years.

Chapter Fifteen

The Quick and the Dead

'Almost upon leaving the station we saw looming above us our future prison; beautiful, serene, majestic, yet forbidding enough to make our hearts sink deep into our boots. It towered above us, dominating the whole village. It was the fairy castle of childhood story books.'

Captain Pat Reid's first impressions of Colditz Castle,
7 November 1941.

O peration Dynamo officially ended at 2.23pm on 4 June. During the nine days of the evacuation 338,226 British and French troops had been evacuated safely to England, a number to which must be added the 26,402 'useless mouths' who began their evacuation on 20 May before Operation Dynamo had begun. The evacuation marked the failure of Allied operations on the continent of Europe and the failure of the German High Command to co-ordinate their air and sea based forces to prevent a third of a million men escape. But the cost to Britain in men and material was high. Official figures indicate that between 10 May and 4 June some 68,111 officers and men were killed in action, died of wounds, were missing, wounded or prisoners of war.

What is often not appreciated is the enormous amount of military materiel that the BEF left behind. The majority of AFVs, transport and equipment had either been destroyed in action or prior to evacuation to prevent it falling into enemy hands intact – for example, only thirteen light and nine Cruiser tanks and 322 Guns out of a possible 2,794 were brought home. Although a large number of the fighting troops returned with their personal weapons many had been unable to do so, or in some cases because they had jettisoned their equipment and much of their clothing as well.

In the naval operation a staggering 288 ships were lost and another 45 badly damaged including the gallant HMS *Keith* of Boulogne fame, which was sunk off the beaches on 1 June. If the naval losses were severe then the RAF losses were disproportionately heavy. Norman Franks in *Fighter Command Losses 1939–1941* documents 372 fighter aircraft destroyed between 10 May and 3 June 1940 with approximately 121 pilots either killed in action or taken prisoner, evidence which destroys the perception that the RAF took little part in the BEF campaign.

Another of the great myths of Dunkirk was that all the troops were evacuated from the beaches by an armada of small boats manned by volunteers from all over England. Although the small boats did help lift 26,000 troops from the beaches over the last four days of the evacuation, two-thirds of those evacuated were lifted directly on to Royal Navy ships from the East Mole at Dunkirk. The other myth surrounding the operation was largely the result of an effective propaganda machine that presented the evacuation as a heroic victory. Heroic it might have been but a victory it certainly was not, a view shared by Mark Henniker who wrote home from Aldershot in June that he supposed 'it would gradually dawn on the generous English people, who greeted us with food, socks, cigarettes and every sort of gift one could imagine, that it was no victory but a crashing defeat'.

As the smoke cleared over Dunkirk the careers of those who had returned home continued. For some, the Flanders campaign was their last active command, for others it was the catalyst which would propel them into the public eye. Sadly a number would not survive the years that lay ahead. Lord Gort left France on 1 June courtesy of the Royal Navy and never again commanded an army abroad, finishing his career as High Commissioner in Palestine and Transjordan. He died of cancer in 1946, a sad end for a man whose courage of conviction may well have saved the BEF from destruction. Another who never again experienced active command was Harold Franklyn who concluded his career as Commander-in-Chief Home Forces. He died in 1963, the same year as Alan Brooke, who returned to France in June 1940 in command of the Second BEF south of the Somme, where he told Churchill 'the French Army was to all intents and purposes dead'. It was Brooke's decision that the battle for France was well and truly over that enabled a further 192,000 Allied personnel to be evacuated through various French ports between 15 and 25 June under the codename Operation Ariel. Sadly Brooke was unable to prevent Major General Victor Fortune and the majority of the 51st (Highland) Division from surrendering on 12 June at St-Valéry-en-Caux. Replacing Dill as CIGS in 1941, he continued to work closely with Churchill – it was Brooke who supported Montgomery's appointment as commander of the Eighth Army in 1942 – and for the remainder of the war took the leading military part in the overall strategic direction of the British war effort. In 1946 he was created Viscount Alanbrooke.

With a war only just beginning it was inevitable that many of the BEF would become casualties over the coming years. One of the most notable was Merton Beckwith-Smith who was promoted to command the 18th Division on return to England and was captured at Singapore in February 1942. Moved to Karenko Camp he died of diphtheria nine months later and is buried at Sai Wan War Cemetery, Hong Kong.

Dublin-born Pat Garstin – who defended the railway station at Louvain – was murdered after his capture on 4 July 1944 near Fontainebleau during Operation Gain when he was serving as a captain with 1/SAS. He is buried at Marissel French National Cemetery, Beauvais.

David Wallis, who served as a second lieutenant with the 4/Ox and Bucks at Cassel, was another who volunteered for Airborne Forces and by 1944 was second-in-command of the 2nd Parachute Battalion. At the Arnhem Bridge he was temporarily in command of the battalion after Brigadier Gerald Lathbury had been posted missing and Lieutenant Colonel John Frost took command of 1 Parachute Brigade. Tragically Wallis was killed by friendly fire on 18 September after two of the A Company outposts had been overrun and he was hit in the chest by machine gun fire. He is buried at Oosterbeek War Cemetery.

Also at Arnhem was Hugh Taylor of 1/Suffolks who volunteered for the Airborne Forces after he had recovered from his wounds received at Watrelos on 23 May. Over Arnhem his aircraft was hit by flak which killed and wounded a number of his men but once again he escaped – this time intact – to take part in the battle with 4 Parachute Brigade. When 5 Parachute Brigade was deployed to the Far East in 1945 he was a company commander with the 12th Battalion and served serving in India, Singapore, Java and Malaya. In 1946 he was with the 6th Airborne Division in Palestine. Retiring in 1959, he died in 1984 aged 66.

Cyril Townsend managed to get home after being wounded at St Venant where he was mentioned in despatches. After attending Staff College he was promoted to major in 1943 and posted to Burma with the 1/North Staffordshires. In 1950 he was in command of 6/Kings African Rifles and heavily involved in the Mau Mau rising in Kenya. He retired in 1956 and died in 1975.

Sergeant Alec Horwood who fought with the 1/6 Queen's on the Escaut was taken prisoner with thirty others from B Company on 21 May. Managing to escape from a building in Antwerp he walked the 110 miles to Nieupoort where he stole a rowing boat and arrived at Dunkirk on 2 June. Commissioned in December 1940 he was attached to 1/Northamptons in Burma where he was mortally wounded after three days of fighting on 20 January 1944 whilst commanding the Mortar Platoon. His action led to the capture of the Japanese position and the award of the VC which was received by his widow on 4 December 1944. He is buried at Imphal War Cemetery, India.

Only three of the five VC recipients of 1940 survived the war. Captain Richard Annand relinquished his commission in 1948 and became a founder member of the British Association for the Hard of Hearing, which became Hearing Concern in 1963. He was also involved in the founding of the Durham County Association for the Disabled and died at Durham shortly after his 90th birthday in December 2004. Stonyhurst-educated Marcus Ervine-Andrews retired as a lieutenant colonel and after the war attempted to return home to his native County Cavan but was driven out by local members of the IRA and later settled in Cornwall. He died aged 83 in March 1995. Lance Corporal Harry Nicholls, the Grenadier Guardsman who won his cross on Poplar Ridge, was informed of his award by the commandant of Stalag XXA and was invested with his VC following his repatriation at the end of hostilities in 1945. Nottingham-born Nicholls died in Leeds in 1975.

Another survivor was Mark Henniker who was promoted to lieutenant colonel in 1941 and joined the 1st Airborne Division as CRE, taking part in operations in North Africa, Primasole Bridge in Sicily and the evacuation of the Arnhem survivors from Oosterbeek. In 1950 he wrote *Memoirs of a Junior Officer* which was followed by *Red Shadows over Malaya* in 1956. His last book, *An Image of War* was published in 1987. He retired from the Army in 1958 with the rank of brigadier and succeeded to the title of 8th Baronet Henniker on 19 February 1958. He died in 1991.

Many of the men who were taken prisoner in 1940 took it upon themselves to give the enemy as much trouble as possible by planning and undertaking escapes from their various POW camps. Although he always denied being a 'proper' escapee in that he simply climbed out of a window of his Lille hospital, Jimmy Langley's subsequent journey through Vichy France to Marseilles was not without its drama, particularly as Captain Phillip Newman had amputated his left arm at Zuydcoote. In Marseilles he met Roderick Brinkman who was taken prisoner on the Ypres-Comines Canal and had escaped from a hospital in Malines. Brinkman eventually made it home in 1941 following a route that Langley used to return to England via Gibraltar. After reporting for duty at Princess Gate, Langley was recruited by MI9 where his first hand knowledge of escape and evasion was put to use in developing escape routes across France and Spain.

After his capture at Dunkirk Philip Newman escaped in August 1941 from a camp in Germany but was recaptured within forty-eight hours. In November 1941 he was transferred to a camp in Rouen from where he escaped again in January 1942. This time he was successful, and returned to Britain in May 1942 via Madrid and Gibraltar. Langley's department was also responsible for organizing the escape of Brigadier George Roupell VC and Captain Charles Gilbert, whom the reader will recall were hiding out in a farm near Rouen. Contacted via a hidden note in a tin of toothpaste, Langley's team eventually deciphered the message and pinpointed which farm the men were hiding in. Confirming the receipt of their message by a coded BBC broadcast the two officers were escorted across the Pyrenees to Spain, arriving home in late 1941. Langley remarked that 'many junior officers found it a pleasant thought to visualize a rather fat and bad tempered brigadier with his austere disciplinarian brigade major working as farm hands'. Langley died in 1983.

Langley was not alone in managing to escape from hospital in the early months of the war. Major Jim Windsor-Lewis who was wounded at Boulogne escaped from hospital in Lille from where he eventually arrived in Brussels. Incredibly, he hitched a lift to Paris in a German Army lorry where he handed himself in at the American embassy. Here his escape plan almost faltered but eventually he was driven by Mary Lindell from Paris to Limoges in a private car. Once in Vichy France he was handed over to another escape organization and successfully crossed the Pyrenees into Spain. Returning to England he took command of 2/Welsh Guards and fought through the remainder of the war. He retired a brigadier and died suddenly in 1964.

Michael Duncan was captured near Watou on 30 May 1940 and was initially sent to Laufen before being moved to Stalag XXI at Posen where he met Barry O'Sullivan from 3/RTR. Both men were moved to Oflag VB at Biberach from where they escaped with twenty-four others on 12 September 1941 through a 145-foot long tunnel. Duncan and O'Sullivan were the first two out and although they initially travelled together, they split up after Duncan injured his knee. O'Sullivan crossed the Swiss border near Schleitheim on the night of 26 September, just hours ahead of Duncan who crossed into Switzerland in the early hours of the next day. Apart from Captain Hugh Woollatt (see Chapter 5) and Lieutenant Angus Rowan-Hamilton, the remaining twenty-two escapees were caught.

In May 1942 Jimmy Langley was joined by Airey Neave who had been captured at Calais and had the distinction of not only being the first British officer to escape from Germany but also the first to mount a successful escape from Colditz. Having reached Switzerland Neave was teamed up with Hugh Woollatt on 14 April 1941 and escorted to Marseilles from where both men crossed the Pyrenees into Spain. Another officer who crossed the Pyrenees was Captain Henry Coombe-Tennant who was captured at Boulogne on 25 May. He was one of the twenty-nine men who escaped from Oflag VIB at Warburg on the night of 30 August 1942. After fusing the electricity system four groups of prisoners rushed the fence simultaneously. Twelve were caught within the camp area and another fourteen over the next two weeks but the first three – Coombe-Tennant, Captain Albert Arkwright (the adjutant of the 2/RSF captured near the Ypres-Comines Canal) and Captain Rupert Fuller – got away. After a long journey through Holland, Belgium and France the three men were escorted across the Pyrenees to Spain on 19 October and were flown from Gibraltar to Bristol the night of 6 November 1942.

One of the unsuccessful Warburg escapees was Captain Dick Tomes who was taken prisoner at Wormhout with 2/Warwicks after the blow on his head had rendered him unconscious. He went over the wire just after Henry Coombe-Tennant and was recaptured near Celle on 10 September after travelling just over 100 miles on foot. Surprisingly he was returned to Warburg from where he was marched east in March 1945 ahead of the advancing Americans. During an attack on the column by Allied fighters he and another group of officers managed to break free and headed towards American lines only to be recaptured near Haideck and imprisoned at Eichstätt, but thirty-six hours later the Americans arrived, a moment Tomes remembered for the rest his life: 'I dared not speak for I knew I should burst into tears if I did'.

Many of those captured in May 1940 ended up at Colditz and were branded as trouble makers for their persistent escape attempts, but as Padre Jock Platt wrote in his diary, 'They would not have been in this camp if they had not been of bolder spirit and larger initiative than their fellows in other camps.'[1] Amongst the first arrivals were Captain Rupert Barry who was captured at Hazebrouck and Dick Elliot of the Irish Guards. Both men had been involved in a previous escape at Laufen and were joined in 1941 by John Hyde-Thompson of the Durham Light Infantry and Captain Cyril Lewthwaite. Hyde-Thompson, who had earlier escaped from Thorn, continued to plan and execute elaborate escape attempts whilst at Colditz, on one occasion getting as far as Ulm before being recaptured. Cyril Lewthwaite was involved in an elaborate plan which involved climbing onto the roof and throwing a rope across to part of the German quarters which gave access to the outer wall. The plan – unfortunately unsuccessful – was devised by the Poles, and even involved building a fake extra chimney stack as cover for the man fixing the ladder.

Gris Davies-Scourfield had escaped from Posen in May 1941 and remained at liberty for nine months in Poland before being recaptured. After arriving at Colditz he again got away by hiding in a basket of waste paper only to be brought back. He retired as a brigadier and died in 2006. In 1943 Anthony Cholmondeley, who was captured near Cassel, arrived with Michael Farr and Tony Rolt. Farr was a serial escaper who had made repeated attempts from a variety of camps before he was finally sent to Colditz. There, he was working on the construction of the famous glider in the castle's roof which was only abandoned when the war ended. He also made wine and ran the castle's distillery. Farr was awarded the MBE in January 1946 for his escape attempts and after the war worked for the family firm in Plymouth making Hawker's 'Pedlar' Sloe Gin. He died in January 1993.

Tony Rolt was also part of the glider construction team at Colditz and had made repeated escape attempts in his previous camps. His first attempt was made within hours of being captured at Calais by diving into a ditch when the attention of the guards was distracted. He was also involved in another attempt with an RAF officer to steal an aircraft to fly to England, but an encounter with a German patrol resulted in recapture. In August 1941 he and a sapper officer walked out of Biberach disguised as German workmen but recapture was followed by fourteen days' solitary confinement and transfer to Stalag XXC at Posen. From Posen Rolt attempted escape again by walking out dressed as a member of a Swiss Red Cross Commission, whose real members had entered a couple of hours earlier. Recaptured after leaving a railway station in daylight, he eventually arrived at Colditz after a stretch at Stalag VIIB at Eichstätt in Bavaria.

Resigning his commission after the war he become one of the great amateur drivers associated with Jaguar cars. In 1951 Rolt came sixth at Le Mans in a Nash-Healey which led to Jaguar recruiting him for the Dundrod race in Ireland.

When the works driver retired halfway through, Rolt took over to break the lap record and raise the car's position from seventh to fourth, winning him a permanent place in the Jaguar team. In 1953 Rolt and Duncan Hamilton in a C-type Jaguar won Le Mans with an average speed of 100mph having beaten the Jaguar of Stirling Moss and Peter Walker into second place. Rolt died in February 2008, aged 89.

Lieutenant Colonel Bill Tod arrived at Colditz in August 1943 and took over as senior British officer and it was under his tenure that the castle was liberated on 16 April 1945. Sadly his 21-year-old son Andrew, a lieutenant in his father's regiment, was killed in November 1943, a tragedy Bill Tod bore with the same stoic resolve he had shown on the Ypres-Comines Canal in May 1940.

Appendix

Order of Battle

Order of Battle 10 May – BEF France 1940
Commander-in-Chief – General The Viscount Gort VC

GHQ Troops

Armoured	Infantry	Royal Artillery	Royal Engineers
12/Royal Lancers	1/Welsh Guards	1,39/Army Field Regiments;	100, 101, 216/Army Field Companies
4/7 Royal Dragoon Guards	7/Cheshire	1,2,4,58,61,63,65,69/ Medium	228, 242/Field Companies
5/Royal Inniskilling Dragoon	1/8 Middlesex	Regiments	223/Field Park Company
Guards	4/Gordon Highlanders	1,51,52/Heavy Regiments	19/Army Field Survey
13/18 Royal Hussars	6/Argyll & Sutherland Highlanders	1,2,3 Super Heavy Batteries	58,61,62/Chemical Warfare Companies
15/19 The King's Royal Hussars		1/Anti-Aircraft Brigade: 1,6,85/Anti-	
1/Light Armoured Reconnaissance	**Pioneers:**	Aircraft Regiments	
Brigade	6,7,8,9/King's Own Royal Regiment	2/Anti-Aircraft Brigade: 60 Anti-	
1/Fife and Forfar Yeomanry	1/6 South Staffordshire	Aircraft Regiment	
1/East Riding Yeomanry	9/West Yorkshire	4/Anti-Aircraft Brigade: 4/Anti-	
2/Light Armoured Reconnaissance		Aircraft Regiment, 1/Light Anti-	
Brigade		Aircraft Regiment	
1/Army Tank Brigade		5/Searchlight Brigade: 1,2,3/	
4 and 7/Battalions Royal Tank		Searchlight Regiments	
Regiment			

I Corps

GOC: Lieutenant General Michael George Barker

Corps Troops

Royal Artillery

27, 140/Field Regiments
3, 5/Medium Regiments
52, 2/Light Anti—Aircraft Regiment
1/Survey Regiment

Royal Engineers

102, 140, 221/Field Companies
105/Field Park Company
13/Corps Field Survey Company

Infantry – Machine Gunners

2/Cheshire
4/Cheshire
2/Manchester

1st Division (With II Corps from 18–23 May)

GOC: Major General the Hon Harold Alexander

1/Guards Brigade GOC: *Gen Merton Beckwith-Smith*

3/Grenadier Guards
2/Coldstream Guards
2/Hampshire

2 Brigade GOC *Brig Charles Edward Hudson VC*

1/Loyal Regiment
2/North Staffordshire
6/Gordon Highlanders

3 Brigade GOC: *Gen Thomas Needham Wilson*

1/Duke of Wellington's
2/Sherwood Foresters
1/King's Shropshire Light Infantry

Artillery

2,19,67/Field Regiments
21/Anti-Tank Regiment

Royal Engineers

23, 238, 248/Field Companies
6/Field Park Company

2nd Division (With 'Rustyforce' from 24–26 May and III Corps from 26 May)

GOC: Major General Henry Lloyd until 16 May, Brigadier Francis Davidson 16–20 May, Major General Noel Irwin from 20 May.

4 Brigade GOC: *Brig Edward Galway Warren*

1/Royal Scots
2/Royal Norfolks
1/8 Lancashire Fusiliers

5 Brigade GOC: *Brig Gerald Ion Gartlan*

2/Dorsetshire
1/Cameron Highlanders
7/Worcestershire

6 Brigade GOC: *Brig Noel Irwin and Brig Dennis Walter Furlong* (after 20 May)

1/Royal Welch Fusiliers
1/Royal Berkshire
2/Durham Light Infantry

Artillery

10, 16, 99/Field Regiments
13/Anti-Tank Regiment

Royal Engineers

5, 209, 99 Field Companies
21/Field Park Company

143 Brigade

GOC: *Brig J Muirhead*
1/Oxfordshire & Bucks Light
Infantry
1/7 Royal Warwicks
1/8 Royal Warwicks

144 Brigade

GOC: *Brig J M Hamilton*
2/Royal Warwicks
5/The Gloucesters
8/Worcestershire

145 Brigade

GOC: *Brig A C Hughes*
2/Gloucesters
4/Oxfordshire & Bucks Light
Infantry
1/Buckinghamshire Battalion (Ox &
Bucks)

Artillery

18, 24,68/Field Regiments
53/Anti–Tank Regiment

Royal Engineers
9, 224, 226/Field Companies
227/Field Park Company

II Corps
GOC: Lieutenant General Alan Francis Brooke

Corps Troops

Royal Artillery

60, 88/Field Regiments
53, 59/Medium Regiments
53/Light Anti–Tank Regiment
2/Survey Regiment

Royal Engineers

222, 234, 226/Field Companies
108/Corps Field Park
14/Corps Field Survey Company

Infantry – Machine Gunners

2/Royal Northumberland Fusiliers (4th Division)
2/Middlesex (3rd Division)
1/7 Middlesex

3rd Division
GOC: Major General Bernard Law Montgomery

7 Guards Brigade

GOC: *Brig John Albert Whitaker*
1/Grenadier Guards
2/Grenadier Guards
1/Coldstream Guards

8 Brigade

GOC: *Brig Christopher Geoffrey
Woolner*
1/Suffolk
2/East Yorkshire
4/Royal Berkshire

9 Brigade

GOC: *Brig William Robb*
2/Lincolnshire
1/KOSB
2/Royal Ulster Rifles

Artillery

7, 33, 76/Field Regiment
20/Anti–Tank Regiment

Royal Engineers
17, 246, 253/Field Companies
15/Field Park Company

4th Division (With III Corps 18–23 May)
GOC: Major General Dudley Graham Johnson VC

10 Brigade	11 Brigade	12 Brigade	Artillery
GOC: *Brig Evelyn Barker* 2/Bedfordshire & Herts 2/Duke of Cornwall's Light Infantry 1/6 East Surrey	GOC: *Brig Kenneth Anderson* 2/Lancashire Fusiliers 1/East Surrey 5/Northamptonshire	GOC: *Brig K L Hawkesworth* 2/The Royal Fusiliers 1/South Lancashire 6/The Black Watch	22, 30, 77/Field Regiments 14/Anti-Tank Regiment **Royal Engineers** 7, 59, 225/Field Companies 18/Field Park Company

50th (Northumbrian) Division (With Frankforce 20–24 May)
Major General Giffard le Quesne Martel

150 Brigade	151 Brigade	25 Brigade	Motor Cycle Infantry
GOC: *Brig C W Haydon* 4/East Yorkshire 4/Green Howards 5/Green Howards	GOC: *Brig J A Churchill* 6/Durham Light Infantry 8/Durham Light Infantry 9/Durham Light Infantry	GOC: *Brig W Ramsden* 2/ Essex Regiment 1/ Royal Irish Fusiliers 1/7 Queen's Royal Regiment	4/Royal Northumberland Fusiliers **Artillery** 72, 74/Field Regiments 65/Anti-Tank Regiment **Royal Engineers** 232, 505/Field Companies 235/Field Park Company

III Corps

GOC: Lieutenant General Sir Ronald Adam (to 26 May) Major General S R Watson

Corps Troops

Artillery	Royal Engineers	Infantry
5/RHA	214, 217/Field Companies	1/9 Manchester (with 5th Division from 14 May)
97/Field Regiment	293/Corps Field Park	
56/Medium Regiment	514 Corps Field Survey Company	
54/Light Anti-Aircraft Regiment		
3/Survey Regiment		

42nd (East Lancashire) Division (With I Corps from 19 May)

GOC: Major General William George Holmes

125 Brigade	126 Brigade	127 Brigade	Artillery
GOC: *Brig G W Sutton*	GOC: *Brig Eric Miles*	GOC: *Brig John Smyth VC*	52, 53/Field Regiments
1/Border Regiment	1/East Lancashire	1/Highland Light Infantry	56/Anti-Tank Regiment
1/5 Lancashire Fusiliers	5/King's Own	4/East Lancashire	
1/6 Lancashire Fusiliers	5/Border Regiment	5/Manchester	**Royal Engineers**
			200, 201, 250/Field Companies
			208/Field Park Company

46th (North Midland & West Riding) Division

(With 'Polforce', 'Rustyforce' and III Corps 20–30 May and with I Corps from 30 May. From 31 May some units served with the 'Beauman' Division)

GOC: Major General Henry Osborne Curtis (Commanded Polforce 20–24 May)

137 Brigade	138 Brigade	139 Brigade	Artillery
GOC: *Brig J Gawthorpe*	GOC: *Brig E J Grinling*	GOC: *Brig H A F Crerdson* (To 22 May)	**Royal Engineers**
2/5 West Yorkshire	6/Lincolnshire	*Brig R C Chichester-Constable*	271/Field Company
2/6 Duke of Wellington's	6/York and Lancaster	2/5 Leicestershire	273/Field Park Company
2/4 KOSB	2/7 Duke of Wellington's	2/5 Sherwood Foresters	
		9/Sherwood Foresters	

23rd (Northumbrian) Division (With 'Petreforce' 18–21 May subsequently with Rustyforce and III Corps)
GOC: Major General W N H Herbert

69 Brigade
GOC: *Brig Viscount Downe*
5/East Yorkshire
5/Green Howards
6/Green Howards

70 Brigade
GOC: *Brig P Kirkup*
10/Durham Light Infantry
11/Durham Light Infantry
1/Tyneside Scottish (Black Watch)

Motorcycle & MG Infantry
8/Royal Northumberland Fusiliers
9/Royal Northumberland Fusiliers

Royal Engineers
223, 507/Field Companies
508/Field Park Company

5th Division (Released to GHQ Reserve and with I Corps 16–19 May, with 'Frankforce' 20–24 May, with III Corps 24–25 May and then to II Corps from 25 May)
GOC: Major General Harold Edmund Franklyn (Commanded Frankforce 20–24 May)

13 Brigade
GOC: *Brig Miles Dempsey*
2/Cameronians
2/Royal Inniskilling Fusiliers
2/Wiltshire

17 Brigade
GOC: *Brig M G Stopford*
2/Royal Scots Fusiliers
2/Northamptonshire
6/Seaforth Highlanders

Artillery
9, 91, 92/Field Regiments
52/Anti-Tank Regiment

Royal Engineers
38, 245, 252 Field Companies
254/Field Park Company

44th (Home Counties) Division
GOC: Major General E A Osborne

131 Brigade
GOC: Brig J F E Utterson-Kelso
2/East Kent (Buffs)
1/5 Queen's
1/6 Queen's

132 Brigade
GOC: *Brig James Stuart Steele*
1/Royal West Kents
4/Royal West Kents
5/Royal West Kents

133 Brigade
GOC: *Brig N I Whitty*
2/Royal Sussex
4/Royal Sussex
5/Royal Sussex

Artillery
57, 68, 55/Field Regiments
57/Anti-Tank Regiment

Royal Engineers
11, 208, 210/Field Companies
211/Field Park Company

Boulogne 22–24 May

20 Guards Brigade	Artillery	Royal Engineers
GOC: *Brig W A F Fox-Pitt* 2/Irish Guards 2/Welsh Guards	275/Battery from 69/Anti-Tank Regiment	262/Field Company from 12th Division

Calais 22–26 May

30 Brigade	Royal Armoured Corps	Artillery
GOC: *Brig Claude N Nicholson* 1/Rifle Brigade 2/KRRC (from 1/Armoured Division) 1/Queen Victoria's Rifles (KRRC)	3/Royal Tank Regiment from 1st Armoured Division	229/Battery from 58/Anti-Tank Regiment 1 Searchlight Regiment 6 Heavy AA Battery 172 Light AA Battery

Notes

Chapter 1: Return

1. Brookes. *Grand Party*. Hutchinson 1941, p13. In 1940 an artillery field regiment of 18 or 25-pounders was composed of two batteries of twelve guns divided into three troops.
2. Montgomery. *TheMemoirs*. Collins 1958, p.52.
3. Dill's discussion with Falls is in Benoist-Méchin, *Sixty Days That Shook the West*, p.12.
4. The Escaut is the French name for the River Schelde. In order not to confuse I have used the French – Escaut – when describing events that took place along the river.
5. Taylor. Suffolk Records Office. GB 554/Y1/252.
6. Duncan.*Underground From Posen*, Kimber 1954, p.9.
7. IWM Dept of Foreign Documents. 11929.
8. Gribble. *The Diary of a Staff Officer*, Methuen 1941, p.9.
9. Nelson. *Always A Grenadier*. The Regiment 1983, p.8.
10. Horsfall, *Say Not The Struggle*, Roundwood 1977, p.26.

Chapter 2: The Dyle

1. Rhodes, *Sword of Bone*, Severn House 1942, p.127.
2. *Youth at War*, Batsford 1944, p.176.
3. Stewart, *History of the XII Royal Lancers*, Oxford 1950, p.348.
4. Taylor, *op. cit.*
5. Ibid.
6. Duncan, *We Marched*, Royal Hampshire Regiment Trust, Chelsea 2001.
7. TNA WO 167/778. David Smith's account at the Monmouth Castle Museum. GB 1578 RMRE/25/6.
8. Walker's diary at KCLMA. The Cointet defences, also known as the Belgian Gate, were a series of heavy steel fences about 10 feet wide and 6 feet high mounted on concrete rollers. Rail obstacles were short sections of railway line sunk vertically into the ground forming a wide belt which was designed to slow any armoured advance.
9. Montgomery, *The Memoirs*, pp.60–61.
10. Forbes and Nicholson, *The Grenadier Guards 1939–1945, Vol.I*, Gale & Polden 1949, p.1.
11. Graves, *History of the Royal Ulster Rifles Vol. III*, The Regiment 1950, p.46.
12. Howard & Sparrow, *The Coldstream Guards 1920 -1946*. p.33.
13. Ibid, pp.33–4. Lord Frederick Cambridge is buried at Hevelee War Cemetery.
14. Farr, Durham Records Office. Farr/DL19/208/1.
15. DLI Newsletter No.8, 1942. I was sent Townsend's diary account by Jim Tuckwell who is the webmaster of the DLI website at http://durhamlightinfantry.webs.com/2dlidyledunkirk1940.htm. He was originally given a copy of the diary by the family of Private Anthony Corkhill who was killed at St Venant and is commemorated on the Dunkirk Memorial.
16. The account of Private James Miller's war is at: www.jameshenrymiller.petermillerphotoworld.co.uk/21.html.

17. There is some discrepancy over who was in command at the blockhouse. David Rissik in *The DLI at War* says it was a Corporal Thompson while Townsend's diary identifies him as 34-year-old Corporal Wilson. I have taken Townsend's diary as the correct version as Wilson's name is on the Dyle Memorial.
18. Farr,/DL19/208/1.
19. Townsend's diary.
20. Farr, DL19/208/1.
21. Miller's account. Private Joseph Hunter died of wounds on 17 June 1940 and is buried at Maastricht General Cemetery.
22. Bell, in *The History of the Manchester Regiment*, reports 9 and 10 Platoons in C Company lost several guns in this engagement before they extricated themselves. Captain Lewis was killed on 19 May and commemorated on the Dunkirk Memorial.
23. Townsend's diary. The majority of the Durhams killed on the Dyle are buried at Leopoldsburg War Cemetery.
24. Henniker, *An Image of War*, Leo Cooper 1987, pp.16 -18. William Thorburn was killed in 1944 serving with the Royal Scots at Kohima. He had recently been promoted to major. He is buried at Kohima War Cemetery.
25. Ibid, p.18.
26. Money's diary. James Bruce's diary is at TNA CAB 106/242.
27. Gaston-Henri Billotte was the French commander of the 1st Army Group.

Chapter 3: Towards the Escaut
1. The diary of L T Tomes. Chipping Campden History Society.
2. *OBLI War Chronicle 1939–1940*, Gale and Polden 1949, p.89.
3. 68/Field Regiment was not brought into action here and would fire its first rounds on 19 May west of the Escaut at Wez Velvain. Arthur Hammond is buried at Waterloo Communal Cemetery. He is the only BEF casualty buried there.
4. *OBLI War Chronicle 1939–1940*, p.242.
5. Smith. *Op. cit.*
6. National Army Museum, 2003-02-277.
7. *OBLI War Chronicle 1939–1940*, p.244. Turner tells us he retired on 18 May, this is probably incorrect as 2/Lieutenant David Wallis writes that the whole of 145 Brigade were across the canal at Hal by 12.45pm on 17 May.
8. *Underground From Posen*, p.17.
9. Forbes & Nicholson. *The Grenadier Guards in the War of 1939–1945*, Volume 1. p.20.
10. Ibid.p.20.
11. Quilter, *No Dishonourable Name*, E P Publishing 1972, p.22. Much of the Rivers Senne and Dendre had been canalised to take barge traffic. The Senne in Brussels was also known as the Charleroi-Brussels Canal and in several accounts the line of both rivers is referred to simply as the 'Canal'.
12. Suffolk Records Office. GB 554/Y1/252.
13. *No Dishonourable Name*, p.22.
14. Guardsman Robert Wriglesworth was killed at Eychen and is buried at Voorde Churchyard Cemetery.
15. Duncan, *We Marched*, Royal Hampshire Regiment Trust.
16. Courage, *The History of 15/19 King's Royal Hussars, 1939–1945*, Gale and Polden 1949, pp.30–31. Cokayne-Frith and seven other casualties of the action at Assche can be found in the Asse (Mollemsebaan) Communal Cemetery. Others are at Adegem Canadian War Cemetery, Hevelee War Cemetery, Mollem Communal Cemetery and are commemorated on the Dunkirk Memorial.

17. Captain Taylor's account of his escape is at TNA WO 208/3298. Guy Courage's older brother, Captain Nigel Courage, commanding B Squadron, was wounded and taken prisoner later on 18 May. He was repatriated in 1943.
18. Farr, DL19/208/1.
19. Designed by Captain H C Boys, the Boys Anti-Tank Rifle (or incorrectly Boyes), was often nicknamed 'the elephant gun' by its users due to its size and large bore.
20. Henniker, *An Image of War*, p.21.
21. The actions of the 4/7 Royal Hussars is at TNA CAB 106/231. Albert Argyle is commemorated on the Dunkirk Memorial. Denis Atkinson was taken prisoner and survived the war.
22. Henniker, *An Image of War*, p.22.
23. TNA, CAB 106/292.
24. Wilkinson, in Daniell, *Cap of Honour*, White Lion 1951, pp.251–2.
25. The majority of the identified men killed in this episode are buried at Merignies Churchyard and Gaurain-Ramecroix War Cemetery. Jones notes that 51 men of A Company were missing of which 8 later rejoined for duty.

Chapter 4: Massacre of the Innocents

1. Giraud escaped from Konigstein Castle in April 1942 and returned to co-operate with the landings in North Africa and the South of France. He died in 1949.
2. The 1/Tyneside Scottish was formed in June 1939 as 12/DLI – a duplicate unit of 9/DLI: known locally as the 'Gestetner Gurkhas'.
3. Ron Stilwell edited Bert Jones' wartime diary *A Prisoner in Poland* and obtained permission from Jones for me to quote from his diary. Ian Laidler sent me a copy of *A Slice of My Life* written by his father James C Laidler and The Duke of Wellington's Regimental Association gave permission to quote from Peter Walker's account.
4. TNA WO 167/765.
5. Captain Edward Hill is buried at Albert Communal Cemetery Extension along with thirteen identified members·of the battalion. Another eight unidentified casualties may well have been killed at Albert. A further seven who died between 20–21 May commemorated on the Dunkirk Memorial.
6. Ibid.
7. TNA WO 167/837. The war diary documents the battalion's arrival at St Roche as 15.15 hours while Lieutenant Colonel Gethin in his 1942 account maintains it was 17.10 hours. Other evidence points towards the war diary being correct.
8. Jacques Mercier is author of *La Gare d'Amiens: 1846–1986*.
9. Dalglish. KCLMA Archive and Doug Swift, *Slow March Through Hell, Arcturus 2006*.
10. TNA WO 167/837.
11. The officers and men killed between 18–21 May 1940 can be found mainly in Salouel Communal Cemetery, Abbeville Communal Cemetery Extension and Pont-de-Metz Churchyard. Major Cassels is buried at Morvillers-St-Saturnin Churchyard east of Aumale.
12. Jones' Account.
13. TNA WO 217/20.
14. Ibid.
15. Jones' Account.
16. Ibid.
17. Huygebeart's account is contrary to some reports that a tank shell was responsible for Lungley's death. André Colliot's account of the battle in *Mai 1940: Un Mois Pas Comme Les Autres* was sent to me by Ron Stilwell.

18. TNA WO 217/20.
19. Two A Company officers, Captain William Findlay who died on 28 May and Second Lieutenant Donald Fergusson who died on 25 May are buried at Mondicourt Communal Cemetery along with 8 NCOs and men of the battalion. John Lungley is buried at La Herliere Communal Cemetery. Others can be found at Saulty Communal Cemetery, Doullens Communal Cemetery and on the Dunkirk Memorial.
20. Swinburne's comments are in the report in WO 167/262 submitted by Captain J B Burr.
21. These may well have been men from 48 Company (Major J S Alston) who had become detached from 5 Group AMPC.
22. Lynch. *Dunkirk 1940: Whereabouts Unknown*, Spellmount 2010, pp.108–9.
23. IWM Dept. of Documents. 94/49/1.
24. The majority of the identified casualties from 70 Brigade can be found at Bucquoy Road Cemetery, Ficheux. Amongst the 162 casualties are Privates Arthur Todhunter and Albert Forster, Sergeant Richard Chambers, CSM John Morris and Captain John Kipling.
25. Walker's Account.
26. Ibid.
27. Ibid. Second Lieutenant Kenneth Smith is buried at Abbeville Communal Cemetery.
28. Ibid.

Chapter 5: The Escaut
1. Chaplin in *The Queen's Own Royal West Kent Regiment 1920–1950* notes the Belgians did not in fact appear on the left flank until 19 May, Captain M Few of the 5/Royal Sussex noted a 2 mile gap between the BEF and the Belgians on the same day, a gap that he says was still apparent 2 days later.
2. Clarke and Tillot, *Kent to Kohima*, Gale and Polden 1951, p.8.
3. Richard Rutherford is buried at Esquelmes War Cemetery.
4. Diary of Edward Sonsonby. QRWS/30/SYSO/1.
5. Arthur Peters died on 26 May 1940 and is buried at Guilford Cemetery.
6. Foster, *History of the Queen's Royal Regiment*, Gale and Polden 1953, p.76.. Blaxland's papers at the IWM indicate he was east of Petegem with 17 Platoon, 2/Buffs at the time.
7. TNA WO 167/762.
8. The Queen's Royal Regiment casualties are at Moregem Churchyard and Ansegem Communal Cemetery. Keane is buried at Bevere Communal Cemetery. The largest concentration of 131 &132 Brigade casualties is at Esquelmes War Cemetery.
9. Riordan, *A History of the 7th Field Company RE*, privately published, p.25.
10. This was a 300 strong party of the 2/Sherwood Foresters under the command of Maj N Temple who had become detached. They rejoined the battalion on 21 May. Lieutenant Colonel Birch commanding the 2/Beds and Herts comments on the degree of confusion that existed at the time and that many units were mixed up at this stage.
11. Jervois, *The History of the Northamptonshire Regiment 1934–1948*, The Regiment, p.73.
12. Captain John Johnson is buried at Kortrijk Communal Cemetery. Lieutenant Colonel Green died of wounds and is buried at White House Cemetery, St-Jean-les-Ypres.
13. Ricketts, *The Final Years 1938–1959*, The Regiment, p.19.
14. Boxhall's account, Surrey History Centre.
15. Finch White in *The Final Years 1938–1959*, p.20.
16. Manley's Account, TNA WO 167/778/1. Lieutenant Colonel Charles Rougier is buried along with 17 other Lancashire Fusiliers at Waarmaarde Churchyard.
17. Medley, *Cap Badge*, Pen and Sword 1995, p.37. Robin Medley was a subaltern with the battalion in May 1940.
18. TNA CAB 106/251.

19. *Cap Badge*, p.40.
20. Suffolk Records Office. Frazer died of wounds in England and is buried at Leigh (St Mary) Churchyard in Kent. John Trelawney died of wounds and is buried at Pecq Communal Cemetery.
21. Bootle-Wilbraham's diary account. The 2/Coldstream Battalion HQ was probably at the Château de Biez. Fane and Boscawen are both buried at Pecq Communal Cemetery and John Burnett is commemorated on the Dunkirk Memorial.
22. Drinkwater, *The Grenadier Gazette*, No.5, 1982. George Button is commemorated on the Dunkirk Memorial as is Major Alston-Roberts-West who may be the unidentified Grenadier officer at Esquelmes War Cemetery.
23. Bollmann & Flörke, Das Infantrie-Regiment 12, Castings 1968.
24. Drinkwater, *op.cit.*
25. *The Grenadier Guards 1939–1945, Volume 1*, p.3. Captain Robert Abel-Smith and Lieutenant the Duke of Northumberland are buried at Esquelmes War Cemetery. Lieutenant Reynell-Pack is commemorated on the Dunkirk Memorial.
26. Major Frederick Matthews is buried at Esquelmes War Cemetery.
27. IWM Sound Archive, Reference: 8192.
28. Ibid. Ernie Leggett's IWM interview, Reference 17761.
29. George Gristock died on 16 May from his wounds and is buried at Bear Road Cemetery, Brighton.
30. Diary of L T Tomes.
31. HFHS Journal. No. 4 May 1993.
32. Lieutenant Colonel Whitfeld's account.
33. Diary of L T Tomes. The 128 Royal Warwicks and 22 Cameron Highlanders that appear on the CWGC database can be found mainly at Calonne Communal Cemetery, Bruyelle War Cemetery, Hollain Churchyard and are commemorated on the Dunkirk Memorial. The 34 Royal Scots and 35 Ox and Bucks Light Infantry who were killed between 20–21 May are mainly commemorated on the Dunkirk Memorial or buried at Bruyelle War Cemetery.
34. Alanbrooke, *War Diaries, 1939–1945*, Phoenix, 2002, p.67.

Chapter 6: Arras

1. Franklyn, *The Story of One Green Howard*, The Regiment, 1966, p.14.
2. English, *Durham Bugle*, Spring 2001, p.9.
3. Macksey, *The Shadow of Vimy Ridge*, Kimber 1965, p213.
4. Perrett, *Through Mud and Blood*, Hale 1975, p.30.
5. Brigadier Peter Vaux in the Pictorial History of the Fourth and Seventh Royal Tank Regiment (www.4and7royaltankregiment.com)
6. Ibid.
7. *Through Mud and Blood*, p.34.
8. Ibid.
9. Macksey. *Op. cit.* p216.
10. Ibid, p.226.
11. Second Lieutenant Thomas Bland died of wounds on 30 May and is buried in Arras Communal Cemetery. Corporal Winder was taken prisoner and survived the war.
12. Lewis and English, *8th Battalion Durham Light Infantry 1939–1945*, Naval & Military Press, p.15.
13. Self. IWM Sound Archive, Reference 10413.
14. Ibid, p.16. Whether this attack took place in Berneville, as suggested in some accounts, is unclear but English's account suggests they were still in the environs of Warlus.
15. Lieutenant Colonel Tom Craig in the Pictorial History of the Fourth and Seventh Royal Tank Regiment (www.4and7royaltankregiment.com

16. *Through Mud and Blood*, p.36. The account is taken from Liddel Hart's *The Rommel Papers*.
17. Royal Tank Museum Bovington (BTM) archive.
18. Ibid.
19. Ibid.
20. Lieutenant Colonel Fitzmaurice is buried in Dunkirk Town Cemetery, Lieutenant Colonel Heyland is commemorated on the Dunkirk Memorial but could be the unidentified officer buried at Wailly Communal Cemetery. Major Gerald Hedderwick is buried at Beaurains Communal Cemetery along with 16 other casualties of the battle. He was killed near the same spot where he fought in April 1917.
21. Weygand's plan mirrored the offensive first mooted by Gamelin which was cancelled when Weygand assumed control of French forces. Had it taken place before 19 May it might possibly have blunted the German panzer thrust and altered the final picture.
22. Norfolk Records Office.
23. From the notes made by Major Llewellyn and given to me by his son, Trefor Llewellyn.
24. From the account of the Welsh Guards Carrier Platoon in France during the defence of Arras, May 1940 compiled by Second Lieutenant Hugh Lister in October 1940.
25. The 8/RNF were intercepted by German infantry just after dawn losing 5 officers and 120 ORs including Lieutenant Colonel F Clarke.
26. Ibid, pp.13–14.
27. Ibid, p.15.
28. Welsh Guards casualties are mainly buried in Arras Communal Cemetery, Guardsmen Daley and Williams are buried at Athies Communal Cemetery and Furness and Berry are commemorated on the Dunkirk Memorial. It is possible that the latter two are amongst the ten unknowns buried at Athies.
29. Moore looks at this phase of the Dunkirk campaign in *The Road To Dunkirk*, pp.40–58.

Chapter 7: The Hell that was Boulogne

1. Behr, in Guderian *Mit den Panzern in Ost und West Vol. 1*, Volk-u-Reich Verlag, 1942.
2. Newbery TNA WO 167/718.
3. Ten identified Guardsmen are buried at the Hook of Holland General Cemetery and one at Gravenzande General Cemetery.
4. TNA CAB 106/226.
5. From an account sent to Jon Cooksey by Boswell and quoted in *Boulogne: 20 Guards Brigade's Fighting Defence – May 1940*, Pen and Sword, 2002.
6. Stanier, IWM Sound Archive, Reference 7175/7.
7. From a tape transcript sent to Jon Cooksey by Corporal Bryan.
8. Hanbury, *A Not Very Military Experience*, privately published, p.10. Captain J Higgon in his account says it was a Boys Rifle that knocked out the church tower sniper, but he was not present at the time.
9. Boswell *op. cit*.
10. TNA WO 106/697.
11. Cook, *Missing in Action*, Trafford, 2013, p.24.
12. From a conversation between Leslie and Jon Cooksey.
13. CAB 106/226.
14. Ibid.
15. Stanier, *op. cit*.
16. IWM Dept. of Documents, Reference 5/2/85.
17. IWM Dept. of Documents, Reference 66/24/1.
18. Ibid.

19. Glover in *The Fight For The Channel Ports*, Leo Cooper 1985, p.82.
20. CAB 106/226.
21. CAB 106/228.
22. Ibid.
23. Tape transcript recorded by Jon Cooksey with Davies.
24. The CWGC Database records sixty-seven identified officers and men from all units involved in the defence of Boulogne buried at: Bolougne Eastern Cemetery, Outreau Communal Cemetery and St Martin Boulogne Communal Cemetery.

Chapter 8: Calais – The Bitter Agony of Defeat
 1. Timpson. TNA WO 217/4.
 2. Kydd. *For You The War Is Over*, Bachman and Turner 1975, p.41.
 3. Recording of Foote's memoirs held by the RTM at Bovington. Already the recipient of the DSO (1942) Foote was in command of 7/RTR when he was awarded the Victoria Cross at the Battle of Gazala in 1942 where he was injured along with Bill Reeves who was CO of 4/RTR at the time. He retired as a Major General in 1958 and died in 1993. SD 7 was the Royal Armoured Corps Branch on the General Staff.
 4. Reeves, RH.87 3RTR 54.
 5. Keller, Report 3.RTR/3N004.
 6. Simpson, BTM Archive.
 7. Reeves, *op. cit.*
 8. Ibid.
 9. TNA WO 167/458.
10. Ibid.
11. TNA WO 167/458.
12. Keller, *op. cit.*
13. TNA WO 217/5.
14. Davies-Scourfield, *In Presence Of My Foes*, Wilton 1991, p19.
15. Evitts. Calais 1940 Remembered. *Journal of the Royal Signals Institution, Winter 1971, Vol X, No.3.*
16. Jabez-Smith, National Army Museum.
17. Ibid.
18. Davies-Scourfield, *op. cit.* p.30.
19. Ibid, p.31.
20. Reeves., *op. cit.*
21. Ibid.
22. Cornwall, BTM Archive.
23. TNA WO 217/5.
24. TNA WO 106/1693.
25. Illingworth, National Army Museum.
26. Evitts. *op. cit.*
27. Ibid and TNA WO 106/1693.
28. TNA WO 217/3.
29. Hoskyns died on 18 June 1940 and is buried in Chilworth Churchyard, Hampshire.
30. Davies-Scourfield, *op. cit* p.54–55.
31. National Army Museum.
32. TNA WO 217/3.
33. There are 105 identified men (killed or died of wounds between 22–28 May) from the units that fought at Calais buried in the Calais Southern Cemetery. Amongst these are Second Lieutenants David Sladen, George Thomas, Richard Warre and Adrian Van der Weyer together with PSMs James Easen, Ivan Williams and Corporal Birt. On the Dunkirk

Memorial are 62 men of the KRRC and RB who died at Calais including Major 'Puffin' Segar-Owen. Major Hamilton-Russell is buried at Burwarton Churchyard, Shropshire. His cousin Lt G Hamilton-Russell was serving with the 3/Grenadier Guards at Pecq. He died of wounds on 2/6/40.
34. TNA WO 167/458.

Chapter 9: The Canal Line

1. TNA CAB 106/217. Woolven is buried at Hazebrouck Communal Cemetery where there are four further casualties from the same battery.
2. Ibid and WO 373/16.
3. Horsfall, *Say Not The Struggle*. Fusilier Connolly is buried at Beuvry Communal Cemetery. The only Fusilier Herbert Wilson on the CWGC database died of wounds on 5/5/41 and is commemorated on the Brookwood Memorial.
4. Ibid, p.101.
5. Irwin, *Youth At War*, p.199.
6. Ibid. Martin in *The Essex Regiment 1929–1950* states that Irwin was accompanied across the canal by Private Clarke who was subsequently awarded the MM. I suspect Irwin's account is the correct version.
7. Kallmeyer's account. Mercian Regiment Museum.
8. Ibid.
9. Hofmann. *Signal*, 1941.
10. Townsend's account.
11. Miller's account. Lieutenant John Gregson is buried at Longuenesse Souvenir Cemetery, St Omer.
12. The War Diary of II/IR 3.
13. Townsend's account. The café referred to was the Café du Nord on the canal bank.
14. Farr, Durham Records Office.
15. Clough-Taylor, *A Wartime Log*, RWF Museum.
16. Townsend, *op. cit.*
17. Miller's account.
18. The St Venant War Crimes, TNA WO 311/97. MI19 was a section of the British Directorate of Military Intelligence and was responsible for obtaining information from enemy prisoners of war.
19. IWM Sound Archive, Reference 11479.
20. Brunnegger, *Saat in den Sturm. Ein soldat der Waffen SS Berichet*, Stocker 2000.
21. IWM Sound Archive, Reference 16972.
22. Brunnegger, *op. cit.*
23. Ibid.
24. Muir, *The First of Foot*, Blackwood 1961, p.69.
25. Ibid. p.72.
26. IWM Sound Archive, Reference 10320.
27. TNA WO 309/1811, WO 309/1371, WO 311/101 & 102.
28. IWM Sound Archive, Reference 10393.
29. Pooley in *The Vengeance of Private Pooley*.
30. Brunnegger, *op. cit.*
31. Jolly, *The Vengeance of Private Pooley*, Heinemann 1956.
32. Miller's account.
33. Ibid.
34. Bell's statement and other material relating to the Nieppe Forest murders are at TNA WO 311/99, WO 208/4647 & TS 26/205.

35. Ibid. Fred Carter, Henry Daniels, Fred Lancaster, Joseph Mills, Ernest Shilling and Horace Theroux are buried at Nieppe-Bois British Cemetery.

Chapter 10: Hazebrouck and Cassel

1. TNA WO 167/804.
2. Gibbens. Soldiers of Oxfordshire (S of O) Archive.
3. Saunders. S of O Archive.
4. Ibid.
5. Le Neve Foster. S of O Archive. The anti-tank officer may have been Major Pedley.
6. Saunders, *op. cit.*
7. Gibbens, *op. cit.*
8. Watson. S of O Archive. *The Ox and Bucks War Chronicle 1939–1940* p.149, states 10 officers and 200 other ranks succeeded in getting back to England. Many of the identified dead who were killed at Hazebrouck are buried at Hazebrouck Communal Cemetery including Brian Heyworth, James Ritchie and Martin Preston. Gunner Ronald Scoates is buried at Steenwerck Communal Cemetery.
9. Perkins, S of O Archive.
10. Gibbens, *op. cit.*
11. In 1940 the Place du Général Vandamme was called Place du Général Plumer.
12. Wild, *The Ox and Bucks War Chronicle 1939–1940*, p.228.
13. Gilmore, S of O Archive 9/3/J/3.
14. TNA WO 217/9, Appendix III.
15. Ibid.
16. TNA WO 167/804.
17. Duncan, *Underground From Posen*, p.24.
18. Wallis, *The Ox and Bucks War Chronicle 1939–1940*, p.199.
19. Mercian Regiment Museum Archives.
20. Gilmore, *op.cit.*
21. 'Hull-down' is a position taken up by an armoured fighting vehicle where the main part of the vehicle is behind a crest or other raised ground leaving only its turret and main armament exposed.
22. National Army Museum.
23. Duncan, *op. cit.* pp.32–33.
24. The CWGC database has only six Ox and Bucks and nineteen Gloucesters buried in the Cassel Communal Cemetery, including George Weightman and Gerald French. More from both battalions, such as Major James Graham, Private William Phelps and Lance Corporal Percy Badnel, are commemorated on the Dunkirk Memorial. John Clerke Brown is buried at Longueness Souvenir Cemetery and Michael Fleming at Lille Southern Cemetery.

Chapter 11: Hondeghem and Cäestre

1. WO 106/217.
2. The time of the German attack differs, from 7.00pm in WO 167/217 to 10.15am (German time) in the German account.
3. From an account held by the 6th Panzer Division Veterans Association and provided by *Oberstleutnant* Schmidt in 1983.
4. Williams, *The New Contemptibles*, Wyman 1940, p.23–4.
5. WO 167/546.
6. Williams, *op. cit.* p.27.
7. Casualties are mainly to be found at St-Sylvestre-Cappel New Cemetery, Terdeghem

Churchyard and Hondeghem Churchyard. Gunner Manning is buried at Longueness Souvenir Cemetery.

8. Hadley, *Third Class to Dunkirk*, Hollins and Carter 1944, p.100
9. Bleach. www.bbc.co.uk/history/ww2peopleswar/stories/04/a2350504.shtml.
10. Longden. *Dunkirk, The Men They Left Behind*, Constable 2009, p.45.
11. Hadley, *op. cit.* p.108.
12. Ibid, p.109.
13. Ibid, p.110–11.
14. Second Lieutenant Desmond Cardwell is buried at Strazeele Communal Cemetery, Sergeant Reginald Cleverly and Private Sidney Bampton are buried at Bertenacre Mil Cemetery, Fletre. Private John Friend died of wounds on 16.6.40 and is commemorated on the Dunkirk Memorial.
15. Few, West Sussex Records Office.
16. Ibid.
17. Ibid.
18. Austin's account in Greenwood *Dunkirk. Bombed, Beached and Bewildered*, privately published, 2011.
19. Other casualties are to be found at Caëstre Communal Cemetery where Second Lieutenant John Hincks is buried, Pradelles Churchyard (Private Ronald Gurr) and on the Dunkirk Memorial.

Chapter 12: Ledringhem, Wormout and West Cappel

1. Priestley, *The Back Badge*, 1946.
2. Guy Rommelaere, *The Forgotten Massacre, May 1940 in Flanders*, Warwick 2001, p.28.
3. Priestley *op cit*. The officers referred to by Priestley were Lieutenant Duncan Norris of D Company, the younger brother of Lieutenant Charlie Norris and Lieutenant Tony Dewsnap. Duncan died of wounds on 28/4/42 and is buried at Hanover War Cemetery.
4. *Firm*, The Regimental Magazine of the Worcester Regiment, July 1948.
5. Diary of L T Tomes.
6. Rommelaere, p.42.
7. Ibid.
8. Ibid.
9. Haywood. Mercian Regiment Museum Archives.
10. 38 Royal Warwicks are buried at Wormhout Communal Cemetery along with the Cheshires and Gunners who supported them including Majors Rance and Chichester-Constable and Lieutenants Dunwell and Padfield. Also there are the dead from the 69/Medium Regiment including Captain Heneage Finch. A further 23 Warwicks are buried ar Esquelbecq Military Cemetery.
11. Cheshire Military Museum Archive and also quoted in part by Rommelaere, p.39.
12. Wormhout Massacre Report WO 309/1813.
13. Ibid.
14. CSM Augustus Jennings and Sergeant Stanley Moore are buried at Esquelbecq Military Cemetery. Captain James Lynn-Allen is commemorated on the Dunkirk Memorial.
15. Norman. KCLMA Archive.
16. Ibid.
17. Llewellyn's account.
18. Ellis. *Welsh Guards at War*, London Stamp Exchange 1989, p.109–10.
19. Llewellyn's account.
20. Haywood. Mercian Regiment Museum Archives. Captain John Farrar is commemorated on the Dunkirk Memorial.
21. Ibid.

22. Norman. KCLMA Archive.
23. Ellis. *Welsh Guards at War*, p.107.
24. Haggas in the Prain papers at KCLMA.
25. Ronald Sharp and Foster Jennings are buried at Warhem Communal Cemetery along with three others of the regiment.
26. Twenty identified Welsh Guards are buried at West Cappel Churchyard, including Guardsman Ivor Llewellyn. PSM Maisey and a number from 6 Platoon were taken prisoner. Ten casualties from the 8/Worcesters are at West Cappel (possibly from the fight at Groenenspriet) and six more at Rexpoëde Communal Cemetery.
27. Haywood, Mercian Regiment Museum Archives.
28. Bailey, Mercian Regiment Museum Archives.

Chapter 13: The Ypres – Comines Canal
1. TNA WO 167/29.
2. *The Story of One Green Howard*, p.29.
3. Holdich Family History Society (HFHS) Journal No. 4, May 1993.
4. Caddick-Adams in *British Army Review* No. 116 and mentioned in Bourgeois *Comines et la Bataille du Canal*.
5. Warner. *The Ox and Bucks War Chronicle 1939–1940*, p.160.
6. Riordan. *A History of The 7th Field Company RE*, p.35.
7. Forbes and Nicholson, *The Grenadier Guards 1939–1945, Vol. I*, p.32–3.
8. Ibid, p.34.
9. Quoted by Kemp in *The History of the Royal Scots Fusiliers*, Maclehose 1948, p.36.
10. Kemp and TNA WO 167/816.
11. Kemp, p.38.
12. HFHS Journal No. 4, May 1993.
13. Smith, Monmouth Castle Archive.

Chapter 14: The Final Line
1. Crang, J, in Bond, B, *The Battle For France and Flanders*, Leo Cooper 2001, p.120.
2. TNA WO 167/778. Furnes is now called Veurne.
3. Smith. Monmouth Castle Archive.
4. Beasley et al, *History of 53 (London) Medium Regiment 1861–1961*, p.56. Thornton is buried at Nieuwpoort Communal Cemetery.
5. Henniker. *Op. cit.* p.42.
6. Christopher Jeffreys and John Lloyd are buried at Veurne Commumal Cemetery Extension and Hercules Pakenham at Gartree Cemetery, Ireland.
7. Howard & Sparrow. *The Coldstream Guards 1920–1946*, p38.
8. Jones, in Wilson, *Dunkirk – From Disaster to Deliverance*, Pen and Sword 2002. John Campbell, Peter Allix and Cecil Preston are buried at Veurne Communal Cemetery Extension.
9. *No Dishonourable Name*, p.30
10. Langley, *Fight Another Day*, Collins 1974, p.45. The Welsh Guards referred to by Langley may well have been those remnants that had survived the fighting at West Cappel.
11. *Fight Another Day*, p.49.
12. Ibid, p.52.
13. *No Dishonourable Name*. p.33. Second Lieutenant Blackwell & Major McCorquodale are buried at Warhem Communal Cemetery. Speed, Dance. Hardwick & Gibbs are commemorated on the Dunkirk Memorial.
14. Ervine-Andrews in Wilson, *Dunkirk – From Disaster to Deliverance*.

15. Ibid.
16. Doll. *British Medical Journal* (BMJ) Vol, 300, May 1990.
17. http://www.bbc.co.uk/history/ww2peopleswar/stories/12/a2281312.shtml
18. Doll, *op. cit.*
19. Henniker, *op. cit.* p.59.
20. Longden, *op. cit.* p.65.

Chapter 15: The Quick and the Dead
1. Quoted by Reid in *Colditz – The Full Story*, Hodder and Stoughton 1962, p.38.

Select Bibliography

The National Archives
Unit war diaries in WO 166 and 167.
Personal accounts in CAB 106 and WO 217.
POW Reports in WO 344, WO 373.

Published Sources
Aitken, L, *Massacre on the Road to Dunkirk*, William Kimber, 1977.
Bell, A C, *The Manchester Regiment 1922–1948*, Sherrat, 1954.
Blaxland, G, *Destination Dunkirk: The Story of Gort's Army*, William Kimber, 1973.
Brooks, G, *Grand Party*, Hutchinson,1942.
Caddick-Adams, P, *By God They Can Fight*, Royal Logistics Corps, 1995.
Cooksey, J, *Boulogne*, Leo Cooper – Pen and Sword, 2002.
Cooksey, J, *Calais*, Leo Cooper – Pen and Sword, 2000.
Chaplin, H D, *Queen's Own Royal West Kent Regiment 1920–1950*, Michael Joseph, 1954.
Cuncliffe, M, *History of the Royal Warwickshire Regiment 1919–1955*, Clowes, 1956.
Daniell, D S, *Cap of Honour*, White Lion 1951.
—— *The History of the East Surrey Regiment, Vol IV,* Ernest Benn 1957.
Davies-Scourfield, E, *In Presence of my Foes*, Wilton, 1991.
Duncan, M, *Underground from Posen*, William Kimber, 1954.
Ellis, L F, *The War in France and Flanders, 1939–40*, HMSO, 1954.
Ellis, L F, *Welsh Guards at War*, London Stamp Exchange, 1989.
Forbes, P, *The Grenadier Guards in the War of 1939–1945, Vol. 1*, Gale and Polden 1949.
Fitzgerald, D, *History of the Irish Guards in the Second World War*, Gale and Polden, 1952.
Franklyn, Sir H, *The Story of One Green Howard in the Dunkirk Campaign*, Green Howards, 1966.
Glover, M, *The Fight for the Channel Ports*, Leo Cooper, 1985.
Gough, G F, *Thirty Days to Dunkirk*, Bridge Books, 1990.
Gribble, P, *The Diary of a Staff Officer*, Methuen 1941.
Hadley, P, *Third Class to Dunkirk*, Hollis & Carter, 1944.
Hart, P, *At the Sharp End*, Leo Cooper, 1998.
Hastings, R H, *The Rifle Brigade in the Second World War 1939–1945*, Gale & Polden, 1950.
Henniker, M, *An Image of War*, Leo Cooper, 1987.
Heyworth, M, *Hazebrouck 1940*, The Naylor Group, 2004.
Horsfall, J, *Say Not the Struggle*, Roundwood, 1977.
Howard, M, & Sparrow, J, *History of the Coldstream Guards 1920–46*, Oxford, 1951.
Irwin, A, *Infantry Officer*, Batsford 1944.
Jackson, J, *The Fall of France*, OUP, 2003.

Kemp, J C, *The History of the Royal Scots Fusiliers 1919–1959*, Maclehose, 1963.

Langley, J M, *Fight another Day*, Collins, 1974.

Lewis, P J & English, I R, *8th Battalion The Durham Light Infantry 1939–1945*, Naval & Military Press Reprint, 2004.

Longden, S, *Dunkirk – The Men they Left Behind*, Constable, 2008.

Lynch, T, *Dunkirk 1940 – Whereabouts Unknown*, Spellmount, 2010.

Mace, P, & Wright, T, *Forrard: The Story of the East Riding Yeomanry*, Leo Cooper, 2001.

Macksey, K, *The Shadow of Vimy Ridge*, William Kimber, 1965.

Mills, G H & Nixon, R F, *The Annals of the KRRC Vol. VI 1921–1943*, Leo Cooper, 1971.

More, C, *The Road to Dunkirk*, Frontline, 2013.

Montgomery, B L, *The Memoirs*, Collins, 1958.

Muir, A, *The First of Foot*, The Regiment, 1961.

Neville, M C, *The Ox and Bucks Light Infantry Chronicle Vol. 1*, Gale and Polden, 1949.

Nicholson, W N, *The History of the Suffolk Regiment 1928–1946*, East Anglian Magazine, 1948.

Perret, B, *Through Mud and Blood*, Robert Hale, 1975.

Reid, P R, *Colditz – The Full Story*, Macmillan, 1984.

Quilter, D C, *No Dishonourable Name*, S R Publishing, 1972.

Franks, N L, *RAF Fighter Command Losses of the Second World War, Vol. 1*, Midland Publishing, 1997.

Rhodes, A, *Sword of Bone*, Faber and Faber, 1942.

Richardson, M, *Tigers at Dunkirk*, Pen & Sword, 2010.

Rissick, D, *The DLI at War 1939–45*, Depot DLI, 1952.

Rodgers, G, *In Search of Tom*, Connoisseur, 2008.

Rommelaere, G, *The Forgotten Massacre*, Warwick Printing Co., 2000.

Sebag-Montefiore, H, *Dunkirk – Fight to the Last Man*, Viking, 2006.

Synge, W, *The Story of the Green Howards*, The Regiment, 1954.

Thompson, J, *Dunkirk – Retreat To Victory*, Sidgwick and Jackson, 2008.

Wilson, P, *Dunkirk – From Disaster to Deliverance*, Pen & Sword, 1999.

Index

Index of Individuals